THE
Quiet
Heart

THE• Quiet Heart

JUNE MASTERS BACHER

HARVEST HOUSE PUBLISHERS
Eugene, Oregon 97402

To
My Mother,
Gussie Owens Masters—
with
LOVE!

THE QUIET HEART

Library of Congress Cataloging-in-Publication Data

Bacher, June Masters.
  The quiet heart : daily devotionals for women / June Masters Bacher.
    p.
  ISBN 0-89081-624-7
  1. Women—Prayer-books and devotions.   I. Title.
  BV4844.B3 1988
  242'.2—dc19   87-82261
                                                                          CIP
Copyright © 1988 by Harvest House Publishers
Eugene, Oregon 97402

Printed in the United States of America.

Contents

My New Year's Prayer

DEAR LORD, we praise You for the beauty and glory of Christmas. We praise You for the loveliness of the world around us—and for another New Year, a chance to try again. You see, we want to continue to give good gifts as the year progresses: to our enemies, we would offer tolerance; to our friends, our service and loyalty; to our children (whether we be mothers, grandmothers, teachers, or neighbors), our patience and a fine example; to our parents, deference and the kind of conduct that will make them proud of their daughters; to ourselves, confidence and respect; to our mates, our love renewed; and to You, our hearts!

But, Lord, we are tired. There is so much to do. Already Christmas seems but a memory (except for the tinsel on the carpet, the drooping Christmas tree, and the leftovers to be wrestled with). And spring seems but a dream. We need Your help, Lord, as we try to navigate through the snowdrifts we yet must climb. You have blessed an old world with a New Year. Now we need hope for old situations and new courage to face them. Give us, we pray, new boots for our weary feet.

Open our eyes to small things. No matter how good our vision, let our hearts probe deeper. Unstop our ears that we may hear the sounds of Your voice in nature. Strengthen our legs as we search out small corners in which we may serve others. Sharpen our intellects and our awareness. Let us ponder the wonderment of our existence, building bridges to the unforeseeable future of this year, leaving a daily heritage for those who come behind us.

Pick us up, Lord, when we falter. Give us the faith and the strength to begin each day anew in service of our families, our friends, the "outsiders," and You. Let us so live that when this year is finished we may say—as we say at life's end—"It is good to have been a woman!"

The Best Year Yet!

A year is the sparkle of snowflakes that January can bring...
The melody repeated by the first robins to sing...
Pink fragrance of June's roses when summertime comes around
And stays till gold of autumn lies shining over the ground...
Three hundred days of beauty and sixty-five days of cheer
Yield three hundred sixty-five reasons to have a wonderful year!

                                            J.M.B.

"YEP, THE BEST YEAR yet," a friend said last New Year's Eve. "Liz is not going to threaten to quit her job, strike in the kitchen, or take a South Sea Island vacation without me. My team will win in the Super Bowl... My hair'll thicken without a transplant . . ."

Tom's bantering monologue came back to me later. "Better for whom?" we had teased him. Now came the answer: *Better for us all if we make it so* Supposing—just *supposing*—it could be applied to the spiritual life of the church. And just supposing the congregation should cooperate? Well, here goes:

"Avocado and citrus groves are going to prosper. Members will sell at a high price and bring their tithes and offerings to the altar (the remaining fruit to be distributed among members at no cost). There will be no cold snaps and what rain falls will come at night so that nobody will miss church because of the weather. Nobody will have colds or flu either, so they can volunteer to serve on calling committees. All persons invited will accept and the congregation will double in number. Crime rates will drop and worshipers can leave automobiles unlocked so that children can play inside them—without bickering. There will be no bickering between members, either. We will work together in perfect harmony. There will be no vandalism or fire, so insurance rates will diminish sharply. Nothing will break down unless it is guaranteed..."

To Think and Pray About: Better for *whom?* Well, Happy New Year, Lord!

Let's Make This Old World Smile!

THE YEAR is still in its infancy. There remains time for those resolutions we all dread so much. Pick up your pencil and jot down ideas with me. Think of it this way: *Together we can make this old world smile!*

This year I resolve to do my best:

To be so at peace with God, family, friends, and the world around me that nothing can shake my tranquility. *Harmony!*

To speak positively of my physical, spiritual, and material blessings. *Healthy attitude!*

To find something good in my friends and tell them, "You are special to me." *Friendship!*

To look on the bright side of every dark cloud. *Philosophy!*

To expect the best of every day, to work for it to happen, and to keep my thoughts lofty. *High expectations!*

To be excited about life and to be as happy about the successes of those around me as I am about my own. *Excitement!*

To put the past behind me—my mistakes and the mistakes of others—and make each stumbling block a stair. *Forgiveness!*

To put on a smile the first thing in the morning and leave it in place until I retire at night. *Pleasantness!*

To spend more time improving myself than criticizing others. *Helpfulness!*

To be too secure to worry, too patient to anger, too strong to fear, and too joy-filled to allow a troubled thought to cross my horizon. *Prayerfulness* (for I will need help with this one, Lord)*!*

To Think and Pray About: "Sow an act, reap a habit; sow a habit, reap a character; sow a character, reap Destiny" (G. B. Boardman). Together we *can* make this old world smile. *Faith!*

Starting Anew at 65

MY MOTHER'S FRIEND had a thing about birthdays. She overcame it at 65.

It rained on Jo's birthday. "That figures," she said. "Gray month. Gray hair. Gray mood." She inspected herself from all angles looking for a bigger bulge or a new liver spot. Always bad, this one was the worst of all—a time (she said) when husbands became interesting "older men" and wives became dull "elderly women."

"Wanting to punish myself," she remembers, "I looked in my scrapbook at the list of advantages of being 21. A glorious day!"

She could vote, date, marry, seek a career, choose her own clothes, travel, live where she wished, read what she chose, forget school routine for a time and *enjoy her freedom!* So?

"That last one did it," Jo admitted. "When had I ever been as free as *now?*" And that was when the dear lady began her list of advantages of turning 65.

Ah yes, she could draw Social Security, ride the city bus free, visit city parks without paying for admission, take Adult Ed courses free, collect MediCare, serve as the sage whose ideas were considered wise and whose services were valuable. There was nothing, in fact, in the first list Jo was unable to do or had not done already. There were countless things she could do now but not then. "Why, I'm a liberated woman!" she cried in discovery.

To Think and Pray About: It is good to pause and count our blessings at every birthday. They pile up with the years. And attitudes are so important: "For as he thinketh in his heart, so is he" (Proverbs 23:7). God is changeless. He has work for us here and each milestone shows that He chose to have us remain to give Him a hand. Resolve this year to enjoy your new freedom. Ask God how you can make it count.

Make Me a Better Christian

UNWORTHY THOUGHTS were nesting in my hair when the newsletter came. It fluttered to the floor and beneath the table. I had to get on my knees to pick it up— about the best position for a prayer: O Heavenly Father, make me a better Christian;

Teach me to understand and have compassion for others and to listen patiently to what they have to say, answering questions and expressing opinions intelligently and kindly;

Keep me from interrupting rudely, speaking condescendingly, and contradicting or antagonizing others;

Make me as courteous to others as I would have them be to me;

Allow me to be self-critical and admit my own faults and mistakes and to have the moral courage to ask forgiveness when I have wronged others;

Eliminate, I pray, all prejudices that have grown within me.

Holy Father, deliver me from vainly hurting the feelings of others;

Hold me from laughing at others' mistakes or resorting to shame or ridicule at their expense;

Let me not tempt or influence others to commit wrong;

And so guide me my every hour that I may demonstrate by all I say and do that integrity and industrious effort which produce happiness, contentment, and Christian satisfaction.

For myself, dear Heavenly Father, I pray that my thoughts be wholesome, my judgment mature, and my actions certain;

Grant me faith modified by tolerance, knowledge tempered by reason, ambition subdued by moderation;

With all Thy gifts make me brave, courageous, valiant, and intrepid in Christian endeavors;

And above all else, give me calm poise and self-control.

—C. P. Huseman

To Think and Pray About: Reread the prayer, concentrating on the title!

Queen for a Day

ONCE UPON A TIME her name was Marjorie. That was 20 years ago when I had her now-grown daughter in class. Now the name is "Marji," the name of a glamorous spa she opened near my city.

Glowingly, Marji told of her many services to pamper women who can afford her fee. Massages, facials, mud baths, manicures, pedicures, and a lot of things I did not understand. "All to soft music, poetry," she said, "and low-cal fruit drinks afterwards."

It sounds elegant all right. Maybe something every woman secretly dreams about. One is supposed to come home with a whole new body and face (experts "style" the hair, "contour" the makeup, and prepare patrons for a grand entrance into the family kitchen).

The chat we had at the supermart was fun. Marji gave me her card and smiled, "Put this in your husband's pocket, maybe for a birthday."

Then came a revelation. "It's a shame, though," my friend said, "how many women received such gifts this Christmas and aren't enjoying them."

"I would think they'd appreciate such luxury." I meant it.

"Appreciate, maybe. Enjoy, no. Invariably, they feel guilty!"

If perchance (some unlikely day) George presents me with such a gift, I shall do more than stick it in my pocket the way I did the card. I shall thank him from the bottom of my heart and go over and live it up as queen for a day. He would want me to enjoy his gift.

To Think and Pray About: Have you ever thought of yourself as queen in your household? You are, you know. And that status is just another manifestation of God's love. How often He surrounds us with gifts we actually reject (or accept ungraciously) because we feel unworthy. Let us thank Him for His gifts of love and enjoy His bountiful luxuries of eternal beauty.

Yesterday's Tides

THE YEAR is a week old and I find myself wondering what I have contributed to it as I walk down to the sea. The sun is warm on my back and the breeze puffs a little as if it has been running uphill. I try to hold onto this silver-blue moment. But something warns: "The time is not yet." Spring makes many false starts in California—even in January—only to retreat through the invisible door it entered—like New Year's resolutions.

Seven days ago I took the filler my last year's schedule had gobbled from my calendar and replaced it with 365 new pages. How clean! As uncluttered as the silver sands I walk on—all scrubbed by last night's tide. As untracked as the dunes. How could the pages fill up with trivia, causing me to erase, smudge, and X-out? How can I leave a trail without cluttering the purity of the sand or my calendar's pages? Would I wish them beautiful—but blank?

My new calendar, though unblemished, looked idle to me—even a bit foolish, like garments on a shop-window manikin. There is little heart in the pages yet. They are unwrinkled by service. The calendar lacks dimension which little tracks across the days of our lives represent. I feel a sense of wonder as the tiny waves lap at my feet. Somewhere, invisible to the eye, the constant moon has changed the course of the tide. The waves and the shifting sands will erase my trail . . .

And, yet, as I turn, I see at the very top of a little knoll my tracks of yesterday. But are they as important as the whole new year of life God has given me? Each day, like this walk, will be adventure-filled. I shall hope that with God's help I can give much which cannot be erased by yesterday's tides.

To Think and Pray About: Take a meditation walk reflecting briefly on accomplishments (no regrets!). Send up a prayer of praise. Trails of love matter more than tracks made in the sand.

Love—and Let Live

ARE YOU a mother? Then it is sure to happen one of these days. You have had it up to here with "Moth-er!" (accent on the second syllable), your child's saying what an embarrassment to have you check with other parents before making a decision . . . rearranging pictures of celebrities, bumper stickers, and autographed stuffed puppies in need of a bath . . . picking up half-eaten Hershey bars and off-the-hanger clothes . . . unsnarling grammar while holding your head over Junior's *D* in the English language.

"I'm sick of this mess," I told my son on one of those days. "You should be more responsible. This room's a disgrace!"

"It's my room. I'll clean it when I have time. Just *leave* it!"

Was I being ordered out or did Bryce mean that I was to leave the disaster area without a promise on his part? Either way, I was displeased. "You will clean it *now*—by yourself!" I marched out.

I am right, I told myself. *Undoubtedly*, something whispered back, *in all but what counts—how you handled it*. I was wrestling with my conscience when I heard the rhythmless click of his sophomore-level, one-fingered typing. His term paper! I should have remembered the progress report warning that his "Be Kind to Animals Week" paper was overdue. I always did his typing, correcting as I worked. I tapped on his door. "I'll type that."

"Don't you think I can do it?" Actually, *No*. But it was I who suggested that he be responsible.

When I returned from my grocery shopping, on the dining table lay the paper and a note: "Will you proofread it, Mother?"

The title caught my eye: LOVE AND LET LIVE. Obviously a typographical error. *LIVE* AND LET LIVE, he had intended. But I liked this better—for myself. The paper would be a mess; the cleaning job, sloppy. But together we could learn . . .

To Think and Pray About: "Love should bend to every necessity"—Luther.

Thoughts for a Rainy Day

Deuteronomy 28:1-12   January 9
Solomon 2:11-13

TODAY BROUGHT a brief clearing after a 12-hour downpour. "Another storm just off-shore," the weatherman
warned. My husband and I donned rain gear and took advantage of the lull for a walk.

The streets were slick. Yellow-line dividers had drowned
beneath layers of mud and rusty rivers roared along the gutters
to clog the drains. Water sloshed over my boot tops. Only
children could enjoy such puddles!

How many crops had been destroyed? How many crops
washed away? All day a storm-formed gusher had been busy
lapping at my own small plot of loam, creasing a frown down
the center of the lawn (and my face!).

George interrupted my thoughts. "Look how quickly the
water clears." Incredibly, what had been ugly, murky rivers
suddenly became crystal-clear streams that laughed playfully
at the sidewalks. How quickly water purifies as it is hurled
against pebbles, driftwood, and other obstacles. This is like
our lives. Right?

My rainy-day mood lifted. We watched the blackbirds
freshen up in little pools after the long drought. We observed
how the rain had rinsed the dusty skirts of the poppies, hosed
off the rooftops, and made clear our polluted air. Yes, there
would be more muddy tides; but they are less frightening and
aggravating when we realize that, threatening though the
storms of life may be, they irrigate the lettuce fields and create
an oasis in the deserts of our hearts. The Master Gardener
knows what is best!

To Think and Pray About: So many ugly and trying incidents
flow into our lives uninvited. But how quickly they clear. Later
we come to realize that we, too, are purified in the process.
Nothing is without purpose—God's purpose. Each time we
strike a pebble we are purified just a little bit more. Praise His
Holy Name!

Cheerful Giving

January 10   2 Corinthians 9:6-11
John 16:33

Minute by minute an hour moves on; hour by hour, the day;
By word or by deed we fulfill a need or chances tiptoe away.
Our highest call is the spreading of joy, so let us be of good cheer;
As minutes, hours, and days move along to make a wonderful year!

                                        J.M.B.

"I'M TIRED of bending backwards to help unapprecia-tive people. Some don't even remember my name!" All of us in our women's group laughed. Stell's one of the most dedicated members. She needed to let off a puff of steam.

"Try borrowing from them," someone teased. It was Stell's turn to laugh. "See?" Julia said. "You just borrowed a giggle."

We are all borrowers and lenders. Or maybe givers and takers? Sometimes we go unsung. But little by little our hearts grow stout. Who is to say the strength comes from the borrow-ing or the lending?

It occurred to me how much I had borrowed from that group. Maybe what I passed on was theirs instead of mine. No . . . actually, God's.

I had borrowed of Julia's faith (what a believer!). And of Ethel's hope (she never "thinks" something but "hopes" it). I wondered if Stell knew how much I had used her model of loving. Jean's courage is an inspiration, a young widow with three children—and a smile. Humility I had borrowed from Bertha—the ghostwriter who prepares just about everything that appears in our church bulletin. The group fills my days with strength that I have passed on to others.

To Think and Pray About: Try calling to mind examples of the living Christ you have borrowed from those around you. Think of ways you can lend it as it returns to its Heavenly Source. It matters little who remembers when we know that the Savior knows. Praise God for others from whom you borrow of Him. And pray that you are always a cheerful giver. Joy never grows thin with the spreading!

Take Your Vitamins!

Numbers 35:30   January 11
Acts 14:17

M Y YOUNG FRIEND, Mike, tells me how he became a
Christian by a reminder to take his vitamins. It was
the "in" thing to scoff at his parents' faith. Any suggestion
constituted "nagging."

"Then along came this impossible lady called 'Miz Evelina'.
She burned comic books I left on the floor and washed my
jeans with pockets full of sand and Kleenex unless I emptied
them. I was enraged when my parents gave me a choice
between attending a church retreat with *them* or staying home
with *her*."

In the mood for a fight, Mike burst through the front door
on his third day at home without his parents. There he found
neighbors standing over the couch where the housekeeper lay.
"She'd fallen and broken her hip—reaching for something.
She was unconscious as the ambulance attendants rushed her
out."

Frightened and completely alone, the boy wandered into
the kitchen. There on the table he saw his vitamin bottle—
the one he had hidden on the top shelf because vitamins were
"kid stuff."

Beside the bottle was a note in the spidery writing of his
archenemy: *Take your vitamins!* And the note was weighted
down with her worn copy of the Bible. "I was sad—then glad. I
mean, I knew that Miz Evelina was reaching for those dumb
vitamins. And now she was all busted up because of me—and I
was busted up *inside* because of her. I had to thank her. The
best medicine she could have would be knowing I took the
medicine from the bottle and the Book!"

To Think and Pray About: We all need our "vitamins."
Strange how we resist the hardest when we are in the greatest
need. If there is something wrong in your life today, look to
God's Word. Search out the most helpful passages, then share
your prescription. Could be that you are the "Miz Evelina."

Color in the "January White Sale"

January 12   Isaiah 1:18
                                              Psalm 51:7-15

REMEMBER when we saved our Christmas checks for the first-of-the-year white sale—back when linens were *white?* Now, shop windows bloom with "color coordinates." Disquieting? Well, no...

It is in the "white of winter" that we discover the spectrum of all other colors: amethyst shadows, scarlet berries, burnished gold of a clinging leaf, quiet green of the gentle-hearted pine with its arms filled with orioles, brown ripples of rabbits in silver brush, and a cobalt jay plucking one last chestnut from its bur.

It is in the white of winter that we rediscover memories, dreams, and truths. Just as there are colors in white, there is white in colors that make up the spectrum of the rainbow—and our lives.

My grandmother used to point out the "white sounds" of January. There was whiteness in the flames which licked at the backlogs... the squeak of snow underfoot... whine of skis mapping out the snowpack... artistry of sparrow tracks ... dumpling babies stuffed inside their furry snowsuits... gaunt silhouettes of hungry wolves... and the disk of sun in its winter solstice. There was a flurry of white in the wings of doves I used to watch, angels I used to hear, and the fairies I used to see as they climbed astride the snowflakes. There was white in the quiet of snow-clogged streets ... church steeples probing the gloom... and in prayer for forgiveness of our sins. This my grandmother pointed out as she quoted layer upon layer of scriptural analogies which piled up in my memory like the winter snow. Remembered truths meld like the colors.

To Think and Pray About: No other season so challenges the senses. Now is the time for memories, dreams, and truths shared by an open fire. Study God's Word together. Enjoy its "white" analogies.

Lower Your Bucket Today!

Mark 4:37-40   January 13
John 7:37

THESE ARE busy after-the-holiday weeks—weeks that can leave us drained, empty, and in need of a refill of faith. How to cope? Maybe you are closer to an estuary than you think.

An ancient ship, blown off course, drifted aimlessly. There remained little food and no water. Men were hungry, thirsty, homesick, and afraid. They talked in low, angry tones of mutiny.

The captain prayed desperately while keeping a watchful eye in search of another ship. "If we don't have water by tomorrow," he whispered, "some of my crew will surely perish." Suddenly on the horizon he spotted another ship. "S.O.S.! S.O.S!" he signaled. "My men are dying of thirst." The reply was immediate. "Lower your bucket. You are in fresh water!"

Hardly daring to share the dubious news, the captain lowered a bucket secured by a rope over the side of the vessel. The contents had no salt! The storm which had tossed the ship about had nosed it toward an estuary where the fresh, sweet water of the river rushed into the sea to drive back the salty water. Who would have thought to test the water before flashing a signal of distress? And, yet, most likely the men had been there for some time and had suffered needlessly.

How like our lives. A storm disturbs our calm. There is no outward sign that, even when the winds have died down, we are in a safety zone. We hunger, thirst, complain. And all we would need do is lower the bucket and drink deeply of the waters of peace God has prepared. Jesus is our estuary. Why grope? Use your rope—of prayer!

To Think and Pray About: Are there days in your life you feel nothing can save? You are adrift. You are abandoned. Still, you fail to test the water? Remember that God is unable to fill your bucket unless you test the waters with renewed faith. Yes, there are refills!

At the Top of the Human Chain

January 14

2 Corinthians 12:7-10
Psalm 31:1-5

A N ENORMOUS poster behind the pulpit of a church we visited frequently when I was a child lingers in my mind. I had never seen a mountain then, so the craggy peak a group was trying to scale captured my attention. *That would be impossible to climb*, I remember thinking. And it would have—alone. That was the whole idea.

Children have a way of identifying with each other, so I looked to the very bottom where the smallest child stood with upturned face. The little boy was reaching toward the hand of an older girl who had begun the climb. She reached down with one of her hands while holding firmly to the hand of the sturdy boy just above her. She looked so loving and kind—unafraid, too, even though she had reached a dizzying height. I was almost afraid to look any higher. What if the picture had changed since I last visited the church? But, to my great relief, each time the protective hand of what must be the father held the woman's hand and it was she who reached to the sturdy little boy. They would all reach the top safely I knew then because the man was holding the hand of Jesus!

At the top of the human chain which Jesus was lifting to safety were the words: *My grace is sufficient for thee.* I always felt warm and safe then, knowing that Jesus was lifting all the people in the congregation—and the whole wide world—up to be with Him.

To Think and Pray About: Have you had a "mountain-climbing day"? "I can't do it alone!" you cry. And you're right; but you're not alone! Jesus is at the top of our human chain. It is good to sit down, close your eyes, and just reach up for that hand today. The weaker we are the stronger the hand of Jesus will feel. Strengthened, we will rise, knowing that we must reach down to lift another—perhaps the little one at the bottom who as yet has not begun to climb. *None* of us can make it alone, but Jesus is reaching! "Our strength is made perfect in weakness" (2 Corinthians 12:9).

Open and Close with a Song

Acts 16:26-31   January 15

"WE'LL OPEN with a song!" Brother Brown always announced at each summer revival meeting. Songs of praise could do just about anything, the old gent said. They could lift us out of prisons, open the doors of the church—*anything*. We children took every word literally. In my fertile imagination I watched the clouds roll away, people march from behind prison walls, and the church door swing open so that people who heard our voices could crowd inside—and live happily ever after.

We used to sing until the rafters shook. And you know what? I have seen people come inside who had never visited before. Maybe they *did* hear our singing.

"Old Brother Brown just never runs down!" We children used to giggle at our private rhyme—loving every minute of the rousing service. Brother Brown opened with a hymn, yes; and he closed with a hymn. What made him special, however, was that he was apt to burst out in song in the middle of a sentence. And, knowing that we were welcome, we would join in. Ours was the singingest church ever.

Does it seem that people sing less than they used to? In some church services there are more announcements than songs; and in some homes, it seems to me, there is no song at all. Not a bad idea, you know—opening and closing with a song. Better yet, what about bursting out in songs of praise in the middle of the day? Maybe it will not send the clouds scudding across the sky; but it can wring the worry out of them. Maybe it will not release all the prisoners (including ourselves); but it can re-lease the spirit. Maybe it will not open the doors literally; but it will say, "Welcome."

To Think and Pray About: Songs of praise must be a great deal more than we give them credit for. Paul and Silas found comfort in them. Let a song of praise open the doors of your heart, untie your tongue, and set your hands free to do God's work today!

A Pot-of-Gold, a Helping of Sunshine

January 16
1 Chronicles 29:3-5
James 1:21-27

"WON'T YOU look in on Mrs. Harper on your way to the convalescent home to see the Vining couple today? She's all alone and a minute of your time would mean so much."

Undoubtedly. But I don't have a minute! Already I feel like the operator of Old MacDonald's farm: "Here a minute; there a minute..."

To Muriel, who'd called, I said Mrs. Harper deserved more than a minute, that nobody could be cheered up that quickly, and that she'd best get somebody who *had* a minute anyway. The usual excuses. I hung up feeling justified, but guilty.

As I dressed hurriedly, I chanced to look out the sliding glass doors in the bedroom. From there I could see the pot-of-gold vine which blooms out like dinner-plate-sized, bronze morning glories in the summer and goes dormant in the winter. Did I or did I not see a trumpet-shaped bloom? In *January?* Impossible—but there it was, protected from the north wind by a tangle of unpruned vines, and exposed—oh, so little—to the winter sunshine from the south.

Well, isn't that all Mrs. Harper needed? If I put my dinner casserole in the oven now, cut my visit with Mr. and Mrs. Vining a bit short (they'd understand), and took the shortcut to the hospital... Impulsively, I ran out and plucked the bright blossom.

Mrs. Harper was entranced with my gift. "It looks for the world like it's filled with sunshine!" And for the lonely lady I knew that it was. Just a single flower had brightened her day—and mine!

To Think and Pray About: It's the "out of season," unexpected deed which often is the most helpful. Just as the flower captured and spread the sun's light, it is up to us to capture and spread the light with which Christ Jesus has lighted up our lives. Any service for Him is a pot-of-gold!

Rise and Shine!

Ephesians 4:1-8   January 17

HERE IN MID-MONTH I received a letter from my friend Bessie, written on New Year's Day. She'd been too busy to mail it! "Soon I shall remove the Three Kings panel from the door, store the little green ceramic Christmas tree, and put the golden angel in her tissue-lined box to wait for a whole year. But I am never sad when I 'un-Christmas' the house, for I accept the New Year and look forward to its challenges... I must not waste a moment!"

Not a word about a solitary breakfast of toast and milk. The retired teacher lives alone and her health demands a stringent diet. *Not a word about how she feels,* although her condition is precarious. *Not a word about having nothing to do,* for she views retirement (even illness) not as a chance to "sleep in," but as an opportunity to "rise and shine" for God!

"I just had my first January devotional. Spiritually nourished, I must wrap some books to mail... deliver magazines to the convalescent home down the street... telephone two sick friends..."

Bessie's annual New Year's letter always reminds me just how purposeful a single life, dedicated to serving others, can be. She refuses to let herself be handicapped by anything life dishes out. She's so busy ministering to others that there is no time for vague aches and pains. Surrounded by those who need her, she has no claim on loneliness or uselessness. And, as Dickens said: "No one is useless in this world who lightens it for someone else." People like my friend in Florida may take down the decorations, but they will never "un-Christmas" the heart.

To Think and Pray About: Benjamin Franklin wrote: "Dost thou love life? Then do not squander time, for that is the stuff life is made of." We're all guilty of doing just that at times, aren't we? Let's resolve today to "squander" our time on others. The Lord will give us strength to rise and shine for Him this New Year—lightening the world for others, hopefully without complaint.

Laying on of Hands

THERE WAS silence in Room #18 each time I walked past on my way to see a friend in the rest home. That seemed strange since there were almost always visitors. Didn't they ever talk?

Then one day I noticed a middle-aged couple taking leave of the tiny, white-haired patient.

"If there's nothing you need, Mother," the younger woman said very quietly, "we must be going. See you next week."

I didn't intend to eavesdrop, spy, or whatever else one might call it. But to myself I thought: *There wasn't even time for an embrace?*

I should be on my way and still I hesitated. "Go in," something urged. And then I heard her crying softly as I stepped inside the door.

"Is there something I can do?" I needn't have hesitated. Her eyes told me that she needed to talk.

"There's something *they* could do," the frail little lady said sadly. "Only it's not their fault really. I spent so much time teaching my children what I thought was right—what was good for them—that I never taught them to show feelings. I need to hear someone say, 'I love you.' I need to have someone just *touch* me again—"

Admittedly, I'd never thought much about touching before. I just took it for granted. We're an affectionate family. But what about all the others I encounter? What are their needs? Like this lady's children, I had offered little material things or had sat with people, but had I neglected speaking of love? Had I remembered to just reach out and touch them physically? Jesus touched others. Undoubtedly, He put some of that power in my hands and in yours.

To Think and Pray About: If Jesus were visiting a rest home, do you feel that He would reach out and touch each patient lovingly? Then, do you think He would speak of His Father's love? Let's follow His example.

My Father's Real Estate

I WAS SAD, remembering the loss of my father. Then came a tender childhood memory that set my heart singing again.

My father never sang solos. Maybe he didn't even have a good voice by critics' standards. But when he sang, holding a hymnal with one hand and my hand with his other, singing: "Oh, they tell me of a land where no stormclouds rise; oh they tell me of a land far away; where the tree of life in eternal bloom sheds its fragrance o'er the uncloudy day," I was closer to heaven than I will ever be again—until I meet him there.

Remembering Daddy's singing—so much of it about heaven—makes it easy to understand why the Book of Revelation became one of my favorites. The other prophecies had come to pass; and, glorious as they were, they were a part of the past. Youth has its thrust in the future (and I praise the Lord that mine still is!).

I pondered Revelation. I am sure, according to the teachings of biblical scholars, that much of the contents went over my head. But one of the beauties of childhood is thinking simple thoughts. I pulled enough from God's promises to "see" what He has in store for us while others struggle with hidden meanings. Heaven is *heaven*, the home Jesus went to prepare for us. That is sufficient.

To Think and Pray About: What is heaven like? Nobody knows for sure. But Daddy's singing gave me a simple childhood faith that nobody has been able to shake or discredit. The "End of Time" means the "Beginning of Eternity." Daddy's Tree of Life surely must stand in the center, for there will be no death. The absence of sickness dispenses with the need for ambulances, funeral processions, and headstones. Light will come from the face of Jesus—so radiant that there will be no shadows, no bars on windows through which no thieves can enter. Our mortal hearts will become immortal! So let not our hearts be troubled. We have real estate in heaven!

Exchanging a Day

EARLY THIS MORNING I heard the touching hymn "Morning Has Broken" over a radio station which usually plays popular music through the day. The words of praise filled my kitchen and my heart. "What a lovely way to start this day, Lord," I whispered.

Something about the words brought back an ancient prayer:

> Lord, this is the beginning of a new day;
> You have given it to me to use as I will:
> I can waste it or I can use it for Your good.
> What I do today is very important,
> Because I am exchanging a day of my life for it.
> When tomorrow comes this day will be gone forever,
> Leaving something in its place.
> I have traded it so I want it to be a gain—Not a loss;
> Good—not evil; success—not failure;
> In order that I shall not forget
> Who gave it to me to exchange. —Anonymous

The sun was chinning itself over our avocado grove. The mockingbirds were chorusing in the still-bare branches of the fig tree—unconcerned that each sang a different song. The scent of orange blossoms sat on the top of the morning. And out beyond the parameters of my private world lay countless opportunities for saying "Thank You, Lord" by serving others in His name. It was as if I had seen and heard the glory of the Lord through song, prayer, and all the things of nature He provides..."In the morning then ye shall see the glory of the Lord" (Exodus 16:17).

To Think and Pray About: Not all people's senses are tuned heavenward any more than all radios were tuned to the "Morning Has Broken" song today. Can you think of some ways you can help others see, hear, and taste the glory of a newborn day? Praise God for another day of life and pray with me that we may "exchange" it wisely!

Safety Tips

I SUPPOSE that the writers of "safety tips" mean well, but reading them is simply not the way to start my day. Take the list I read this morning: 1) Beware of sharp knives in your cupboard drawers (Now I'm afraid to look for a dull one); 2) Watch out for poisonous chemicals stored with your foodstuff (Which ones are they?); 3) WARNING—Keep paper towels, dishcloths, plastic utensils, and electrical cords away from stoves and outlets (But where else would I use them?); and 5) Always keep a fire extinguisher in hand (Do they really expect me to use only one hand for household tasks?). I suddenly remember that most accidents happen in the home, so I'd best get out anyway.

But another item alongside this one caught my eye: *Running and jogging can be dangerous!* I started to lay the paper aside (having decided to crawl to safety) when the bottom line of the jogging item captured my attention: "Don't try to 'tough it out' and stop running before you're in agony." That's the best advice I gleaned.

There *are* hazards in this world—within our homes and on the outside. But we don't have to "tough it out" alone. We should learn the rules of safety, practice them as sanely as we know how, and stop senseless worrying (like mine!). I don't need to run, jog, or even crawl. I need to strengthen my legs by kneeling and asking God to remove unnecessary fear from my heart whether it's about knives, chemicals, or explosives—or maybe something quite different. I can't outrun hazards—no matter how conditioned I am to jogging. So right now, at this very moment, I must stop and talk to God before I end up in agony. I know that agonizing is not God's plan for me either—and I'm glad!

To Think and Pray About: Do you find yourself worrying unnecessarily about your problems or overly concerned about things over which you have little control? Ask. Believe. Receive! That's the best "safety tip" of them all.

Sometimes I'm a Magpie

FABLES were a literary favorite with me in my growing-up years. I especially liked "Why the Magpie's Nest is Unfinished."

Wise Owl called together all the birds of the forest. "It's time," said he, "that we learned to build homes. You will need a foot and a bill."

"I already have both!" piped Myrtie Magpie.

Wise Owl ignored the interruption. "Some of us use sticks—"

"I know that," Myrtie said irritably.

"And some of us use mud and straw—"

"Ho hum."

"Since so many birds have good ideas on building, I think we should share. Rennie Wren, will you begin?"

The little Wren brought a marsh reed and began constructing a side-opening nest—good, said the owl, because it had a roof for protection. "First," said Rennie, "lay two strong reeds crosswise."

"I *know* that," Myrtie again interrupted. And she kept interrupting as the Wren, the Warbler, and the Oriole demonstrated.

At last Wise Owl had enough of her rudeness. "You know it all," he said. "so why bother with us? You will know how to roof."

Only Myrtie did not know. And so to this day the Magpie's nest is an architectural eyesore. The foundation is shapeless. The walls are irregular and drafty. And there is no roof at all.

Sometimes, like Myrtie, I am a poor listener. I tune out important details with silent *I-know's* when listening to recipes. Result: A culinary disaster. Then I remember the fable.

To Think and Pray About: The concept of being a Christian know-it-all hits home with me, too. I can never help others who are building their lives in Christ unless I listen. Think of some creative listening skills as you build God's temple within your heart.

A Diet for Gaining—Happiness!

Psalm 31:19-24   January 23

ALL OF US gasped when Freddie, our twiggy friend, told the group she was dieting (Why do we assume all diets are for weight loss?). Freddie's diet was for *enrichment!* Don't try it unless you want to gain—happiness, that is.

Breakfast: An appetizer of exercise—preferably a brisk walk—just as the sun rises. Let the dew wash your face and the breeze brush your hair. Try a slice of prayer while the kettle steams. Fill your nostrils with perfume of the season; your ear, with birdsong; and your heart with lovely thoughts. Hum a stanza of a favorite hymn as you butter your daily bread—fresh from the Father's field.

Lunch: Stretch out on the grass with a bowl of fruit, the *Good Book,* and the morning mail. List those who wrote; pray for them; try counting your blessings like others count sheep— until the beauty of the moment . . . the warmth of the sun . . . and the length of the list allow you to doze . . .

Coffee break: Between the demands of a busy schedule, take time to lift your eyes and feast on an in-between snack. Watch the shadows lengthen and give praise. Watch the bees in the honeysuckle, the butterflies on the forsythia, and give praise. Smell the aroma of the evening roast . . . observe the line of fresh laundry . . . call a sick friend . . . wave to a going-home child . . . and give praise. Flex those muscles and enjoy your renewed strength.

Dinner: Put a log on the fire in winter. Move into the backyard in summer. Draw a loved one close . . . open your heart to your neighbors and your door to the sojourner. Dish up large portions of love, sprinkled with kindness, and garnish with smiles. Drink in the sunset together and choose for yourself a wedge of sky drizzled with stars. Sip from the vastness of the universe and know that God's love is greater—so sweet, so filling, so satisfying that no dessert is needed.

To Think and Pray About: Praise God for His love. Fill your cup to the brim!

On Being an "Only Child"

A SCHOOL "staffing" was in progress—a practice which always set me on edge because there's an air of negativism. One of my students was the subject and I saw little wrong that love wouldn't cure. Unfortunately, however, I'd be the last to speak—after the "evidence" was in from the principal, the psychometrician, playground teachers, and all other school personnel associated with David.

Almost immediately the discussion bogged down over the child's family status. "He's an only child," one teacher commented, "and behaves that way!" *Just how's an only child supposed to act?*

But I was on the outside looking in. The others were of one voice. "Right!" I heard all around me. I said nothing. You see, I'm an only.

"Have you noticed that it runs in families?" (I'd never thought of "only children" being a genetic thing, contagious, or whatever the implication was.) They began to cite cases and I felt my face reddening. My husband and I have only one child through no fault of our own.

I will never know how Leta knew my feelings. I only know that underneath the table she reached and placed her hand over mine. Her clasp was warm, firm, and supporting. My courage returned. I was able to go through my report objectively. And win! Because of a gesture of love.

To Think and Pray About: The incident led me to make a list of questions to use professionally and in my personal relationships: 1) Do I tend to generalize or categorize because of a personal theory? 2) Do I offer understanding and support to others when I see their courage waver? and 3) Do I lose sight of the measure of love in one person, God's only Son? Read today's suggested passages and pray with me about them.

To Do a Blessed Thing

NELLA PAUSED from sorting her late uncle's few possessions. "You know, I'll wager Uncle Thad never did a blessed thing for anybody."

"He got you and me together this year," I reminded my friend.

Nella smiled. "For that you get *this*."

"It looks used," I observed of the ancient King James Bible.

"By *him*?" Nella looked skeptical.

Everybody knew Thadeus Perkins—or thought they did. He'd stayed on at the town's one hotel since the death of his wife, although nobody knew how he afforded it. His small World War I pension would do well to cover his daily "refreshments" at the local bar. Probably both owners chose to forget his bills. He was a natty dresser and carried a cane (although later I was to learn that the clothes were kept new-looking by spot cleaner and that the cane was to hide a limp from a service-connected injury). That's about all I knew about Thad— except that he shied away from other people except "the boys" with whom he played pool. Well, I knew something else. He had no relatives except Nella who came every five years or so. "My *half*-uncle," she'd sigh. "How apt!" And then he died.

Curiously, I opened the worn Bible. Automatically, it opened in the middle where lay the key to so many things. I could have wept. There his marriage, his wife's death, and the date of his baptism were recorded. But there was something more: "On January 25, 1920, I (with 14 others) was put out of the (and he gave its name) church without trial. I am so lonely. Will whoever gets this Book pray for me?"

I kept the old Bible. It is good for me to review the incident and to think about Jesus' warning when I am tempted to be judgmental. "Uncle Thad" did at least one blessed thing!

To Think and Pray About: *Lord, remove stones from my hand; malice from my heart; and unworthy thoughts from my mind today.*

Open My Heart, Lord

Open my heart, Lord, to small daily things;
Each blessing You've shaped that blossoms and
*   sings...*   J.M.B.

THE HILL presented no problem. I left my three hiking companions and hurried ahead for no reason I can recall. I regretted it 300 yards later. Feeling foolish, I sat down on a rock to pant. When my heart stopped beating like a tomtom, I heard voices. Children's voices filled with squeals of glee. The sounds belonged, I discovered, to a Brownie troop which spied me at once. "It helps to rest," one volunteered. I agreed.

"Did you plant yours?" The child reached into her uniform pocket and brought out a bulb. "We plant flowers as we go."

"Maybe you're a pick-up person?"

I guess the child knew she had lost me. "Sometimes we stop and clean what litterbugs leave. Want a cookie while you enjoy the view?"

I accepted, ashamed to admit that I was neither planter, pick-up person, nor even a viewer. I had been in too much of a rush to reach the top. I was exhausted and what good had I done along the way?

Reducing my speed to a sensible pace, I stopped here and there to inhale the rare, thin air of the higher altitude. I marveled at the shadowy valleys. I picked up two discarded bags. I had no bulbs to plant, but I moved two stones from the path my friends would travel. My heart picked up speed again—this time with joy.

To Think and Pray About: Consider how important our journey through life is. At the end, let us be able to say, "Lord, I helped others, maintained tranquility—and enjoyed the view! Thank You."

Burying My Sins

1 John 1:6-10   January 27
Colossians 2:6-17

GOD REASSURES us repeatedly that forgiveness is ours. He removes our transgressions "as far as the east is from the west" (Psalm 103:12). Why, then, do I insist on going back to rehash my guilt after He has removed it? It's a human frailty of mine—one I'm working on. This recent incident helped.

We were discussing forgiveness at a Bible-study class. Question: *How do we rid ourselves of guilt and shame?* Answer: *Turn them over to God.* Question: *Will He bury them forever?* Answer: *Yes, unless we choose to exhume them.* Question: *How can we avoid that?*

We pray, obviously, but one of our guests from another state told of this exercise. "I know a man who paddles out into a lake daily so that God can bury his sins there. Then, when he comes ashore, he posts a sign saying: *No fishing!*"

It's a helpful thought. Rowing out on the water where all is still and peaceful to have a talk with God! It's a wonderful feeling to know (even vicariously) that my doubts, fears, and misgivings are buried at sea. How wonderful to "Take my burdens to the Lord and leave them there," as the old hymn says. But that's precisely what I have to do: *Leave them there!* Back from my imaginary trip, I am free—if I go one step farther. I must not go back to fish for those problems; and that's the part I must remember.

To Think and Pray About: We are to ask God for forgiveness. We are to believe ourselves forgiven. We are to *know* we are. God has promised and He never breaks a promise. Would it not behoove us then to *thank* Him for forgiving those transgressions and to demonstrate our faith in His promises by never, ever again fishing for those buried sins? *Father, remind me that I am not to "fish in troubled waters" in search of my wrongdoings. Teach me to forget as You have forgotten. To You I give all honor and glory!*

The Feel of the Potter's Hand

January 28   Jeremiah 18:1-6
                                                        Isaiah 64:8

M Y MOTHER shared a meaningful incident with me a long time ago. It remains today one of the best ways of dealing with stress that I know.

At a women's missionary meeting, the ladies were to respond to roll call by giving the title of a favorite hymn, reciting a stanza if possible, and telling why the hymn was a special inspiration.

Mrs. Aldridge, a lady well into her eighties and a member of everything worth joining in the community, smiled when the secretary called her name: " 'Have Thine Own Way, Lord!' and I love the first verse:

> Have Thine own way, Lord; Have Thine own way!
> Thou art the Potter, I am the clay.
> Mold me and make me after Thy will,
> While I am waiting yielded and still."
>
> A.A. Pollard

And then Mrs. Aldridge gave her testimonial. "I think of my body as common, unwashed clay. But the Creator put inside me a certain quality which is yielding, ready for the potter's wheel of God's mighty hand—providing I don't allow myself to harden. I must wait for Him to mold me into a rounded vessel when I would rise too high! Then, when He is finished, He will put me through the trials of the fiery furnace—not to melt me down, but to glaze me into His finished product."

To Think and Pray About: We know we must keep our hearts pliable, yielding, and waiting. God is shaping us for His purpose. There's no time to squat sullenly. There are days when I am tempted to feel a little too smug, too self-sufficient, too able on my own. Then I try to imagine the Potter's hand pushing me gently down into the rounded vessel He would have me be. There are trials, but it will all be worth it when we see ourselves finished with God's "final glaze." We know we will be pleasing to His eye!

Up from the Snow

Could anything be longer or colder than this day?
Who said if winter visits can spring be far away?
And then I saw the blossom, much like a winter star,
Ah, foolish little flower, how very brave you are!
A tiny thing of beauty—white courage on a stem—
Somehow God's fragile snowdrop had brought me
    thoughts of Him.
The day grew warm and lovely for there will be a spring
As long as winter snowfalls can raise a Perfect Thing.
                                                J.M.B.

"HOW BEAUTIFUL," you may have breathed reverently when the first flake fell. The grandeur and the solemnity of the moment brought excitement to the children; peace and harmony to your heart. You stood suspended between the world where snow has begun to change familiar shapes into things of beauty and the universe of stars hidden by a thin layer of clouds. Only no stars were visible. They were falling. . . falling. . . falling.

How is it that so suddenly such warm moments must melt? Tree branches, so lovely just seconds ago, sag beneath their unaccustomed snowpack. You realize that the mailman will be unable to find your door unless someone shovels a trail through the chilling drifts. There are frozen pipes, wet boots, and the threat of a power outage to be dealt with. The children's snowball fight has to be halted because of an injury. The older folk complain of the chill. The wood gives out. The dog smells like wet wool. . . and a sense of frustration sets in.

To Think and Pray About: How can we reclaim the spiritual attunement we felt at the first snowflakes? They will irrigate the gardens and the parks, bring up the snowdrops, and ultimately return to the vast ocean from which they came. Compare that mission to ours.

Our Neighbor to the North

A S I MADE some notes for tomorrow on my daily calendar, something in the date seemed familiar, so I checked my diary. Familiar, yes! On January 31, 1980 I had penned: "I am proud of the world today." Americans, I remembered, hoisted Canadian flags, swamped consulates and radio stations with calls cheering our northern neighbors in proclamations, billboards, and newspapers for spiriting six U.S. diplomats out of Iran. It was a noble act—one we'll always remember as the ultimate in friendship, something we too often take for granted.

It's easy to be patriotic at times like this. We need so desperately to *believe*. Or, as a full-page Citicorp advertisement in the *New York Times* expressed it: "In a world filled with hatred, anxiety and spite, you (Canada) showed unwavering compassion, reason and courage." But what impressed me most were the words of a Canadian diplomat: "I like Americans! They let you know when you do something wrong; but when you do something right, they let you know, too!" We grew.

To Think and Pray About: I grew, too, and I plan to keep on growing. I liked Utah's idea of a Friendship Day proclamation—liked it so well I have tried to make every day a Friendship Day. My child's teacher should know I am appreciative—whether One-Son is (or is not) doing well. My doctor should know how invaluable his services are when I am (or am not) responding to his treatment. My friends should know that I treasure them in every circumstance. My family deserves to be smothered with "I love yous." And, most of all, I must thank my loving Lord for His blessings. Life is too short to count. It's easy to love in "great moments," but what about the low points? Can you think of them as situations God set to help you grow? Can you praise Him for *everything* that comes your way, knowing there's a reason? Let's *tell* Him. God should know He's "done something right."

A Secret Shelf

I RAN ACROSS the Red Satin punch recipe today. It reminded me . . .

Millie's "Come in" was muffled when I rang her doorbell on New Year's Eve. "I need your Red Satin punch," I called. "The one using cranapple—" I lowered my voice as my friend, dusting her hands, emerged from the entrance closet. "Good riddance!" she said.

I wasn't sure what she meant for a moment. Then Millie continued. "The little shelf in the closet is a secret place. I dump all my petty grievances there—daily, weekly, whenever they're too much, but *always* on New Year's Eve. Now, I'm ready for a clean start."

The idea had come when Millie was a little girl, she told me. "I used to play a game called 'Nobody Knows But Me and God' when I had a problem that only He and I could resolve. I found that if I talked to Him and then tucked it away, pretty soon nobody knew but God!"

I sort of wondered if she was serious. "It works?"

" 'Hey, Look Us Over'!" she said. "Twenty-five years married and the roof's still on. Shelving those grudges beats nagging Jack about the rising cost of living or kicking the terrier. It's a new *me* you're looking at. I don't even remember what the problems were!"

I left Millie's house with two tried-and-true recipes. The punch I knew was a combination of ingredients and the secret-shelf idea sounded worth a try. I trusted God with all else. Why not my problems? George built me a little shelf (until then I'd been using a small corner of my mind). I wish I could offer an example of the problems I shelved; but, you see, they are in God's hands!

To Think and Pray About: *Father, such a short while ago we sang "Another Year Is Dawning." Remind us that once we turn a calendar, old things are past; and, as we turn over an old concern to You, we put on the new self through Your grace.*

A Prayer in the Silver Silence

ALMIGHTY GOD, Creator of the snowflake's intricate design, how silently the snow fell last night. Heaped high on the picket fence, bundled in the trees, and frosting the rooftops, the lacy miracle has transformed the world in quiet innocence and muted its voice to a silver silence.

How quiet Your love, Lord. Yet everywhere You are speaking to us, reassuring us, telling us that earth's pulse, though slowed in rest, continues to beat. We hear the twitter of the birds that winter here whispering of spring. Now and then we see a frisky squirrel's tail flirt playfully as he braves the trackless snow to garner that last acorn clinging to the oak. Cautiously, comes the timid deer . . . testing the pond and finding the water quilted in ice. Its thirst unquenched, the graceful creature nibbles at the bark of a slippery elm, cautiously licks at the snow, and is satisfied. And the visiting birds have found the red-berried bush!

Again You have provided, Lord. You have quenched the thirst and satisfied the appetite of the forest creatures—just as You provide for us in time of need. The birds are right! You have watered the whole earth—and spring *will* flourish again. Soon the white page of February will bear Your signature spelled out in the green quills of the crocus, curled catkins on the elders, and a million golden daffodils. Yes, You have provided for them all and added a promise of spring.

And You have provided Your images with yet another promise—one so wondrously deep that science is unable to explain. You have shown us that life on this planet is more than a bubble that floats but for a moment then sinks to nothingness. But there exists a realm where the snowflakes which leap like angels retain forever their pristine beauty, festive stars in midnight's dance never fade, and spring reigns eternal—because You are there—after the silver silence of winter's brief grave.

Six More Weeks of Winter!

If you are unhappy and feeling alone,
Try thinking of others and blues will be gone.
Write someone a letter—a thought for the day—
The words can be simple (they're better that way).
Enclose something special—an old recipe—
You'll find yourself smiling; just try it and see.

J.M.B.

I F THE DAY is dark and gloomy, be happy! An overcast sky will keep the groundhog from seeing his shadow! And your happy countenance will light up the gloom for less-happy friends. Say "Happy Groundhog Day!" to everyone you meet. That will bring a smile for sure. Then both of you will feel better.

Maybe the critter overslept anyway...but undoubtedly somewhere candles are glowing. Are you familiar with the celebration of Candlemas Day? Old World tradition placed the presentation of the Infant Jesus in the Temple of Jerusalem on February second. The Candlemas ceremony marked the end of the Christmas season by lighting windows throughout the cities with bright candles. Hopefully, so the lesser-known legend goes, there would be dark clouds and rain on the festival day—an omen that winter was ended (perhaps by the glowing candles and the arrival of the King in the Temple).

A newer and more familiar legend has it that the woodchuck awoke during one of the Candlemas Day celebrations, came sleepily from his burrow after his winter's sleep, saw his shadow, and hurried back to bed. (Go ahead and smile!)

To Think and Pray About: No matter what the weather, this is a good day to ask ourselves some questions: 1) Am I a timid woodchuck? and 2) Do I burn candles for Christ (this can be any small deed in His name)? Now, let's "do" for others and have a happy Groundhog Day!

Wonderful World of Words!

February 3

*Nobody ever outgrows Scripture; the book widens
and deepens with our years.*

Spurgeon

M Y REFERENCE material spread over the den floor
like a wordprint carpet. I was wishing that I had more
room than my desk afforded when my husband walked in to
announce that he was ready to paint the walls—*now*. It had
taken an hour for me to set up shop.

George was already rolling my typewriter out the door. I did
a quick survey. What did I actually need to have moved into
my temporary quarters in the dining room?

"Just bring the dictionary and the Bible," I instructed Pan,
the neighbor boy who was mine for the morning and who
always wants to "help" in a domestic crisis.

The six-year-old scooped the books up in sturdy arms. "You
must need to know a lotta meanings!" he said with round eyes.

Need to know a lot of meanings? I'd never thought of it that
way; but, of course I do. The dictionary is more for spelling
than definitions. But my Bible is strictly for "meanings"—
checking on accepted definitions and making sure of proper
quotes. But there's a bonus to such research. There is just no
way to read a passage from God's Word without finding a new
dimension. I look for one meaning and half a dozen new ones
open up to me.

Later (in a better mood—the wall *did* look nice!), I shared
with my husband that I would know what to take along in case
of a necessary evacuation. My Bible is a necessity: in my
Christian writing, yes, but in my Christian life, too. I need to
know *lots* of meanings. And God's Word provides them all.

To Think and Pray About: "Have you hugged God's Word
today?" *Thank You, Lord, for the new meanings we find in our
daily lives with every reading of Your Word. Thank You, too, for
continued revelation.*

Stay Away from the Lowlands!

THE FEBRUARY SUN is brilliant today. Just yesterday, though, when we thought the rainstorm that had pounded this Southern California town was over, a deluge put us temporarily awash again.

I say "temporarily." Who knows? The daily paper is filled with articles claiming that drainage projects are light years away. "Construction's not expected to begin for a year for the environmentally fragile and flood-ridden lowlands..." says one report. And another's abandoned because of the squabbles among property owners.

One of our former councilmen (not noted for long-suffering silence) says no ditch is going to solve the problem. "Why in tarnation folks keep building in the low-lying areas beats me. They know the river will come back to claim its old course."

It's hard to understand why engineers would select such building sites as river beds—unstable at best and disaster areas in case of rain. They flood out every year; and people go right on cleaning up and being flooded again and again until their homes are washed away completely.

Why? I ask—knowing at the same time I make similar mistakes in other areas of life. I make some unwise decisions, regret them, ask forgiveness—all well and good, until I turn and make the same mistakes. Finally, a part of *me* is washed away in the process. How can I avoid this "lowland" pattern?

To Think and Pray About: In today's reading Jesus meant that Peter was a strong apostle, a good foundation. Nothing could be stronger than the rock of His love. No floods can destroy what we build in Him. This old hymn has a message for me:

> Lord, lift me up and let me stand
> By faith on heaven's tableland,
> A higher plane that I have found;
> Lord, plant my feet on higher ground —J. Oatman.

Lord, lift us from "former things" that would reclaim our lives!

A Prayer for All Broken Hearts

AT FIRST, we felt shocked; then sad; and now partly responsible. Why didn't we see the danger signals before two members of our family announced that they are seeking a divorce? How could we have failed to see the quiet desperation in which they were living so that we could have somehow shared the burden that devitalized their energy and affected their happiness to the point of parting? I find myself feeling strangely guilty—guilty because I wasn't there when they needed me; guilty, too, because of my own successful marriage. Maybe I feel just a little afraid, too, for their marriage once was as stable as ours.

It is entirely proper to cry at weddings. How many, I wonder, cry at divorces? Only those directly involved, I guess, and none of us know how much; for, unlike weddings, the couple weeps in solitude. What can we do? There is no need for a best man and matron of honor in a divorce court. But there's need for friendship, love, understanding, and—above all—God! Maybe our loved ones need us even more in times of defeat than in times of sorrow or of joy. There's no dignity in defeat. Nobody wins. But God can scoop up the losers in His loving arms. And I must take no sides, make no judgments, offer no advice—just offer love and more love.

I'm preparing a special message for my loved ones today. Dear Ones: "Are you willing to believe that love is the strongest thing in the world . . . and that the blessed life which began in Bethlehem 2000 years ago is the image and brightness of Eternal Love? Then you can keep Christmas—no matter what the season brings"—Henry Van Dyke.

To Think and Pray About: *Lord, whatever the tragedy of yesterday, we beg that You mend all broken hearts with Your mercy. Let them meet this day with confidence and goodwill. Replace bitterness and malice with tolerance and compassion. May in time all scar tissue be removed, each tear be wiped away. This, Lord, we pray for the brokenhearted.*

It's Hard to Be "Hardened!"

WHAT "hardens" us into being good soldiers for the Lord?

George Washington became known as the father of his country even during his own lifetime (I recently learned). But he is revered more as a human temple than loved as a fellow human being.

Was that the whole story? Hardly. Modern research has uncovered the warm man beneath the formidable legend. It has shown him to be a man of faults, but with a certain greatness that allowed him to rise above them.

- As a soldier, he made mistakes but won the war.
- As a statesman, he spoke seldom; but, when he spoke, he made sense.

And so our first President came to be admired for his "soldierhood" of courage, energy, judgment, common sense, granite character, and honor.

Now, what about *me*?

- Can I rise above my faults?
- Can I accept my failures, get up, and continue the fight?
- Can I hold my tongue until it has healing words to share?
- Can I *endure* (crying quietly, if cry I must)?

Then the Lord has need of me.

To Think and Pray About: Try getting together with family or friends and formulating a list of questions which probe into your private selves. Comparisons and discussions will make the project all the more rich. Then together let us enlist for service with the Father of the world! *Here we are, Lord. Harden us into good soldiers for Your cause.*

Unsigned Valentines

Matthew 6:1-4   February 7
Proverbs 17:17

I found it last night, quite hidden from sight—
A valentine trimmed with a rose—
Repeating a past that rushes so fast,
Not pausing to tell where it goes...
It's yellowed with age, that single-line page,
(How I thrilled whenever it came!)
I recall my blue dress... a first shy caress...
And still love the sender the same.

J.M.B.

"I LOVE YOU!" What sweeter words ever strummed the human ear? And, yet, the world is starving to hear somebody say them. Not in a general sense. Directly to each individual. Valentine's Day is coming. What better day?

The true identity of St. Valentine remains a mystery. But it's no secret how friends and lovers celebrate the holiday the world over. The tradition dates back to Charles Duc d'Orleans who, from his confinement in the Tower of London in 1415, sent his wife rhymed love letters. And always they were unsigned!

This Valentine's Day I plan a few anonymous love notes. They will lack the bleeding hearts, lovers' knots, and turtledoves. You see, these notes are not going to my "one true love" (although he will receive one all his own). But the recipients I have in mind will be lonely persons, shut-ins, or persons who are just downright "unlovable" and probably never received an "I love you" before. Sign them? Of course not! That would spoil my fun.

To Think and Pray About: A little love note could turn a life around—particularly if it is unsigned. Jesus told us that "secret alms" pleased the Heavenly Father. Who knows where your gesture could lead? My first valentine was unsigned—and led me to the altar.

"Hallelujah!" Days

FEEL the day's falling apart? Maybe this will help.
"Aunt Emma" (we children called her) had "Hallelujah! Days."

"Why is this?" I asked. She explained that it was a "Hallelujah! Day" when the neighbors came to patch up the leaky roof of the three-room house Aunt Emma, her husband, and their two unmarried sons shared in near-poverty. It was a "Hallelujah! Day" when the tomatoes came up in the hotbed, when she finished transplanting them, when they bloomed...bore fruit...and when she finished canning them. Small things like that.

When the great events came along, it seemed to me that Aunt Emma forgot to go to bed. I could hear her singing across the fields as I went to sleep and when I woke up. The "great events" were when her boys made a profession of faith, when they took wives for themselves, and later when the wives accepted Jesus.

All this I could understand, but one thing puzzled me. Aunt Emma was deathly afraid of storms (so was I!). I was caught at her house in a thunderstorm one sultry summer day and both of us were terrified. She held me close and rocked me back and forth, singing, "...Praise Him, ever in joyful song!" She would jump when there was an element-splitting bolt of lightning, only to call out a shout of joy by the time it thundered. How could she be afraid—and happy?

"Couldn't we be struck?" I whispered.

"Not by *that* bolt!" she consoled.

To Think and Pray About: Do you feel it's possible to be afraid and happy at the same time? Would God understand if you explained your fear? Storms will enter our lives; but, so far, we've come through safely. How many, many times we are made to realize that their frightening "bolts" didn't touch our lives, after all. Try to recall a specific incident. Give God the praise and expect a "Hallelujah! Day" today!

Gifts Nobody Returns

1 Chronicles 28:9,10   February 9

WHAT IN THE WORLD was I going to take to Mrs.
Beard's birthday party? When the Bible-study group
decided we should do more than serve brownies and coffee
after class, I thought it was a poor suggestion. "She has
everything money can buy," I pointed out.

The 84-year-old lady is about the doing-est person I know
(and never mind the "for her age" bit—she can hum a ring
around the rest of us). She heads every committee and—being
a practical nurse—is the first to pop in when there's illness.
"Can't retire 'til folks quit getting sick," she says. As to her
family life: "The doctor left her a fortune but no children,"
one of our mutual friends told me. "Could be she's a little
lonely." I doubted that. But what in the world could I take?

I keep a gift list of "possibles," but nothing sounded right.
As I started to file the gift-list envelope, a note dropped out—
something somebody had tucked inside a Christmas card enti-
tled *Gifts Nobody Returns:*
- Praise for a job well done
- Consideration—offering to wear another's shoes
- Gratitude—a word, a note, a smile with meaning in it
- Inspiration—being what you want another to be
- An offer—to share a bit of your time, your heart, and your
  love willingly, behaving as if it no longer belonged to you!

—Anonymous

It occurred to me suddenly that in all the years I'd known
Mrs. Beard, I had never told her what a great job she's doing.
She and I don't wear the same "shoe size" when it comes to
committees, but couldn't I offer to give her a hand even if only
occasionally? The inspiration she has given made it easy to
write a love letter; and, true, the words I shared no longer
belonged to me. They were God's.

To Think and Pray About: How can you become a real giver
of what others will want to keep? God's gifts—wrapped in His
Love? Study the list and see in what areas you can serve most
comfortably with a willing spirit.

Let There Be Rainbows

Fill up my cup, Lord, from Your vast sky;
Bless me with showers—my cup is dry.
Let there be rainbows born of each rain
Painting the clouds with sunshine again.
Let there be laughter after each tear;
Let there be courage following fear.
When there are storm clouds over the land
And my cup's empty I'll understand
If I see rainbows born of each rain—
Painting my soul with glory again.   J.M.B.

THEY SAY you can't walk through a rainbow. But I did; at least, I stood in one for a moment—long enough to see the flip-side of the day.

"Another dismal day...We need to pick avocados... The leaves need raking..." How many ways can one complain about the weather? I exhausted them all at breakfast.

George took his dishes to the sink. "Come see the little rainbow," he invited.

The rainbow looked like a remnant of ribbon suspended from the sun-brightened cloud that hovered briefly in front of our house.

I was fascinated. "I've always wanted to stand in the middle!"

"Only if you stood on the little hill you wouldn't see the rainbow. There's a scientific explanation, but it's easier to say you'd be blinded by the sun—or looking at the clouds."

How true. When the world's bright I don't look for rainbows. Blinded by tears, I can't see them either; and yet it's those very tears that form the phenomenon which scientists try to explain and miss the glory of life's sun and showers. Suddenly, it was as if I did stand in a rainbow. You see, I'd stopped sniveling and begun smiling.

To Think and Pray About: *Lord, let us reflect the rainbow of Your promise.*

Happiness Is a Choice

NOW, *what am I going to say to him today?* I asked in half-prayer. Nothing I'd offered Mr. Smith during my twice-a-week visits had seemed to help. Circumstances were admittedly dreadful. His wife was paralyzed from a massive stroke. He'd had three major operations. They had little money and no family.

Still, they were together in the rest home, I reasoned. The State was helping. Our church kept the couple on the prayer list. Friends visited. My husband and I took care of their business needs. None of these things lifted Mr. Smith's depression. He talked of suicide—almost cheerfully when he saw my look of dismay. *So what am I going to say to him today?* I repeated on the way to the mailbox.

I tossed the mail on the dining room table and busied myself at the sink, my thinking place. Maybe I should skip today's visit. If the attending physician was unable to help, not to mention the minister, and eventually the psychiatrist, what could I do? I felt a throb in my left temple. Another headache! "I'm depressed, too," I admitted aloud and began opening the mail.

Happiness is a choice! The title almost smiled when I opened a review copy of the book. An accompanying letter from the author, Dr. Paul D. Meier, explained that the book dealt with depression and how to cope with it. The title alone seemed to be God's answer at the moment. "Happiness is a choice for me, too," I whispered.

A little later I laid the complimentary copy of the book in Mr. Smith's hands. The title caught him off guard and I saw tears fill his eyes. I reached to touch his hand. "God wants us to be happy," I said. "It's a choice He gives us." Amazingly, he smiled! So did I.

To Think and Pray About: Meditate on the title. How can you share Pascal's philosophy: "Happiness is neither within us only; nor without; it is the union of ourselves with God"?

The Seeds of Abraham

Sharp winter winds brought killing frost and took
*   away the weeds;*
And though it took my flowers, too, frost left the tiny
*   seeds.*

                            J.M.B.

TODAY our nation pays tribute to Abraham Lincoln. It seems appropriate to reflect on the simple dignity of the closing words of the former President's Gettysburg Address:

> The world will little note or long remember what we say here, but it will never forget what they did here. It is for us, the living, rather, to be dedicated here to the unfinished work which they who fought here have thus far so nobly advanced . . . that these dead shall not have died in vain; that this nation, under God, shall have a new birth of freedom . . . and shall not perish from earth.

But the world *has* remembered what Lincoln said and will long remember it. Children seemed to sense the tenderheartedness behind his actions and the words. No living creature was to suffer, he told them; and once he spent an entire afternoon trying to help them rescue a hedgehog caught fast in the crevice of a rock. Unable to pull the animal out, he walked a long way to borrow a pole with an iron hook from a blacksmith. With the instrument and a tender hand, he was able to set the little creature free. The greatness of his soul and spirit planted seeds of freedom. For "if a house be divided against itself, that house cannot stand," he quoted St. Mark (3:5).

To Think and Pray About: Do you recognize some parallels in the heritage that President Lincoln left and that of Jesus Christ before him?

Jesus, the Pattern for My Heart

WHENEVER I make an art assignment requiring a pattern, I will try to remember a story Muriel Leeson wrote for *Guideposts*. She told of expressing a desire to be a "real Christian" like one of her church leaders. Muriel's husband suggested that she make use of the "Original Christian," Jesus Christ.

Tomorrow my students will be making valentines for their parents. So I will put Muriel's idea to work.

Last Valentine's Day the children in my classroom gave up in frustration while trying to cut heart-shapes from red construction paper. I was disappointed, too. Just a few minutes before I had been as excited as they and now I was gathering up scraps and scissors, admittedly in irritation. *What did I do wrong?* I whispered. The answer showed up in *Guideposts*.

"Children, I've brought a pattern for a heart," I remember saying. "I'll hand it to Joe. Joe, when you cut a pattern, pass this to Nan." Fine. They did just that. And the pattern found its way back to my desk. There it lay—unused again.

The problem, of course, was that Joe cut his second valentine using *his* pattern (as did the others). From then on, it was downhill all the way. The children cut new hearts from the pattern most recently cut out. Results were lopsided and shapeless, bearing little or no resemblance of the near-perfect pattern I'd provided. There were tears of anguish and only a few (and I wasn't among them) discovered that the secret lay in returning to the original heart.

To Think and Pray About: Yes, this year I will provide better cutting guides. More importantly, I will remember the lesson for myself. Jesus gave us the perfect example. We must pattern our hearts from His heart. Think of ways in which you can follow His pattern. And remember that tomorrow's holiday is shaped for love! How can you love like the "Original Christian"?

How to Say "I Love You!"

February 14   1 John 4:7-12

VALENTINE'S DAY is no longer reserved for sweet-hearts alone. The idea is to let everybody you love know it! Any day that reminds us to love is worthy of celebration.

In my little-girl prayers, I begged God to fill my life with love. "Make Mama love me...Daddy, too...my grand-parents, aunts, uncles, cousins. Neighbors, too! And friends ...Make the whole world love me!"

February fourteenth was the day I set aside to see if my prayers had been answered. Each valentine said "I love you," whether the verse was sentimental or comical. Numbers counted. Cards received must, in my mind, exceed numbers sent. They didn't and I was sad—until my grandmother made me see things differently.

"It's what we *give* that counts," she said. "Your heart is a valentine when you share its love. Love grows when it's shared."

God has answered my prayers. He answered most of them before I asked. My family loves me as do my friends. My life is filled to the brim. I try to measure love and I'm unable. I need never ask for more. All this God has given because He loves me. Looking back, I realize that even then I knew His supply was unlimited—a giving kind of love that asked no valentine in return.

To Think and Pray About: "Love is a basket with five loaves and two fishes. It's never enough until you give it away"— Author unknown. Have you ever noticed how the little bits (and big chunks) of love multiply when we divide them? We need ask God for no more love than He has given us through His Son and our daily blessings. But we need to think of ways to thank Him, praise Him, and share what He has placed in the hearts of us all. It's more than enough. Deep down inside, do you ever feel that you give more daily "valentines" than you receive? Then thank God for being your source. He has given you a "valentine heart"! And its giving says "I love you."

Love's "Inside" Sticker

Romans 8:35   February 15
1 John 4:10; Jeremiah 31:3

I ♥ U. I ♥ AMERICA. I ♥ ROCK... And from there to the unmentionables. Ho hum... bumper stickers. But wait! Those are for posting on the outside for the benefit of others. It occurs to me that some *inside* stickers might be worth exploring. I could post several right onto my heart. All day and all night they would comfort me.

Be my guest. I want you to join me for a pretest:

- What do I ♥ most of all in life?
- Does what I ♥ meet all my needs?
- Does what I ♥ return my ♥?
- How long will what I ♥ last?

Now let's come up with some answers (look inside your ♥).

- I ♥ Jesus.
- Jesus ♥'s ME.
- Jesus ♥'s ME.

Forever and ever! ("...I have loved thee with everlasting love..."—Jeremiah 31:3).

To Think and Pray About: Today's suggested reading includes only a few of my favorite love verses. Check your reference Bible and see how many verses you find concerning the love of Jesus, His faithfulness, His promises, and His sacrifices so that we can know that one day we shall join Him in glory. Until then, we have the blessed assurance that once He walked as we walk, in the flesh, and He continues to walk with us through the Holy Spirit. *Love!* It's a beautiful word. Wear it close to your ♥.

Selecting the Right House

One needs a house where children can grow;
A big living room where fires can glow;
A quiet backyard where neighbors can meet
Away from the noise of the busy street;
Big front windows that let in a view,
Roses scented with early dew;
With doors that open their hinges wide
To welcome God and stranger inside.

J.M.B.

MY FRIEND Ellie and her husband own a lovely home in the suburbs—the kind one dreams about with room to walk without stepping on the dog; one bath per capita; roses that grow without mildewing—*everything!* Why then, should she call and ask if I'd like to see what she called "our house"?

Ellie swung the car expertly into a lane of traffic that led to a part of town obviously familiar to her. "I knew it was right the minute I saw it. And I kept praying that the other couple couldn't swing the loan—just sort of bossing God around, without promising Him what I'd do with the house, or giving any thought to the strangers who wanted it." She paused to look at me. "I know what you're thinking—that I should have said, 'Thy will be done,' but I was so busy fretting I couldn't sleep trying to hurry up the deal." What in the world was this all about?

Ellie smiled. "When the other couple got the house I realized I hadn't been asking for His Will at all—just mine. So I drive by now and then to remind me the Lord's Prayer does not say 'My will be done'—and I've made our house an altar."

To Think and Pray About: How do you find ways of saying "Thy will" and not "My Will"?

Leaning on the Everlasting Arms

W E HAVE a new dog named "Desi." Desi is much like our previous boxer except of a more gentle nature and inclined to be shy.

"Look!" one of the neighbor boys pointed out to his younger brother, "Mrs. Bacher's new dog is a *leaner!*"

I glanced down at Desi who was surveying the distance between herself and the cat perched on the fence across the street. She stood statue-still, the picture of bravery— leaning against my right leg with all her 60 pounds.

That night I mentioned the dog's stance to my husband. "Sure," he said. "That's her security." And since then I have observed that whenever there's the slightest tension (sudden noise, scolding tone, or the presence of another animal), Desi bristles but safely positions herself to lean against either George or me.

I have read that animals pick up signals from their owners. Probably. I can see why any dog of mine would be a leaner, all right. I need my family's approval, my minister's prayers, my friends' love . . . and from God I need *all* those things—and more! Without Him, I can do nothing. With His help, I am not sure I can do "all things," but I'm willing to try, knowing He's at my side offering security.

As a child I used to enjoy singing the old hymn, "What a Fellowship, What a Joy Divine!"—Elisha Hoffman. I find myself going through my day's work better when I use the chorus as a prayer.

To Think and Pray About: Whether you consider yourself a leaner or whether others lean on you, you have God as security. Lean on Him. Oh, the old hymn? It goes like this:

> Leaning, leaning, Safe and secure from all alarms;
> Leaning, leaning, Leaning on the everlasting arms!

Thank You, Father, for Your support. Let us ever lean on You!

YIELD!

THE NIGHT George and I hosted our block's Neighborhood Watch, a traffic safety officer surprised me by saying, "The chief cause of accidents within the city limits is the failure to yield right-of-way."

I wondered aloud why this would be. "I don't know," he said. "It seems to trigger a desire to race in some drivers—or to prove a point. And sometimes," he added sadly, "they're right—*dead* right!"

Today I'm paying more attention at the stoplights and the intersections, where, heretofore, I've taken it for granted that most drivers know the law. Actually, I suppose they do. It's just that they forget, get careless, or—like the officer said—feel put down when they have to surrender. Then it happened! Careful as I was, some guy revved up and roared out on his cycle right in front of me. *Who do you think you are?* ran through my mind but would be foolish to say for more reasons than one.

I realized that there are situations in life in which I push for right-of-way in my thinking. Oh, unintentionally, but I push all the same. The result's the same no matter what motivated the action. I can be *dead* right and lose a friend, wound a loved one in my family, offend the stranger who crosses my path in the supermart line. And it isn't always the driver who's injured. The victim may be the one who suffers. Thoughtlessness on my part can snuff out the "spiritual life" of someone else.

To Think and Pray About: Aren't there times when we fail to surrender ourselves to our Heavenly Father? We know His laws and His wishes. We know the consequences of guilt and remorse when we are disobedient. But when I am wrong, He never says, "Who do you think you are?" He is patient, gentle, loving, and kind. Even when I am stiff-necked, He understands. Wouldn't it follow that He expects the same of me with His other children at life's intersections? How can we make *living* right more vital than *being* right? YIELD!

The Thousand-Year Rain

T HE MINISTER finished a rousing sermon on the millennium. Troubled by the phrase "millennial reign," a small boy tugged at his mother's skirt.

"What does *millen-yum* mean, Mama?"

"A thousand years, honey," she replied.

The child frowned then let out a whistle. "Mankind! That's a lot longer rain than when Noah was in the ark!"

The doctrine of future events varies, to be sure. I was unaware just how much until our Bible study group attacked Revelation objectively. Believe me, it's a weighty subject.

In an oversimplified version, let me tell you what definitions we came up with from the literature. Be reminded that theologians debate—sometimes heatedly. No wonder the child was confused!

1. Postmillennial view: The Second Coming of Christ is *after* the millennium (an era of peace and abundance brought about by the church).

2. Amillennial view: The Second Coming of Christ is *at the end* of the Church Age (and there is no earthly millennium).

3. Premillennial view: The Second Coming of Christ will occur *before* the millennium (His kingdom lasts for 1000 years, etc.).

(Oh, there is more—*lots* more. Consult your minister, read your Bible, pray for interpretation. Today's time together with you has to do with the outcome of our study . . . and I urge you to do more than "Take a Number" on the matter.)

At the close of the study, one of our guests pinned our pastor down. "Which position do you take?" she asked. ("Pinned him down," did I say? She *tried* to and failed.)

"Our church has a position, but I go beyond it," he smiled. "I take a *pan*millennial view—meaning that whatever God has in store will all pan out!"

To Think and Pray About: Praise God for His promises, just and true, paving the way to Eternity. And, yes, it will all "pan out" when He reigns in our hearts.

Birthday Hope

February 20   2 Samuel 23:3,4
Psalm 146:5

A FRIEND whose home is in a snowbound place sees a dripping icicle as the first hint of approaching spring. "February, the birthday month, is truly a month of hope," she wrote in yesterday's letter, "no matter which days we observe the anniversaries!"

Ah, spring. Soon we'll be enjoying warmer days and green, grassy slopes. We await with joyful expectancy the blossom-laden boughs of trees and bushes and the bright yellow trumpets of daffodils popping up for the first glimpse of the warming sun.

The letter set me thinking how absolutely vital hope is in our lives. Does anything wonderful happen without the precedent of hope? No matter how buffeted we are by the wintry storms of life, there is ever with us the hope of spring, the birthday of a brighter season. God promised in the beginning that "While the earth remaineth, seedtime and harvest, and cold and heat, and summer and winter, and day and night shall not cease" (Genesis 8:22).

To Think and Pray About: Have you read this beautiful inscription on Washington's tomb?

> Washington, the brave, the wise, the good,
> Supreme in war, in council, in peace.
> Valiant without ambition, discreet without fear,
> Confident without presumption.
> In disaster, calm; in success, moderate; in all,
> himself.
> The hero, the patriot, the Christian,
> The father of nations, the friend of mankind,
> Who, when he had won all, renounced all,
> And sought in the bosom of his family and of nature,
> retirement,
> And in hope of religion, immortality.

February's Silence

Ecclesiastes 3:1-13   February 21

The earth seems hardly breathing—its heartbeat is so faint—
The river's tongue is silent . . . all's ice-bound in restraint.
February's resting in white hands of the frost
And though there is no motion, its pulse has not been lost.

                                                    J.M.B.

"HEAVEN is under our feet as well as over our heads," (*The Pond in Winter*, Walden). Walk in the snow in reality or in memory . . . muse . . . marvel . . . meditate in the pristine silence; knowing that our silence is pleasing to God.

What could be more beautiful than the "white heaven" we walk upon? The snow's beauty alone would be enough to praise God for, but there's much more! The vast prairies seeded with winter wheat, the apple orchards which ache to bloom, and the tall snowcaps preparing to irrigate the valleys in the spring thaw, need the snow's protective blanket tucked beneath their chins. It holds the sun's warmth to the breast of the earth until time for them to rise to their calling.

Furry woodland creatures whose heartbeats are slowed for hibernating need the covering of the snow. Tulips and daffodils, too, need rest, so walk with caution! They are light sleepers. Be careful lest you bruise a tiny crocus, so joy-filled it's unable to wait for spring.

Songbirds, too, need a winter vacation, so they have come South to bless those of us who live here. We cherish them, knowing that they, like the snow in other places, will leave us when winter is through.

To Think and Pray About: *Lord, we praise You for the silence of winter. No other season so challenges the senses. Let us rejoice that the world is at rest with You.*

Faith That Keeps Our Boats Afloat

February 22   2 Corinthians 4:18; 5:7

EIGHTH-GRADERS in my junior-high history class decided to make use of patriotic posters for one of the bulletin boards. "Washington Crossing the Delaware" centered the arrangement which they entitled "The Father of Our Country." Open House was on Washington's birthday.

As I walked by the display at the close of the evening an elderly gentleman tapped the poster with his cane. "That's what we need more of, Lass. Faith! Somebody must have known that boat would float!"

How right he was, I thought. How different the history of our country might have been had there been no crossing. George Washington took the crew across the troubled waters without a dampening of the American spirit, a cramp in the muscles of courage, or a case of hyperventilation. That must have been the first health program of the new nation. And its policy was faith. It came to me that evening as I looked at the little party with its strange three-cornered hats that I simply fail to take into account the full coverage of the policy I hold. Maybe at times I even lack conviction that I can collect. How could I doubt when faith is the root of all Christian blessings? "Believe," Jesus says, "and you shall be saved." I could live happily with that even were there nothing more. The very vision of "walking through the valley of shadow" is less startling with faith to light the dark, building a bridge across the gulf of this life, and landing me at Jesus' feet on the farthest shore. But there's more. Faith sees me through the little bumps of daily life. Faith makes me know that I have a great God. Faith never lets me sink. It keeps my eyes on the land. Faith lets me know that my boat will float!

To Think and Pray About: Praise God for faith—faith in Him, in others, in yourself, our country, God's world! Tell others. Their boats may be sinking.

A Great Imitation

Isaiah 30:21   February 23
John 13:15

YESTERDAY there was no time for baking. My husband and son made no secret of their disappointment. But there was Open House at school. Anyway, the cherry tree has no fruit for the traditional pie to celebrate our first President's birthday. In fact, it has no blooms. But a mockingbird is perched on a bare limb, singing his heart out.

I listen. Some of the bird notes I am unable to identify. But I recognize the call of a lark. And there! Unmistakably there is the loving coo of a mourning dove.

We are told that the head only reproduces what the heart creates. I guess the fellow on that lifeless-looking limb is a good illustration. No song of his own; but he can follow the leader happily.

I move from the window, searching the pantry shelf for a can of cherry-pie mix. My family will expect the dessert to make up for last night's transgression. And I think, as I open the filling and pour it into the pastry shell, of the patterns set down by some of the great men before our time. Specifically, I think of Washington. His victories, with final triumph, were bought with sacrifice and bitter strife when he crossed the ice-clogged Delaware in the picture my class hung up for Open House. What was the cost of Washington's answer to freedom's call? It was to strive, to endure, and to strive again . . . leading the way to "freedom's holy light." Isn't that what God asks of us all?

I set the pie in the oven. I can never be so great. But I can "imitate." I am thankful for such models. They lead me to better understand the true meaning of following the greatest Leader of all! Come to think of it, my out-of-a-can pie is not the real thing; but my men don't require perfection. Neither does God.

To Think and Pray About: We have great leaders. How can you and I be great followers? *We would imitate You, Lord, all the way!*

Need of Contrasts

*If the world had known no winter and the time were
    always spring,
Would we watch the birds fly over; would we listen to
    them sing?
If our hearts had known no sorrow and our bodies known
    no pain,
Would there be the same rejoicing as when lives are whole
    again?
If the earth had seen no storm clouds or perhaps there
    were no night,
Would the sunshine of the morning fill our souls with such
    delight?
Life, it seems, has need of contrasts and my heart with
    rapture thrills
When on dark days I remember every valley has two hills.*
                                            J.M.B.

MY FRIEND Betty dropped by this morning—a welcome
burst of sunshine. I had "cabin fever" just because
a day's rain had deprived my husband and me of our daily walk.

Now Betty's family has undergone a series of crises. Their
younger daughter suffered Guillain-Berre (polyneurities). There
has been a death in the family and a separation of another
daughter from her husband. Through it all, Betty has kept her
courage and her faith—doubled them, in fact. "Contrasts
help us appreciate," she says.

I looked up at the leaden sky—such a temporary thing, so
inconsequential. How could I let a series of small storms spoil
my conviction that only a thin layer of clouds separates me
from the sun? And then it occurred to me how fortunate we are
that God sends us a variety of friends, too, His ambassadors of
peace and good will.

To Think and Pray About: Let us give God praise for people
He sends to brighten our lives and double our faith because of
life's contrasts.

Measuring a Miracle

THE VERY MENTION of the word *miracle* was exciting to me as a child. I stood in wonder and awe at the stories that nobody could explain away. One by one my funny, little childhood friends (fairies, elves, Santa Claus, and the Easter Bunny—in that order) took their rightful places in the world of make-believe. They had been fun, but I felt no pain at their departure. It was like putting away my dolls. But miracles were different. They were my real world!

Small wonder then that I didn't restrict my definition of miracles to the accounts in the Bible—although they were my first loves. I saw every good thing as a miracle God sent (and I still do!), but where I ran into difficulty was in cataloging them (Mrs. Whitney said).

"How's your toothache?" my mother would ask.

"Gone," I would say and call it one of my "minor miracles."

"Major miracles" were those in which a prayer was answered when the odds were against it two-to-one. It might be a healing, a change in a never-before-changed situation— something wished for but unexpected by others. Only *I* expected it. That was the key.

Basically, my beliefs are unchanged. They're just refined. I've dispensed with categories at the suggestion of Mrs. Whitney.

The little lady, who is ninety-fivish, spent a quarter-hour telling me how she'd sprained her ankle swatting a fly on the ceiling. Someone had seen a red, woolen blanket she'd tossed across a shrub to air, taken it as a distress signal, and come to her rescue.

"A minor miracle!" I exclaimed, meaning it.

"Young lady, miracles don't come in sizes," she replied.

To Think and Pray About: Just a twist of words sometimes can cause us to take a new look at God's ways in the world. Look around you for miracles as you go through this day.

Being Clean Underneath

I WAS at a very impressionable age when I took a mini-course in something called Charm School. At 13 one's shoulders seem to droop, one's hands feel too large for pipe-stem arms, and what is one supposed to do with long legs except tie them in a knot when seated? I clung to every word the dainty, well-groomed teacher had to say, but the answers I wanted didn't come. Now, I know that Miss Evelyn knew we girls would grow out of the awkward stage. She was more concerned with what we should grow *into*. So, she spent her time talking about good grooming and helped me to form habits which linger to this day.

"Every girl can be beautiful," she declared. (I listened then!) "And beauty begins inside." That launched her program for good nutrition and exercise. Dewy-eyed with dreams of radiant skin, a "crown-glory" of hair like Paul talks about, and teeth like freshwater pearls, I was probably the teacher's most cooperative student.

I began to feel good about myself. In my new image, I began to walk taller and some of my feelings of awkwardness went away. By the time we got around to studying about right clothes and caring for them, I was ready for a whole new wardrobe. Only that wasn't what she had in mind. I was bitterly disappointed when Miss Evelyn began with personal hygiene. But she had a way of making things come alive. She made me listen again with only a brief example.

"Mary was the prettiest girl in the senior class," she told us, "and by far the best dresser. She captured the attention of the new boy his first day of school because she wore her becoming red dress. He invited her for a soda—just once. As they talked, a dirty strap slipped from underneath Mary's short sleeve—" *Oh, how awful!* I thought. "Girls, I can't overstress the importance of being clean underneath!"

To Think and Pray About: *Being clean underneath!* Does this concept carry a message for us all?

A Stronger You

BUMP, BUMP! goes your heart. A warm glow sets fire to your cheeks and courses to your fingertips. Here he is in the flesh. The man you have waited for all your life. The man you will marry!

The courtship moves on schedule, mutual attraction blooming into interests shared. You are pursued honorably and seriously in a way that will lead to the altar, a home, and family. God brought you together!

And then He tore you apart (or so you think in your heartbreak). For suddenly the relationship explodes, leaving you torn apart inside, bitter, and unable to love again—*ever.*

Your family means well. Little brother, hurting for you, jeers and calls it "puppy love." Mother and Dad, angered, say "the scamp didn't deserve you." And your friends try (too soon) introducing you to every eligible bachelor in town. None of them know that you are ill. Yes, *ill*, so be patient with yourself. Psychologists compare "withdrawal" from love to that of withdrawal from a powerful drug. Among the symptoms may be depression, anxiety, a period of grief, and a lack of purpose in life—even wavering of a once-strong faith.

Do these emotion-packed words sound familiar: "But I didn't want it to end" . . . "I'll never let anyone get close to me again" . . . "I am unworthy, unlovable—even God no longer hears my prayers"?

Would it help you today to know that all of us experience heartbreak at one time or another, that we understand? This kind of trauma can come when one breaks with a once-cherished friend or loses a loved one through death. The symptoms are similar and the cure is the same. Rest assured that heartbreak never goes unnoticed by God. He watches and waits until the bitterness lessens. And then He puts His arms around a stronger *you!*

To Think and Pray About: Whatever the circumstances, God will heal. "It is better to have loved and lost than not to love at all"—Tennyson.

"Me First!"

FEBRUARY is drawing to a close. And, asked what song they would like to sing, school children continue to call out, "First!"

I doubt if that is the complete title, but it fits. The words go like this:

> First in war, first in peace
> First in the hearts of his countrymen...

Other than the story of the hatchet-death of the cherry tree, boys and girls most often remember George Washington as our nation's first President. And that he was.

That thought used to bother me a little. After all, General Washington had other accomplishments. And "first" is not always "best." Maybe I overstressed that point at times for fear there would develop a kind of "me first" attitude.

Then one day it occurred to me that "me first" may have its merits in some circumstances. Supposing, I decided, I got in the last word with a friend in one of those summer-storm word exchanges? "Let me be first to tell you I was wrong..." I might begin. Or, if there is a desperate need for someone to do an untidy job at home, in the church, or in the neighborhood? If I am first to volunteer my services, perhaps the others will follow my example. And that new person at church... Shouldn't I be first to offer a hand? I believe that God would have us be "me first" people sometimes.

To Think and Pray About: Yes, Mr. President, you left us a precious heritage. Your job took courage. And so will ours. Perhaps some of us are not as brave as you; but in our weakness we are made strong. You, as "Father of our Country," will remember from your Bible study that the Father of the world tells us so (Hebrews 11:34). And it is to Him we pray: *Lord, we tend to hesitate. Let us step forward and lead the line for You!*

An Unbargained-for Bonus

What do you think of when someone mentions a "bonus"? A raise in salary? Fringe benefits? Usually it's some kind of premium, gift, or dividend. But how hard did you have to bargain? We live in a day of negotiating. But God is untroubled by "fair labor practices." He goes on handing out bonus after bonus: seasonal gifts which only the ticking of His Great Clock can offer—and every four years a bonus day, unique to the month of February in leap year.

Somewhere it is snowing. Here a warm breeze blows. Both are bonuses from God who knows what each section of His footstool needs and embroiders it with the design found pleasing in His eyes. I find myself thinking that this day has a greater purpose than its "divisible by four" explanations. Maybe God sets it aside for us to use in meditation, observing His ways in nature wherever we are.

And so I go down to the sea where the wind moves among the palms. One by one they fan themselves, sigh, settle back to silence; and the wind goes back to the sand. Ahead lies a silver dune waiting to be climbed and beyond that the restless blue of the sea. I climb, looking down on the tufts of grass that keep the dune from being bald. Low tide has left a wide stretch of hard, white sand lightly tinted by the sea's vegetation. From California through Washington, Florida through Maine, and along the Gulf of Mexico, our country has over 50,000 miles of shoreline. How many will walk this way today collecting shells and driftwood and fail to see God's purpose?

To Think and Pray About: Treasure the work of the Master Designer and give praise for this bonus day.

> The trees in white prayer lift their hands this silent
>   winter day;
> They seem to know though smooth the snow that
>   God has walked this way.   J.M.B.

Let Me Slow Down, Lord

Let me slow down, Lord, so that I see;
The bud of a rose, a nod of the tree;
Laughing of children in innocent play;
The brightness of morning and closing of day.
Let me slow down, Lord, so others may see
Your Perfect Example shining through me.

J.M.B.

LORD OF HEAVEN AND EARTH, we stand on the doorstep of spring. New sap rises in the hidden root transforming winter's stark, misshapen things to Your intended shapes. Ancient trees—old, crooked, and bent with the years—reach fragrant arms to welcome the homecoming songbirds whose golden voices bring us Your message: "It is spring!" *Let me slow down, Lord, so I can hear.*

I know, Lord, that no blind force brings forth this beauty from barren sod. The same Mind which sowed the stars in the Milky Way of Your heaven has planted the earth with tiny seed and made them grow, has breathed new life into each lifeless limb and petaled it with blossoms and new leaves, and has changed a world of cold indifference into a garden of love. *Let me slow down, Lord, so I can see.*

I see Your signature on the eternal hills. The forest moves. The crayoned walls of the canyons echo with mighty rivers emerging from their ice-locks and rushing out to sea. The clouds back away from the peaks whose time-layered hands reach up to touch Your face. *Let me slow down, Lord, so I may feel Your presence.*

And, please, Lord, free my heart of winter's indifference. Release the ice-locks within me. *Let me move toward you slowly, Lord—slowly because I am bringing another along.* Amen.

The Message

Snowfields look thinner since yesterday;
Birds call shyly, not sure what to say;
Velvety buzz of first bumblebee...
Winds awaken every young tree...
Eyes of the mountains and valleys below
Flutter green lashes...
And God whispers, "Grow."

                                              J.M.B.

NOTHING STIRS. The earth is breathless... weight-less... motionless... "without form and void." And then there is light, faint at first, but enough to bring a jack-in-the-pulpit from beneath a sun-warmed stone. The hickory nut tree dons a wig of catkins... a lilac uncurls its purple fist... and the chirp, twitter, and mating calls of wild things turn winter into spring. The earth takes shape, breathes, and moves again.

   Although spring comes on wary, hesitant feet in some sections, there's a growing feeling in the air these days. Go outside. Inhale and you'll sense it. Does it occur to you that the return of spring is like the first act of Creation? Three long months the earth continued its circled orb of a sun which buried its face in a blanket of clouds. But now there is a band of brightness and the warm, energetic fingers of returning sun probe the dark places, shooing out the cold. Clouds tiptoe to the mountaintops and vanish. It is a daylight world of faith and courage. Doubt, fear, and dread (all born of darkness) are gone.

To Think and Pray About: Is it not the same in our spiritual lives? God is the Light which transforms the unknown into the known. His love dissipates the clouds that obscure our vision. Praise Him for the sunlight of His love. Listen! Did you hear Him say "Grow"?

Chatting with Our Lord

HELLO! I have a little springtime gift for you. May I come inside your heart to present it?

Don't stop your work, worry about the newspapers on the floor—and, most of all, don't worry about grammar and sentence structure. You don't have to be clever to please, but I would like to have you talk to me—and love me. I'm your closest neighbor, you know.

Just talk to me as you would talk to anyone else of whom you are very fond. Tell me the names of persons you're concerned about and I'll speak to my Father about them. I want to know their needs. Just show your love for them and for me by trusting me to do what I know is best.

Are there any poor people in this neighborhood? What about widows and orphans? And I want to know about the sick and the sinners, for I have good news for them.

And what about your own needs? Have you lost a loved one, damaged a friendship, or had a misunderstanding with a stranger? If it's easier, you can make a list of your needs and read them to me. I'll understand. Just tell me about your little shortcomings. Are you sometimes afflicted with pride, touchiness, selfishness, meanness—maybe even laziness? Don't be ashamed to confess.

Tell me about your plans. Is there a job that looks too big? A person you have trouble pleasing? Someone you need to do something special for? I can help you meet those needs.

And tell me about your failures. I can show you the cause. What is worrying you? Who has caused you pain? Talk about it all. Tell me you are sorry. Tell me you are willing to forgive and forget. I will bless you!

And, oh, I do want to know about your joys! Tell me about your happiness. Show me your gratitude. The gift I promised? *Love!*

To Think and Pray About: Imagine that Jesus enters your home for just such a visit. Can you arrange a talking-prayer response?

Learning to Live (by Losing)

I ALWAYS like the writings of the "Quaker poet." He was a reformer at heart, fighting social wrongs of whatever kind. Yet today the poems in which he expressed social conscience are but a memory. Maybe that's one reason I passed them along to my son.

From the "Hickory, Dickory, Dock" rhymes, Bryce went to some of my favorites. I took a secret pride that he committed to memory all 11 stanzas of Whittier's "In School Days."

Gradually, though, as Bryce grew older, he lost interest in poetry—even Whittier's sacrificial narrative of the little girl who spelled the word in a spelling bee and (tearfully) had to pass to a higher position in line than the boy who was her friend. Bryce had other interests in high school. One of them was chess.

The campus chess club was a service organization. Its members participated in civic activities; and Bryce took to visiting the Senior Citizens' Center and playing with the older members there. He matched wits with some fine minds and was proud of his accomplishments there. As he moved towards the top of a tournament, he clipped newspaper articles which gave the scores and posted them on his bulletin board with pride.

Then one evening Bryce came home looking ready for tears. He must have lost, but tears? He hadn't used them for years!

"It's not what you think," he said. "I have to play a man who's dying of cancer—and I plan to 'lose' like in Whittier's poem."

To Think and Pray About: What is your definition of "winning"? How do you think you can win for Christ by losing to others when the need arises? Nobody loves a loser? God does!

Let's Go Fly a Prayer!

Psalm 123:1   March 5

ONCE A YEAR here in Escondido, California, we observe Kite Day. Young and not-so-young gather in one of the shopping centers to enjoy the all-age sport. There are kites that fly high and steadily, kites that fly low and fast, kites that lift... tail-less kites... kites with tails... strong, delicate, shaped in squares, circles, diamonds, triangles, rectangles, hexagons, trapezoids, and shapes I'm unable to pronounce. There are kites made of paper, silk, plastic, nylon, polyester, bamboo, wood, or combinations of those materials for Kite Day.

Last March our local newspaper made quite a to-do about the annual festivity. Maybe it was all the publicity which attracted Frank Oberman, an expert on kite facts, to visit. He told the history of kites to children who clustered around him. Then he suggested that they do as the Korean children do: print their names and birth dates on the faces of the kites and send them up with a wish. Locally, the children were excited as the playful wind caught up their wish-bearing kites. They held onto the silk lines (the kites' last ties with earth), their eyes lifted intently heavenward where their names were suspended.

"Now!" Mr. Oberman called. "Let out your lines! Lift up your eyes! It's a wonderful day. Let's go fly a wish!"

The kites climbed until their strings played out. The wish-flyers had a choice of reeling in their strings and retrieving their wishes or letting the kites go up into the vast blue where (according to the myth), the wishes reached Sky's Answering Service.

To Think and Pray About: It's good for me to be caught up in a moment such as this! *How like my deeds; how like my prayers,* I thought. I must let go of my deeds if I wish to have them reach others; and I must let go of my prayers if they are to reach my Father's Answering Service. Let out your line. Lift up your eyes. It's a wonderful day to "go fly a prayer!"

The Process of Spring

March 6

Psalm 104:30,31
2 Corinthians 4:16

To cultivate a garden we must uproot each weed
And prune the branches gently lest blossoms go to seed.
To make a heart more lovely we must do much the same,
Removing pride and envy selfishness and blame.
Thoughts flourish like the flowers and one day will unfold
With fragrant joy and beauty as great as hearts can hold.

J.M.B.

THE ALMOND TREES have come alive! Their branches are strung with feathery, pink blossoms. The air is loud with bees. A spring-sweet perfume—light and elusive—rises up to greet the new season. The scene, so Genesis-fresh, brings with it the promise of harvest. This is what my grandmother would have referred to as a "fruitful spring."

I look upon those old almond trees (they are the senior citizens of the orchards in temperate climates) and wonder who planted the kernels and who grafted or budded the sweet-almond branches onto the bitter-almond stock. Who watered them and fed them? Some thoughtful person . . . and yet, on a day like this, one just has to know that we who live upon this planet only tend God's garden, a garden whose process began before mankind was created. And then hearts such as mine rejoice that we are a part in a plan so great, a part so great that we have dominion over it all.

As a child I used to think that spring happened suddenly. Now, I know that spring emerges gradually, as new as dawn—and as old. And inside our hearts there is a newness of life and an oldness of promise. We, like the trees, will emerge triumphantly as we allow our Creator to graft the sweet wood of faith onto our bitter stock.

To Think and Pray About: Renew our faith, Lord. Give each heart a "fruitful spring."

Good Intentions

I T WAS our first home and we chose every board with care. My husband did most of the work, but he needed a carpenter to do the roof.

Most of the carpenters were busy on contracts, but finally one man said he would help as he was out of work for three days.

George hesitated. "That's a lot of roof in that length of time."

"This kind of shingling's easier than some. I'm able to overlap and use only one nail. We can always go back and secure shingles."

Only we didn't—not until the terrible storm.

Our toddler was watching clouds build up from his favorite picture window in the living room when he suddenly let out a shout of glee: "I'll huff and I'll puff and I'll blow your house down!" I heard the splintering noise and ran to where Bryce was pointing to what looked like millions of flying shingles. Suddenly our entire roof was gone.

We were talking about the incident recently—remembering how much it cost us in the long run. George had to lose a week's work to replace the roof. We had to buy new shingles (up in price by then). And the rain damaged the interior of our new house—"All for the want of a nail," my husband said.

To Think and Pray About: These things happen, don't they? Maybe not with nails, but with other good intentions. We nod (later we'll visit). We say, "Sorry" (later we'll make things right). Then there's a storm. How can you "nail down" relationships today? Pray!

> There's more to life than living; the two are not the
> same;
> For life means deeds of kindness that words cannot
> explain.
> There's more to love than loving; Altho' they're
> close, 'tis true;
> But if a heart is loving, there will be action, too.

After the Storm

I WONDER how agnostics or atheists deal with mornings like this. But then, I (a believer!) had had trouble dealing with yesterday.

Following days of drenching rain, killer floods, and general chaos, there came a freak downpour. Without warning, a black curtain of rain simply swallowed our city. I waded a lake that came to the hem of my skirt trying to find my car in the teachers' parking lot. Paperwork for the day was a total loss. My freshly done hair was soaked. I dripped in the front door to hear three children screaming like banshees (one mine, two somebody else's); a cold-nosed dog demanding dinner; and a husband who announced cheerfully that the roof was leaking in five places and the septic tank was overflowing.

"Let me in the door, *please!*" So began our evening. When my husband and I crept into bed, exhausted (at midnight), the boys were still giggling. The roof was still leaking (into pans and buckets). The rain was still raining. And the septic tank would have to be dealt with tomorrow.

I awoke with a start, wondering if once again the power had failed and our electric clock had stopped. It was full daylight, surely seven o'clock on a March day, and far too late to hope to get everybody off on a weekday morning. The clock appeared to be working, but how could it be so light at 4:30 A.M.?

I ran barefoot to the window and there hung the most breathtaking moon I've ever seen, suspended in a sky so clear that it appeared blue even in the pre-dawn. I watched in prayerful wonder until it was time to get the day on its feet. Only God could create such a day from yesterday's chaos—and put my heart back together!

To Think and Pray About: Do you think this kind of beauty follows chaos by accident? In what other ways does God, through nature, cleanse the world, the spirit? We walk through storms that strip us bare or cleanse us so we can grow again— according to our faith. God assures us that He's in charge. We can cope through prayer.

Close Your Eyes and Think about Him!

Proverbs 20:12,13   March 9
Revelation 22:4,5

"I DON'T want a recess. I want to stay inside and play," a little buttercup of a girl declared when the bell signaled a break in the second-grade reading class.

"It's like this all the time," the young teacher, whose new reading program I was observing, told me.

I could understand why. I played the game right along with the children as the teacher explained the assignment. It was an exciting experience—one which I put to use in a spiritual way in my Bible reading. Here's how Miss Zale encourages creative thinking.

"Today we'll be reading about cats," she said as she wrote the word on the chalkboard. "Now, think of a cat. Not just any cat. A very special one—special because it's your personal cat. Close your eyes and think about your cat!"

There was pin-drop silence. A creative sort of silence in which I felt a multitude of warm, friendly animals rubbing against my legs. But I was new to the game and was unable to pick out one of the imaginary kitties as my very own the way the children did.

"My cat's a Persian with tiger-colored eyes, but he sings because he loves me." That was the buttercup child.

"Mine has four white feet—like he has boots on. He only cries when I'm mean to him" . . . "Mine's kind" . . . "Mine is warm and alive." Imagination took over, all inhibition gone.

To Think and Pray About: Children are bombarded with so many pictures, which, in a sense, is having someone else do their thinking. And you and I are so bombarded by a busy world—its noise and its petty irritations—that we have too little time to think. Or maybe we let others tell us what God is like instead of taking time to seek Him in that quiet place. Today, remember how special He is—a personal God who loves you!

Positive Thoughts Should Ride Up Front

I ALWAYS admired the way Mr. Fitzsimmons drove his ancient Hudson. There was something so decisive about his manner that his bobbles seemed to be the other driver's fault. He took no unnecessary chances, but once he made up his mind to leave an intersection or overtake and pass another vehicle, he didn't dawdle. In the 28 of his 82 years I'd known him he had been involved in no accidents to my knowledge.

One day I overheard an examiner at the Department of Motor Vehicles say, "Do you wish to renew your license, sir?" It was just a routine question, but Mr. Fitzsimmons took it as an affront.

"Of course I do!" he said.

The examiner looked a bit apologetic. "It's just that—well, a lot of folk your age have given up driving. But," he smiled, "you seem to be able to stay out of trouble on the freeway."

"Sure do!" Mr. Fitzsimmons responded. "I put all my positive thoughts in front and lock negative ones in back with the spare tire!"

And that applies to more than freeway driving, I thought. Any task I undertake is much less awesome when I get my thinking straight. I'm sure that if I took an on ramp with the conviction that I was going to come home with a pleated fender, it would happen. It might anyway, but (with my thoughts under control), it's much less likely. And what about household tasks? Everybody knows you can't make pastry if you let the stuff know you're scared of it. So I put my doubts under the sink. And who would accept an invitation to church if I prefaced it by, "Now, don't be offended—"? When I put my confidence in Christ, I can put away all negative thoughts. I can behave boldly, knowing He will sustain me.

To Think and Pray About: Check your symptoms: Negative thoughts? Doubting faith? Wavering opinions? Indecisive actions? Faintness of heart? Have a talk with God. He'll help you put positive thoughts up front.

Windows of Gold

"THE WINDOWS of Gold" is a lovely old legend. It serves to remind me just where my "guiding light" is. Each morning at sunrise a small boy looked from the front window of his cabin high on a mountaintop into the gold-filled windows of a great cathedral in the valley. Some day, surely, his legs would be strong enough for him to travel the long distance so that he could get a better view.

At last he felt strong enough. "Surely," those around him insisted, "you can wait until the winter is past."

No, he could not wait. Indeed! It was the promised warmth in the golden windows below which begged him to begin his search. All day the child traveled down the rugged mountainside. He was cold and hungry. His shoes were worn thin. None of this mattered, however, for below him the welcoming beams reached out to guide his steps—until suddenly the lights went out in the church.

The boy looked around in dismay, realizing that he'd reached the valley just at sundown. He reached out to a stranger. "Please, sir," he begged. "Can you help? I've lost my guiding light. Can you show me where the Golden Windows are?"

The stranger touched his hand gently. "It is dark here in the valley. You must look to the mountaintop for the windows of gold."

The boy raised his eyes and there in his own front window high above he saw the last rays of the setting sun reflected. "I need not have searched," marveled the small boy as he turned toward home.

To Think and Pray About: God the Father is our Guiding Light. We need never travel to far, distant places to see His bright glow. It is just a breath-of-prayer away. The glorious message is that He is sending out His search light morning, noon, and night. We need but follow. *Father, thank You for Your always-shining light. May each of us reflect it.*

Thankful for an Appetite!

"THIN IS IN" the television commercial sang out. A certain health club was promising instant weight loss (they never said how). The point I found depressing was their reassurance to the listening audience that they would no longer crave food. "As a matter of fact," the announcer said glibly, "you won't feel hungry because you will lose all desire for food." *How awful!*

In our family, mealtime is special, a time of togetherness. A time for placing the day and our lives in God's hands. And a time for enjoying the bounty of this wonderful land. Breakfast would lose its excitement without our orange juice, English muffins spread with my mother's special marmalade, and our briskly-perked coffee. Lunch is sometimes a scattered affair; but come what may, we're together at dinner again, relishing every mouthful from crisp salad through a favorite dessert!

I look with pride upon a well-appointed table with flowers in season. I enjoy feeding my family and eating with them (even when it's leftovers). How dreadful it would be if they came to my carefully prepared meals and said, "Sorry. No desire for food."

Personally, each time I give thanks for the food which the Heavenly Father provides, I add another "Thank You" for the appetite to enjoy it! I know that God would want me to eat moderately and to curb an appetite which went out of control, but I think that pleasure in food is one of His bonus gifts.

To Think and Pray About: Are you grateful for the appetite God gave you? Think about it and then ask yourself: *Am I grateful for my appetite for spiritual food?* Without it we would starve, you know. Thank God today for the physical appetite which provides a means to nourishment and a "togetherness" time with family and friends. Thank Him for the spiritual appetite which allows you to feed upon His Word. We know He feeds the hungry.

Hidden "Lint Traps"

"HOW LONG has it been since you cleaned this lint trap?" That's my husband during an inspection of my washing machine which developed a wheeze in mid-cycle.

How long? That's me—thinking. Aloud, I answer question with question: "Was I supposed to? Do washers have them—like dryers?"

You know the look I received if you're the wife or the friend of a do-it-yourself man. You know they're very thorough. Very exacting. Very apt to find the trouble with household appliances. *And* the user!

George reads every instruction book from cover to cover the way I read a good novel. He tests every nut and bolt before plugging a piece of equipment into an electrical outlet. Then, when an appliance wheezes, rattles, or balks, he knows what to look for.

I watch in fascination as he expertly reaches toward an innocent-looking tray (existence of which I knew nothing) and pulls. *Maybe just this once he'll be wrong.* He isn't, of course. A fat ball of gray fuzz testifies to that.

Now, if I had read the instruction book, I would have known where the lint trap was and that it required emptying in order for the machine to get its breath. When a filter's clogged, the washing machine is unable to do its job. Hence, the wheeze; and hence, the services of a well-paid repairman had George not been watching out for such emergencies.

My husband replaces the part and the machine spins away merrily. All of us are happy. But I make a mental note to empty the little gadget as soon as this load of laundry is finished.

To Think and Pray About: How many hidden "lint traps" do you suppose we have inside that need emptying? There's so much in our lives that needs daily filtering. God's Word is our instruction book. With daily prayer let's empty the "fuzz" that clogs our spiritual lives. Emergency? The Lord is our repairman!

Tuning In

March 14   Matthew 11:15

EACH TIME I twist the little "on" knob on my portable radio, I'm mystified. It seems incredible that somewhere out there a giant transmitting system is beaming messages that make no sound until I tune in. I was baffled by it all when I took a survey course in physics. I'm still baffled. The professor explained the relationship between something called "transmission of desired intelligence and reception by an appropriate antenna system." All those signals are busy day and night—bombarding each other through space, just waiting to bring me the latest news, words of wisdom, and soothing music. There's so little I have to do. And yet it's essential that I turn the little knob. Otherwise, for me, the signals have gone to waste.

There was a time, before television took over, when a radio kept our family in tune with the world. We set our clocks by it. We listened to the morning news at breakfast and to the evening news before retiring. I remember with what care my father selected a tall antenna that he teasingly said would "reach out and grab the programs before they went into the neighbors' boxes." My little radio has a built-in antenna, of course, but the need for the knob remains.

Sometimes when I'm listening, especially to a particularly inspirational program, I close my eyes and think of all the signals that God is sending my way. His is the greatest "transmission of desired intelligence" the world has ever known. Thoughtfully, He equipped us each with a marvelous built-in antenna. We can reach Him day or night by turning the knob of our hearts and letting His presence enter. Otherwise, all those wonderful things He has to offer are like those meaningless signals which are trying to reach me and failing—until I switch to "on."

To Think and Pray About: God has a message for you! Tune in today to His "morning news" to start your day and to His "evening news" just before falling asleep. And set your clock by His time for tomorrow.

In the Beginning Was the Word

I STOPPED in to see Sadie, my 90-year-old friend, yesterday. She always makes me feel good about life. Yesterday we talked about literature.

"I never heard of a 'nonreader' in my day," Sadie told me. "The teachers expected us to read and we read. Good literature, it was—like *Aesop's Fables*, *A Tale of Two Cities*, and *The Ancient Mariner*. We had to memorize a lot, too—little phrases that come back to me unexpectedly to light up the corners of my mind."

My friend's eyes sparkled. "I go on like Tennyson's *Brook*, don't I just? But that's the idea. An *analogy*! I wouldn't think thoughts like that or appreciate them from other people unless I'd been exposed to the original."

Unless I'd been exposed to the original. I latched onto the phrase and brought it home with me. There are so many ways of becoming nonreaders, only one of which is improper grasp of reading skills early in life. Faulty habits tend to develop— skimming newspapers, letting church literature pile up, or skipping our "reading assignments" in the Bible. Assignments? Yes, they are. God wants us to be avid readers. He, like the teachers of old, expects it of us. He wants us to be exposed to His "original."

To Think and Pray About: God has prepared an entire library for our minds to grow on—history, adventure, discovery, love stories—all with "happily-ever-after" endings, based on His promises. It is important for us to read and to commit some key verses to memory so that the bright prisms can fall into a meaningful design in a gloom-filled moment. It is important, too, to be able to enrich our lives with analogies, similes, and parodies taken from God's Word—being ever conscious of those which might be used erroneously. Like my friend Sadie, we need exposure to the "Original." Think of ways in which you might improve your reading habits today. Your Father will be so proud of you!

Binding Up Wounds

I WAS only four years old when Cornelia introduced me to her doll "Flora." Maybe the little girl will forgive me for remembering the doll better than its owner. The doll's medical history intrigued me.

"Flora," eight-year-old Cornelia said that Sunday afternoon my parents were visiting hers, "show our new friend your scars."

"She's my very favorite doll," Cornelia explained as she gently removed the small china figure's dress. "She was broken into a jillion pieces when she fell off the shelf. I cried and cried—till Daddy told me to stop crying and start looking for the pieces so he could put her together again!"

It was a beautiful story, I decided, even before I saw the magical job Cornelia's father had done with glue. "Flora doesn't look busted," I marveled, for there were hardly any scars at all.

"You needn't be so careful," Cornelia smiled when she noticed how cautiously I held the doll. "Flora's stronger than the rest of my doll-family since Daddy glued and bandaged her. She's all healed. Daddy's a good fixer-upper." There was pride and love in the little girl's eyes for a father who had healed her toy and heart.

Sometimes in life I'm a Flora, I think. I say that because I'm prone to fall off shelves. And when I break into "a jillion pieces," I need a loving Father to bind up my wounds. Afterwards, I am stronger than before.

And sometimes I'm a Cornelia. I see a loved one who is suffering from compound fractures sustained from everyday living. I want to cry and cry—until I remember that if I'm going to help, I must stop crying and help pick up the pieces. God will attend to the rest. He's the best "fixer-upper" the world has ever known!

To Think and Pray About: God sent His Son to bind up the brokenhearted. How can you help others know of His Love?

Spring's Pattern

1 Peter 4:8-11   March 17

Trees that wear new dresses and little birds that sing
Reveal the same bright pattern God uses every spring.
If your lips are smiling and singing just a bit,
You need not search for springtime—you are part of it.
                                                    J.M.B.

TODAY is St. Patrick's Day. My Irish stew is bubbling away happily. Irish things are always happy (aren't we!). My grandmothers (both sides come from the Emerald Isle) used to say that there could never be tears in the eyes of an Irish potato. That's good. Who needs tears when the hills are wearing green?

There are a good many legends and half-truths surrounding St. Patrick. Oh, he existed; but if he said as many words of wisdom as my maternal grandmother in particular credited him with, he certainly talked a lot. She did say something about the legendary character which lingered in my mind, however—something which is good to think about whether St. Patrick or someone you and I know had the characteristic. "He had a love-touch," she said, "that caused the heart to sing."

I wonder if I have that love-touch? I wonder how many hearts I have caused to sing? We meet people who do that. We feel a certain warmth of mind and heart even after they've gone. Sometimes we read a good book that reaches out and touches us. I even recognize these people when they're actors in a fine performance. I laugh with them and I cry with them. I've felt this love-touch in the hands of a nurse's aide. I've sensed it in my mail carrier's voice. I've heard it in my minister's prayers...a child's laugh...a friendly "Hi!"

To Think and Pray About: The "love-touch" came from God. Wouldn't this St. Patrick's Day be a nice time to pass it on and cause some heart to sing?

Leprechauns Mustn't Be Thanked!

March 18   Romans 15:1-7

I T BEGAN the day I came home from the hospital, wondering how we'd manage until I was on my feet. Dinner, for instance. But there beside the front door sat an enormous pot. "Stew!" my husband declared without looking, for no lid could restrain the odor of herbs.

"Good eating!" George read the unsigned note beside the pot.

"Leprechauns do things like that," our son (the believer) told us. "They never sign their names. Just put the empty pot back."

The next day there was a fat apple pie and on the third day there was a big bouquet of garden-fresh flowers. The anonymous donor knew we had no need for a main dish or dessert.

After we'd polished off the leftovers, George scrubbed the containers and wondered aloud how to return them. Bryce, wise to the ways of the "wee people," set the pot and pie tin outside the door. He was unsurprised when, instead of picking the containers up, they refilled them with chili and apricot cobbler. By the time we'd licked the platters clean, I was up and about. It was I who set the utensils out and tucked in a "Thank you!"

"You shouldn't have," Bryce said sadly. "They'll not be back."

"They've met our needs, whoever they are," I told him.

"Does he believe that stuff?" George asked with concern. Three days later his question was answered. A young couple moved into the house next door. As I watched the moving van unload, I spotted a small figure climbing the fence between their house and ours. In his arms was a basketful of tangerines from our tree. He wore blue jeans and a familiar T-shirt with a "B" on the back; but I was sure the note he carried was not signed. Now I'm doubly indebted to those kind people whose name I may never know. They gave our son a greater gift than they know. To this day he "gives in secret."

To Think and Pray About: Do a secret kindness today. Discuss the value of silent "need fillers."

Return of the Swallows

"They'll be on time," the children said
Though winds blew strong from clouds of lead.
Against the storm the swallows flew
Arriving as they always do.
How much alike the child and bird,
With faith in things unseen, unheard.
The sky's so wide; their wings so small;
Yet neither questions God at all.

J.M.B.

YES, the swallows have come back to Capistrano. They've nested in its ruins (and partial restoration) since the 1782 earthquake here in California. Watching the little feathered creatures, so fragile and yet so sure-of-flight, brings a lump to the throat of the onlooker. As I watched them sweep down gracefully one St. Joseph's Day, I thought: *All these tourists with cameras believe the swallows will come; but it's the little birds that have the fire of faith in their tiny hearts.*

Sort of a disturbing thought. It was a picture-perfect day, just right for flying. But I remembered other March nineteenths that were far less favorable—days when grumbling spectators said, "They won't make it..." "I'm tired of waiting..." or, on occasion, "Who cares about birds?"

God cares. He cares about the sparrow, so He cares about the mission-dwelling swallows. And we know how much He cares about us, His children. How, then, could we let the fire of faith burn low and finally turn to ashes? It is good for me to remember this when I tend to question or demand proofs as if God's love were some geometry problem needing a corollary.

To Think and Pray About: It was Joseph Fort Newton who said, "Belief is truth in the mind; faith is fire in the heart." *Lord Jesus, give us the faith of the child and the bird.*

The Bridge that Leads to Heaven

THE WINTER FLOODS in California have been devastating. Residents watched rich, fertile farmlands washed out to sea as dry riverbeds became roaring bodies of water.

Sightseers were asked to stay away from the flooded areas so they wouldn't hamper rescue units. However, there were a number of vantage points from which we could survey the damages. One of the points was a rocky avocado-clad hill which overlooked a dam just outside our city. From there, I watched the murky water below rising and falling—almost angrily, it seemed—towards houses in the lowlands. What means, I wondered, could the Red Cross and Disaster Units employ to get aid in or the residents out? No boat would test such rapids surely.

And then I saw an arching bridge, built high by some far-sighted engineer. It was shaped like a rainbow; and, remembering God's ancient promise, I took comfort in seeing that bridge. God said our world would never be destroyed by water again and He sealed that promise with a rainbow. The people below me would walk on that bridge. The flood waters would recede. Skies would clear and, once again, there would be so much to be thankful for.

To Think and Pray About: One of the blessings we can all be thankful for is the Holy Spirit, sent by God, our Father, as a "bridge over troubled waters." God knew when He took His Son back to Their heavenly home that we would have need of this Presence in our lives. Have you ever considered how wonderful it is that we can walk out, unafraid, knowing that we are never alone or unattended as we move toward the "other shore"? Nothing can quench God's eternal love. Nothing can drown it. Shouldn't we thank Him for His promises and their fulfillment? How will you apply them to your life today? *Father, we know that floods will come into our lives, but we thank You for an avenue of escape. You are the engineer who provides us with a bridge in troubled times. We praise Your name!*

Believing in a Spring

I love the things of nature that zig-zag in the blue:
Birds—and wings of lightning, for storms are
*   nature's, too.*
I do not hide from sadness; I know it has to be
For it's a part of wisdom that God has given me.
My tears are only showers like nature sends the rain;
And then a rainbow tells me the sun has shone again.
                                                    J.M.B.

THE PLANET EARTH stops snoring, turns over slowly, and shows its face to those of us in the northern hemisphere. Warmed by its direct beams, we flex our muscles and stretch ourselves out full-length—body and soul. It, then is good to say "I told you so!" to those who said spring would never come.

If I didn't trust spring to come with its wonderful sameness year after year after year, I'd be admitting that I denied the whole life process. And if I did that, wouldn't I be erasing all God has taught me—His promises, His loving concern, even God Himself? For one of the ways God reveals Himself to the human race is through nature. Those who understand and appreciate nature—its seasons and its processes—are understanding and appreciating a bit of their Creator. It's sort of the subconscious leading to the conscience He also equipped us with. God reveals Himself in so many wonderful ways in the Bible, where often His teachings are enriched with lovely nature-thoughts. And, finally, He reveals Himself to us fully through the gift of His Son.

To Think and Pray About: As the sun reaches the equator today, winter officially ends. For this brief day, day and night are equal; and, then, the vernal equinox marks the stretching out of our days.—It also marks the stretching out of our spirits toward the glory of Easter, God's greatest promise fulfilled— giving us love, triumph over death, and eternal spring.

When Embankments Are Steep

I HAVE a skinned knee, a bruised elbow, and a pair of snagged nylon hose. Besides, I have a skinned, bruised, and snagged ego. I slid down a hill yesterday because I refused help which was right under my nose (on which I landed).

It happened on one of those divided downtown streets—a steep one. I took a handful of daffodils to an ailing friend and proceeded on foot to the post office.

"That side of the street's narrow," my friend cautioned.

"No problem with the steep and narrow," I assured her.

"Why don't you use—"

Caution, I was sure she'd say. I just waved and turned uphill.

Wow! The street *was* narrow. And it would be impossible to see an oncoming car. I decided it was wiser to go over the embankment to the broader street below. I stepped into the grass (taller than I thought—and slippery), lost my footing, and landed at the bottom. It was there that I discovered a nice, wide set of concrete steps leading right down beside where I had slid.

Foolishly, I realigned my branches and limped home. But, on the way, I did some thinking. How like me to go my own way without waiting for a well-meaning friend to so much as complete a sentence. And how like me to go my own way in little everyday things when I should seek some advice from God. He has planned this world so perfectly that I know He remembered to add "steps" that allow us to go up and down life's steep embankments with a little more grace.

To Think and Pray About: By the time I reached home, I was smiling at my childish behavior. I had a feeling God smiled with me—and that He knows I will try to avoid some of life's needless hurts today. But I wonder why we veer off without so much as looking right or left for all that He has prepared for us? Today, as you approach little inclines (whether you're going up or down), ask God to show you the steps He has provided.

Faith Can Begin with a Recipe

James 3:17   March 23

EMILY CALLED early this morning. "Heat up the coffee," she said. "I've finally mustered the courage to try Great Aunt Tilda's Scripture cake!"

My friend trotted across the lawn leaving a trail of spiced smells. The cake was delicious. "Why would you hesitate to bake this?" I asked.

"At first I didn't want to look up all the references," Emily smiled. "My aunt brought the recipe from Europe and said all the makings are in the Old Testament. We were to read for ourselves!"

Understandable. But I was sure there was something else and there was.

Emily held a forkful of the feathery spice cake up. "Any idea what 'Judges, Jeremiah, and Samuel' cost by the cup these days?" (The ingredients translated into butter, eggs, and honey and yes, I *did* know about costs.) "Not to mention the other ingredients..."

As Emily chatted about the recipe's inclusion of exotic spices, dried fruits, and chopped almonds, I could see the figures running up on the cash register. "A very expensive cake."

"Well, yes—but there's more than price. I was afraid the cake would be a flop. All that money from the week's grocery allowance—and Joe mad at me—you know?"

Instead, there had been instant success. And any husband would welcome the dessert. Emily was fairly glowing. "She couldn't have known about mixes and how much Joe detests them. Still, I wonder if Aunt Tilda didn't want me to develop some faith in myself?"

To Think and Pray About: Life offers so many opportunities to exercise faith and to develop more than we have. God's Word is a book of faith. Like my friend, we need to turn to the Scriptures. Ponder this: *Fear knocked at the door. Faith answered. No one was there*—Old English legend.

Signs of Spring

March 24   Matthew 5:14-17

Spring crept through my window,
Perched upon the sill,
And kindled flames of yellow
Upon a daffodil.

J.M.B.

HOW DO YOU KNOW when spring is "just around the corner"? Some people chart temperatures and declare that winter's ending when the mercury climbs to 60 degrees for three straight days. Others watch weather maps or listen to forecasters; and, of course, the most common expression is "Watch for a robin." My father used to test the bark on an elm branch. If it would slip off to expose a smooth, white limb beneath, it was "bleeding with sap." My grandmother used to say she knew it was spring because folks were "feeling the gypsy urge." Those were the days when rural people were more nomadic than they are today. I don't know why we feel a need to look for "signs," but it seems that we need to document things in order to proceed to the next step.

Maybe that's good. I recall so vividly all the activity around my childhood home once we decided it was spring. There were new fields to plow, feather beds and winter woolens to air, lazy hens to cull, cuttings to set out, gutters to clean, and (alas!) sassafras tea for those of us who looked peaked. In short, my parents and grandparents attended to everything that had a need.

The world has changed a lot, and yet I need to see the old "signs" even here in California where only the calendar tells me it's spring. But, do I pay enough attention to the signs around me—no hope of spring, until I bring it? I'm looking at the daffodil blooming outside my window—so like the sunlight—and calculating how many bulblets it will produce. Even a bulb shared in Jesus' name would be a "sign."

To Think and Pray About: Look for a need today—and fill it!

The Anvil and the Hammer

Psalm 119:66-69   March 25

EDWIN MARKHAM was one of my English teacher's favorite writers because, she said, he could say "much in little." Sometimes when such meanings evaded us, she'd elaborate on the brief lines until they bloomed with new meaning.

"You know," she said the day she told us to memorize "Preparedness," "Mr. Markham knew we'd take many forms in this life." I read the lines:

> For all your days prepare,
> And meet them ever alike:
> When you are the anvil, bear—
> When you are the hammer, strike.

Maybe I looked puzzled for she continued: "When life's heavy with sorrow, bear it—like the anvil. When fortune smiles, strike like the hammer! This is the armor for success in the world—success of the spirit. For this is no gospel for worldly souls."

I pondered Miss V.'s words. I wasn't sure of the distinction of worldly souls . . . weren't all souls of the spirit? But I was an idealist—and I knew something about blacksmith shops. If I could bear up like the familiar anvil and strike out at all the injustice (words would be my hammer, I supposed), this world was sure to be forged into something more wonderful than before I entered it.

To Think and Pray About: Let's think of the poem in different terms. God has need of us to be anvils, but are they restricted to times of sorrow? When we feel that others have misused us, can we bear it? And must words be used only as weapons? How can we best serve our Lord in restraint? Restraint, for me anyway, would be true "success of the spirit." We know there are times when we must bear and times when we must strike out. Let's ask God for the wisdom to know the difference. I need to learn the skill of saying "much in little" in time of stress. Can you pin down your need? Pray about it.

Even an Onion Has Power!

"I DON'T WANT to be an onion," I told my teacher flatly when she announced the character parts for the third-grade play. MariJane had long, yellow curls so she would be a tulip. Felda had hyacinth-blue eyes so she would be a crocus. Iris (with such a name) was bound to be an iris... and so went my reasoning about "The Little Bulblets" skit. All would be beautiful—except me.

That was the whole point of the plot, of course. All the bulbs shared a drawer for a home and did a lot of talking about what they were going to be when they "grew up." The bulbs looked very much alike without the sprouts, leaves, and flowers they would produce one day. The little onion, dissatisfied with being an onion, said, "I'll be more yellow than the tulip, more blue than the crocus, and more purple than the iris. I'll be the biggest, the best, and the most beautiful of you all!"

Of course, the onion can never be a tulip, or a crocus, or an iris. The onion sprouted blades instead of leaves. And there was no bloom at all. So the flowers laughed, because of all the silly boasting. Embarrassed, the little onion sank down into the garden soil—too ashamed to reach its full potential, that of being a great onion.

"What's so great about being an onion?" I asked the teacher. "An onion's beautiful in its own way. It's tall, straight, and green. It has no spectacular bloom, but flowers which bloom for beauty alone can't spice foods the way an onion can," was her reply.

The onion really had the leading role and the wise teacher told me she'd assigned it to me because I could memorize the lines. That made *me* special—like the onion—and I could utilize my talent. The same God who created the lovely flowers created the lowly onion as He created you and me—each with a special power.

To Think and Pray About: There's a need for you exactly as you are—whether you're an "onion" or a "flower." God expects us to use our talents.

A "Bakker's Dozen"

Matthew 10:8,40   March 27

THERE WERE pastry shops scattered up and down the street where my cousin lived when we were children. There were big, fancy shops where the waitresses wore costumes of their native lands and there were shops which served special gourmet pastries with afternoon tea prepared especially for wealthy patrons. But there was only one Friendly Bakker's Shop. "You'll see," my cousin said secretively. "It has a *heart*."

Mr. Bakker was a wee, squat man with a foreign accent. But there was nothing "foreign" in his attitude. He wore an enormous gold-toothed smile and loved strangers as well as friends. He took my hand and showed me the back of the tiny shop where he'd worked all night baking and frosting, but it was the shape of the cookies that took my eye. "Where did you find such a cutter?" I asked.

The little man smiled. "Me heart," he said. Later I wondered if perhaps that might be true, after all.

My aunt had ordered a dozen pastries and while I tried to figure how many that would be for each of us at dinner, I noticed Mr. Bakker's error in counting. "That was 13," I told him.

"Sure was. A Bakker's dozen!"

Times were very hard. His shop was small. I'm sure Mr. Bakker had a hard time making a living. Still, it was he— not the owners of the fancy shops—who "miscounted" heart shaped cookies for little girls. It was he who left a lovely memory in the hearts of us both. God blessed him with a "giving heart" for a pattern.

To Think and Pray About: Is yours a giving heart? We're created in God's image. We know He used His own heart for a pattern when He created our hearts. In what ways does He give to you a "Bakker's dozen" each time you ask for a blessing? You can never repay (neither does He expect repayment), so think of ways in which you can give in like manner to those around you today. Make yours a giving heart for Him.

Strength to Lift a Stone

THE PLOWMAN in the old legend, "The Lifted Stone" learned a lesson worth remembering. Year after year he said to himself, "Someday I'll be able to harvest enough from this field to pay for help to move this stone." Alas! Each year his yield decreased. Weeds, grass, and bushes grew up around the enormous rock. He tried to hack them away, but the roots went deeper and deeper. Each season the circle of wasteland increased as the farmer plowed around the barrier. At last, although he could scarcely see the top of the rock, he realized that there was very little land left to cultivate.

What could the man do? There was no choice but to attempt to roll the stone out of the field by himself. He cut a path through the growth and made a way for the object which had robbed him of his rightful harvest for so long. To the farmer's amazement, he found the rock flat underneath and so light in weight that he could carry it out of the field single-handed.

So many times I've postponed jobs I dreaded because I felt they would involve more strength than I had. When I buckled in to do them I was surprised at the ease with which I accomplished the tasks. The same is true in my spiritual life. All too often I know there's a "rock" that needs to be removed and I walk around it instead. *I'm not strong enough to move it*, I tell myself. So I neglect it or wait for a committee or a study group to solve the problem. I stumble over the barrier and (worse!) I know that others may stumble over it, too. I must conquer this temptation. It is frightening to think of what might have happened had the angels thought the stone was too heavy at Jesus' tomb.

To Think and Pray About: Is there a stone that needs removing in your life? What is the first step you feel you should take? Do you walk around it, stumble over it, wait for others to do the job, or ask God to help you move it? There's nothing He can't lift!

To Gladden the Earth

My soul blesses the great Father every day that
He has gladdened the earth with little children.
                                        Mary Howitt

THE FIRE DRILL did it. We were in the midst of achievement tests and any thinking principal would ignore the
one passage in the state code that says there has to be a fire
drill every month! So what if this was the last school day of the
month? The children scattered like the Twelve Tribes of
Israel. Would I ever get them settled again?

"Get in line!" My voice was unnecessarily loud, but didn't I
have to get them shaped up before returning to the classroom?

"No talking!" The children reacted badly to my unaccustomed sharpness. Somebody in back of the line pushed. The
one ahead of him, a born clown, faked a fall. And even the
"good guys" fell domino-fashion just as the principal walked
out to check our progress.

I'm not sure why his presence angered me. No teacher, as far
as I know, was ever dismissed because children behaved like
children. I only remember seeing red; and back inside, I read
the riot act. "If you finish these assignments, there will be
more," I concluded and plunged into work myself that could
have waited like the fire drill.

Benny's hand went up. I ignored it. It went up again. I shook
my head and went on with my work.

Suddenly, he was beside my desk. "Sit down!" I whispered.
"You can see I'm busy."

But Benny, with eight-year-old perseverance, said, "This
won't take long," and placed a little note on my desk. Inside
was a lopsided heart holding the world's most treasured message: *I love you!*

Loving is our most important job!

To Think and Pray About: Thank You, Lord, for children to
gladden the heart!

A Second Opinion

A PAIR OF mockingbirds nested in my grandmother's front-yard umbrella tree (right above my swing) the spring I was seven. She and I had an exciting time watching what a bird can build with a beak, a foot—and bit of song. For a while the newlyweds worked diligently together, weaving twigs, strings, and straws into the just-right architecture for raising a family. Then, Papa Bird took to sitting on the lightning rod in the middle of the roof, singing away while Mama Bird seemed to be fussing a lot with some finishing touches to the nest.

Occasionally, Mama would call up to her mate in a scolding sort of way which he ignored—until the day of the red string! It looked like a piece of yarn from my grandmother's afghan—pleasing to my eye, but repulsive to Mama Bird's! Such a ruckus—and it went on for hours. The string in question would drop nearby my swing and Papa would retrieve it. There would be a terrible commotion. And then they would start all over.

"It's a pretty string," I said to my grandmother. "Why doesn't she want it in the nest?"

"Most likely because he did all the choosing. Or maybe because he sang while she worked. There needs to be more than one opinion when two people work together."

The little bird story had a happy ending. Mama and Papa flew off together as they used to do and brought back something they both liked. Then, without warning, Mama flew down, picked up the red string, and took it to their nest!

The real implication came home to me years later when my young husband and I set up housekeeping. I wasn't sure he appreciated it with my first telling; and there were times when I regretted sharing it. He, too, used it as an example. But compromising paid off.

To Think and Pray About: Can you think of situations when a "second opinion" has paid off for you? Let's listen to others—and seek God's way.

Joys Unopened

IT IS RAINING. Big silver drops splash my windowpane. Between the little rivulets on the glass I see the clustered lilac buds, their purple just beginning to show, pouting at the storm.

Somewhere a clock chimes the hour as it hurries toward April. *Tick-tock . . . Tick-tock . . . Sadness-joy . . . Sadness-joy . . .* Rain, with its mixed blessings, stirs the emotions of us all. Last fall it was welcome. The mouth of the earth was dry. Rain watered the late gardens. It rinsed the dusty skirts of the poppies and formed little pools for the complaining blackbirds. It hosed off the rooftops and made the gutters roar—all in a laughing sort of way.

But the rain overstayed. Grown-ups grumbled. Children, yesterday's puddle-splashers, became today's complainers. "Rain, rain, go away . . ." they chanted. The earth, once satisfied, refused to hold another drop. It peevishly spewed the water into little streamlets which rushed their burden to the brimming river, flooding the lowlands, drowning the crops, and sweeping the buildings out to sea.

I am sad for the tillers of the fields and the inhabitants of the lost buildings; but I know that the Master Architect will reshape the terrain. Though it is watered by tears of sorrow, it will bloom in joy. Every storm forms a new kind of beauty, whether the raindrops fall silently or hurl themselves against the wind. Each drop will touch an unopened bud to help God decorate His world with another spring. And so it is with our lives. We weep so we can bloom.

Gibran, in his book *The Prophet,* wrote that sadness and joy go hand-in-hand. That which causes us sorrow will be our source of joy.

Sadness-joy . . . Sadness-joy . . . The clock ticks on toward April. I look back at the lilac buds. A little more purple shows!

To Think and Pray About: As you turn your calendars today, anticipate the "unopened buds of joy." Our Lord will see that they bloom.

Give Me the Spirit of Easter, Lord

L ORD, there is wonder in my heart. I see life returning and life renewed and I marvel at Your handiwork. Something deep inside of me responds much as the winter-brown bulb responds to the new warmth of the sun. A fire is kindled in my heart, lighted by the flame of hope and faith. It is as if my being struggles to reflect Your warmth like the earth sends its warmth back to the sun. Spring's green fire of gladness lights up my soul.

This is a time of great humility, Lord, for once again You have fulfilled Your promise in a way which my human heart is unable to comprehend. Even the agnostics must feel their denial of Your existence falter. And surely the scientific-minded must find new evidence of a Force Beyond—by whatever name—in every new leaf and bird song. Humbled, can they not see spring as both a "result" and a "cause"? Resurrection in nature lies all around them, but You are the ultimate truth. "I am the Resurrection," Your Son told us that first Easter. Let those who doubt reach, like the leaf itself reaches for the light, for something beyond—and find *You.*

Your Spirit is upon the face of the earth, Lord—under the earth and below it. We feel Your presence everywhere. Perpetual youth blooms around us in the green ribbons of spring because You have shared with us its secret: *eternal life!* Even now, last year's hay is speared by fresh life from far below. Soon the hills will pasture a thousand cattle and we will know that summer is nigh. The reapers will come when autumn is at its most glorious. But the long winter sleep to follow is not death's Grim Reaper. It is only the pause for resting of the grass and the tree. Beneath is the living root waiting for the sparrow of spring. We accept with gladness, Lord, Your promise that we, too, put forth the green blade to eternity in the promise of Easter!

Bridges to the Sky

April 2   Genesis 9:13-16

Hebrews 10:23,35

The rain fell intermittently, not pausing once for sleep
(Sometimes the wind was silver-toned; sometimes 'twas hoarse
*   and deep)*
Until the storm had washed the clouds and tumbled each one
*   dry;*
Then spread them on clean bannisters of bridges to the sky . . .
We know that storms will come our way, yet there's a reason
*   why:*
When we are tossed about, we seek God's bridges to the sky.
                                                J.M.B.

MY GRANDMOTHER used to point to a rainbow and say, "That is God's bridge to heaven." And then she and I would talk about its creation in the month of sunshine and showers.

God created the earth beautiful and washed-clean. He planted the flowers, set out the trees and filled each bough with birds. How sparkling and fresh it must have been. Then Satan, through mankind, created ugliness and uncleanliness. But God, in His mercy, washed it clean again for the new generation. And with a new start, He made a promise never again to destroy the earth and all within it by flood. His sign of "good faith" was the magnificent rainbow He arched across the sky—His bridge to heaven.

And my grandmother was right, wasn't she? God's covenant, like all His other promises, has remained through the ages as a reminder of His relationship with His images, all of us who inhabit His footstool. His Bridge of the New Testament was His Son, who waits to receive us and purify us from the floods of sin.

To Think and Pray About: Imagine a rainbow! Can you see Jesus extending His hand—not with that proverbial pot of gold, but with something infinitely more precious: eternal life?

A New Image

Acts 2:28   April 3
John 16:33

Haye you heard the story about the man who shaved
off his beard and mustache as an April Fool's joke?
Bear in mind that these whiskers had been his shield for 10
years and you will understand why the joke was on him.
Alas...

- His nose looked longer than he remembered.
- His eyes were closer together than he once thought.
- He had no chin (Remember "Andy Gump" of the fun-
  nies?).
- His ears were lower than they should be.
- His face was shorter than he thought.
- He had no upper lip...

Pick any two above (and there were more) and it was easy for
him to understand why he'd grown the mask in the first place.
It was cheaper and less painful than cosmetic surgery. But:

- His children (6 and 8) asked Mother who the stranger
  was.
- His dog barked.
- His friends did not recognize him (except the creditors).
- The postman asked for the address of the previous resi-
  dent...

There is more here, too, but you get the drift. Maybe the
little story will amuse you (and doctors are telling us what the
Bible has told us all along—a good hee-haw is a painkiller!).
What's more, with all those endorphins released (the body's
natural "ease medicine"), you are conditioned to look into the
mirror, reverse the situation, and ask: "Hey, you, what would
result if I *added* something instead of shaving it off?" That
something is a smile.

To Think and Pray About: Want to cheer others today? The
best thing you have up your sleeve is your funny bone. Choose
a victim for your smile!

The Little Lost Princess

THE STORY of "The Little Lost Princess" (author unknown) touches me with each reading as it touches the children with whom I share it. A little orphan girl wove a beautiful fantasy to share with children more fortunate than herself. "I have a real father," she told her few friends. "He is much stronger and taller and kinder than any of your fathers."

"How would you know if you have never seen him?" the others scoffed.

"Oh, I have seen him! He comes to me each night in my dreams. He sits and watches over me while I sleep. He holds my hand when I'm afraid. He awakens me when I have bad dreams. He speaks to me in the still of the night and teaches me how to call out his name when I'm lonely, hungry, or afraid during the day when I'm alone."

"Likely story!" the children jeered. "If he loved you, he'd come for you."

The Little Princess was not to be discouraged. "He's waiting for me to find him. Some day I will."

In a way which can happen only in fairy tales, one night the child ventured farther into Dreamland than usual. And, calling out, she opened her eyes to find her father waiting with outstretched arms—more handsome than she had believed and far more powerful. What's more, he was a king! *If only the other children could see me,* she thought. And then she realized that it didn't matter anymore. She was surrounded by love— love which had been there all along, hers for the reaching and taking. Around her was the sound of many choruses: "The Little Princess is home!"

To Think and Pray About: Do you believe that God and His host of angels rejoice just this way when we take the step that brings us closer to Home? Perhaps it is a person who has never known the Savior—or maybe it's you, or I, as Christians who are willing to go that extra mile for the cause of Christ. God waits with outstretched arms to receive us all. How can we spread the Good News today?

A Triangle of Love

THE PRINCIPAL announced at a faculty meeting that cardiopulmonary resuscitation might be a course required in the classroom by the State of California. Several teachers raised their eyebrows. Viv groaned audibly. On the way out, she commented, "The three R's weren't enough. We have to add R for resuscitation! I feel completely boxed into a square by the four R's."

Myrtie nodded. "I guess we all do sometimes. That's when I teach creative thinking."

I asked my friend what that was.

"An invaluable skill. We look, listen, live and write down our thoughts. I call it the three L's."

The three L's. Clever—only she'd left out the L of loving!

Myrtie read my thoughts. "It's called a triangle game."

Of course! A Triangle of Love. Now, wouldn't that be a nice thing to think through in my Christian living?

Angle One: *Look to God for help.*

Angle Two: *Listen to His voice.*

Angle Three: *Live for Him!*

Now, when I feel "boxed in," I review the Triangle of Love. It is wonderful to know that I have but to look and I will see that God is ever beside me. It is good to be still and listen to His voice which I'm unable to hear above the tumult that rushing and fretting can bring. It follows naturally that I want to live creatively.

To Think and Pray About: Write down as many passages as you can think of in regard to God's boundless love. How can you pass them along in deeds today? What power there is, what energy eternally unspent, in the Blessed Trinity! *Father, thank You for Your Triangle of Love. Teach us to look, listen, and live for You.*

A Dish for the King!

FRIDAY was "hash day" at our house when I was growing up. Since then I've seen dozens of exotic recipes for all kinds of hash—none as good (or as simple to make) as my mother's. She simply tossed all the week's leftovers into a buttered skillet, blended them together and set before us a dish fit for the table of a king.

Strange thing. I used to look into the icebox (no electric refrigerators in those days) and say, "Yuck!" How could anybody—even an accomplished cook like Mama—come up with anything appetizing from cold cabbage, a greasy sausage, string beans (which I loathed), and a few unidentified objects that might be turnips, yams, or "poor man's casserole"? She could. And she did. Even before my mother served my plate, the matchless aroma set me to salivating.

Once I asked if she had a recipe of any kind. She laughed. "How could I when the ingredients are different each time? But there's a sort of secret that even I don't understand," she admitted. "Put together, the ordinary, tasteless ingredients take on the flavor of the others. They sort of complement each other to make a good dish."

How true of life, I thought today as I wrestled with some drab pickings I'd hidden in the freezer after New Year's dinner when I could no longer look a turkey carcass in the face. *God gave to each of us a special little something—often unidentifiable—which we can share with each other.* He intends that each of us add a bit of zeal!

To Think and Pray About: Like my mother's dish, don't you think that each of us contributes to the other—putting together our little ordinary gifts to blend into something *extra*-ordinary? Just why we are as we are is God's secret, but He reminds us over and over that we can do our bit to make a dish worthy for the table of our King! *Father, remind us how, through our blended efforts, we become one in Your service.*

It Feels Good to Give!

Hebrews 9:11-14   April 7
Luke 11:10-13

T HE BLOUSE simply took my breath away. So did the price! Hanging the garment back on the rack, I walked out of the dress shop determined to give no more thought to the purchase.

That was a hard decision to stick by. The exquisite detailing came back as I grocery shopped, banked, and drove home. To rid myself of the temptation to go back and buy the blouse, I surveyed my blouses-on-hand. I had more than I could wear out, I told myself firmly. But I simply had to have it.

Before I could telephone to have the blouse put aside, a friend—one of those special persons I would "do anything for"—called. "May I leave Joey with you long enough to take Millie to the hospital?"

"The *hospital?*" I'd known the daughter was to have an impacted wisdom tooth extracted, but why in the hospital? (Few went in those days.)

"X-rays showed four teeth must come out instead of one." My friend hesitated then said in a low voice, "There goes her birthday party—because the car payment's due and Dan has lost his job . . ."

Later, I did some mental arithmetic. How much would a birthday party cost—cake and ice cream, favors, the things little girls love? And there had to be a suitable gift. Yes, I could do it for the cost of a blouse. It was a "sacrifice" (emotionally); but yes, a little girl's joy was worth it! It hurt, actually *hurt*, and then I remembered the real sacrifice that Jesus made.

To Think and Pray About: Some of you make Lenten sacrifices. I trust that those sacrifices are not like one shared with me by a neighbor. "I never mind Lent," she said. "I give up chocolate as I never eat it anyway!" Is that a sacrifice? A true sacrifice has naught to do with the season . . . and certainly it is not characterized by going without what you do not want. What did Jesus give? *A sacrifice must hurt.*

"Free Love"?

1 Corinthians 16:20
Proverbs 22:6

DO YOU sometimes resent your doctor's advice—even when you ask for it? You know—curtailment of this and that. Restrictive.

Debbie and her mother were practically in hand-to-hand combat the day I returned a borrowed book. Mayo's an open person. She made no attempt to gloss over the tension between her and her daughter.

"This young lady thinks society's going through a sexually-informed lag! Says that's her body and she'll do with it what she pleases if she's so inclined."

The college girl's chin jutted out defensively. "I didn't say I was *so inclined*, did I? But the choice is mine—not yours!"

"Correction," Mayo said, toning down an octave. "Not yours. Not mine either. It's the Lord's!"

Debbie could fight her mother, society, or city hall—but not the Word of God. That is, of course, due to her early training. (I shudder when I hear people say we are undergoing a "moral revolution." Horsefeathers! Running scared is not to be confused with cleanliness of spirit.) But, back to Debbie and Mayo. Things quieted down and the three of us enjoyed coffee.

My grandmother used to say that nothing in this world belonged to its inhabitants: not the money we work for, what we buy with it, or our talents. All these (and more) are given to our stewardship to use for our happiness, enrichment of the lives of others, and glorification of God. And that includes our bodies—which calls for some restriction.

To Think and Pray About: Mothers and daughters, talk openly about the most formidable disease to confront modern medicine. AIDS compares to the medieval plague. But God drew up sound policies regarding faithful marriages and cleanliness of mind, spirit, and body before the problem. Review what wearing the white bridal veil represents: virginity! How can we all purify our bodies?

Definition of a Friend

Proverbs 17:17   April 9
Psalm 40:1-5

It seems to me if friendship lies
Within the heart and mind,
Our deeds will show and make folk know
It need not be defined...

                                        J.M.B.

BOBBY, an energy-filled boy in the third-grade, hopped happily along his way to school. He's always counting things. The number of oranges on each tree. How many cars he meets. Or how many times he or a companion begins a sentence "Well—" But this morning he was chatting with an adult and counting friends, telling what made each of them so special.

"Mickey has three dogs and they're all smart. Smarter than Lester's, but then he has a Siamese cat. It's Sam's dad who takes us fishing." Bobby's list of friends went on and on.

"You certainly have lots of friends," his companion commented.

"Well—yes," the child said slowly, "but just one *true* friend."

Interesting. Would he define "true friend"?

He did. "We trust each other," he said simply. And what could be more special than that?

To Think and Pray About: Are you a true friend? Am I? What are some qualifications? A true friend would give abundant love, 24-hour service, an always-open line of communication. A true friend would suffer with us, rejoice with us, and give us the heartiest counsel. A true friend would make the noblest sacrifice asking nothing in return for the trust—except that it be returned. Noble qualities? Yes, so how can we work to become that kind of friend? Well—we have a perfect example: *Jesus, blessed Jesus!* What are some ways in which we can show others that we trust Him?

What Machine's Can't Calculate

"Then sings my soul,
My saviour, God, to Thee:
How great Thou art,
How great Thou art!"

                              Carl Boberg hymn

THE LITTLE BOY was watching his grandfather attempt to master the use of a pocket calculator he had received for his birthday.

"Can you count to a million on this, Grandpa?" the child asked.

"Well, I guess I could if I put my mind to it, Sonny."

"But the machine doesn't show millions, Grandpa. Why?"

The elderly gentleman scratched his cloud of silver hair and pondered a moment. Then, with a smile, he answered: "Well, now, I guess there are some things in this world that are just too great for most of us to calculate."

Today as I listened to the lyrics of the century-old hymn on the radio, my heart turned over with the awesome wonder of the world our Lord has created . . . the stars . . . the rolling thunder . . . the beauty of the *here* and the *there* He has prepared for us.

Yes, oh, yes! There are some things that are just too great for most of us to calculate. If scientists ever figure out how many stars there are and what is causing the dark hole in the ozone layer, perhaps they will tell us. Until then (and afterward!), let us sing with the psalmist: "Great is the Lord—and greatly to be praised; and his greatness is unsearchable."

To Think and Pray About: Concentrate on the beauties of the universe. There are millions around you (with or without a calculator!). Zoom in on a few and share with a friend. Anxieties will melt away.

My Creed

SOMEBODY wiser than I said that a creed is no more a person's religion than the backbone is the person. But I hasten to add that subscribing to a good creed is as essential to the total being as a healthy backbone is to the skeletal frame. It holds it together. And aren't there times when the mother of a teenage son needs both?

First, the object of the creed needs a definition:

His arms are too short to pick up dirty socks, but they are long enough to reach tonight's dessert in the back of the fridge, all of next week's orange juice, and enough boiled ham to serve a wrecking crew.

His mind is as keen as Einstein's at points; at others, a mass of whale blubber. In other words, he can remember the name of every rock star since it all began with Elvis, but is unable to remember math assignments. He telephones a friend who has lost his notebook; then both forget what he called for.

His feet tangle whenever he is near the china cabinet, mirrors, or the sliding glass doors but maneuver him gracefully through a double dribble on a freshly waxed basketball court.

He has no time to read but stays in the shower till the water runs cold and dishes are done. He has little time for a haircut either (15 minutes) but spends half an hour blobbing on mousse and shaping tufts into spikes that rival porcupine quills.

His artistic talents are limited to painting the outdoor furniture (when pressured). For this, he wears designer jeans so splattered that he could roll on the table and put the brush aside after ten minutes.

His "allergies" have left him too weakened to run the vacuum sweeper. But he can prepare the gear for backpacking with friends up dusty trails bordered by poison ivy.

To Think and Pray About: Parents of a teenage son, he will leave your household soon. Ask God to bring him home safely—either to you or to Himself.

The Story of Our Lives

Malachi 3:8
Matthew 5:42; Mark 10:21

M Y HUSBAND's head bobbed up from behind the stacks of receipts and W-2 forms that he was sorting. "These kind of tell the story of our lives, don't they?"

"Not really," I started to protest. But memory of something my grandfather used to say stopped the words: "Your checkbook tells more about you than the hymns you sing or the creeds you recite."

We'll see about that, I thought, picking up a checkbook. Quickly, I thumbed through the stubs and canceled checks.

Now, I certainly could defend all those supermarket stubs. An itemized list would show staples, not caviar. (But Isaiah asks, "Wherefore do ye spend money which is not for bread?")

Well, books. One needs to improve the mind. (Of course, I had planned a new Bible. Mine's a disgrace. This year, for sure.)

Doctor bills. We all have those and at what a cost! (Of course, the doctor couldn't have done all he did without prayers—and I am trying to remember if I thanked the Lord properly.)

Looks like a lot for shoes. Of course, we walk eight miles a day (but not in blue bedroom shoes). I hurried past "shoes" and went to "vacation." We needed the rest. Everybody knows how hard we work. (Of course, we would have camped in the mountains again—that's real fun—but the cruise looked so exciting.)

I laid the checkbook aside, thinking that my husband had a point. It's not that I'm a spendthrift. Fact is, I'm frugal. And the comparative figures on the stubs marked "church," "missions," and the like testified to that. Grandpa was right!

To Think and Pray About: Do you feel you should contribute more by way of tithes and offerings? But what about time and *self*? Think of other ways we may be robbing God.

Lost?

John 14:16   April 13
Luke 9:57-61

So ALL is going wrong. But what could you expect on the thirteenth day of the month? A lot unless you get lost in it.

"We're lost," my husband told the service station attendant once when we were on a trip.

"Most folks are," the man in overalls grumbled good-naturedly as he crawfished from beneath a pickup he was tuning. "Leastwise them that come to me."

Inside the cluttered room our host wiped his hands on the bib of his overalls and pointed a greasy finger at an ancient wall map. "She's old," he said of the map, "but the way ain't changed."

He gave us directions. The day took on a new sheen through the fly-specked window. We'd been lost; but somebody had shown us the way.

Now, the way wasn't new. It had been there all along. Roads don't get lost. People do. So let's not lose our way in this day. Jesus showed us the way to the Father and He's waiting for us to follow. What a glorious opportunity His example set for those of us who are His followers already to point the way to others.

To Think and Pray About: There are so many opportunities—as countless as birds in flight. And gone as quickly. It does not behoove us to waste a second. The lad who knocks at the door—no job for him? Then say so with a smile. That non-Christian neighbor probably likes gingerbread. Is there a poem you especially liked in your church bulletin? Share the bulletin with the newcomer on the block, underlining the time of the Sunday worship service. Reread the Words of Jesus in the New Testament. Like the map, though old, it's unchanged. Let's point it out to others this April thirteenth! See? It can be the "luckiest" day of our lives!

Go for the Best!

April 14

Luke 12:29-34
Luke 10:38-42

"NO!" my neighbor closed the door on a closetful of party trays, damask cloths, a punch bowl, and a hostess gown.

Then "Yes!" she continued as she sorted plastic dishes, oil covers, coffee pots, and warm sweaters.

Marta was packing the camper she and her husband were taking on a first trip to the mountains. "Kind of good for me, you know, having to choose between essentials and things I can do without."

"It sounds so cold-blooded," I ventured, remembering her love for the "better things" in life.

"Not really," she laughed. "It's just an uncluttered way of thinking. You go for the best!"

Go for the best. That's the key. But how—

Watching her, I began to understand. One says "Yes" to things that work, fit, uncomplicate life. One says "No" to things that take unnecessary care, time, and space when you don't have it. In other words, the things that take more than they give in return.

Now, there are X number of years meted out to us. We do not know how many, but we know how many days in each year and how many hours in each day. We know, too, that our "best" is God and the promotion of His kingdom. So to Him and His children (all people) we say "Yes!" to their needs. And we close the door on all nonessential activities before they take up squatter's rights in our lives. What better way of putting it than "Go for the best!"

To Think and Pray About: Think of ways to uncomplicate your life today. What will you do with the time this allows you? Take a leap in faith forming miraculous partnership with your fellowman. Like Mary, you will have "chosen the good part."

Tribute

DON'T WALK. *Run!* To your nearest post office, that is. Unless, of course, you sent your tribute to Uncle Sam (on your husband's side surely!) before the 12 o'clock deadline tonight.

What? You don't have the report finished? Why not use the "simplified 1040 form"? Just follow two easy steps: 1. *How much did you earn last year? 2. Send it in!*

Did you smile? If so, give yourself a plus. Did you laugh outright? Then you are entitled to a double plus. But that's not all! You've improved your physical condition. Your heart, circulatory system, lungs, brain (and maybe other internal organs) have gone through body-building push-ups. Your spirits soared momentarily. Oops! Your elation is gone? This, you say, won't pay what you owe the Internal Revenue Service? No, but it will put you in better shape to earn more next year, so you can impress the government even more! Maybe you'll even be audited. Can you top that?

"Does she glory in paying income tax?" I hear you gasp. No, I don't. But I glory in being able to work so that I earn enough to qualify. Taxes have a long history and one look at the government's attempts to balance the budget (while we at home budget the balance!) tells us that there are more to come. We have no choice. We are bound by law and we are told to obey the law of the land (Titus 3:1).

Ecclesiastes speaks of a time to weep, and a time to laugh; a time to mourn, and a time to dance. We might as well be philosophical and add "and a time to render unto Caesar." Which is now!

To Think and Pray About: Back from the post office? Meditate on Ecclesiastes' arrangement of "times." Sum it up and you have darkness before dawn. So the time has come to laugh with overpowering relief. It is over for a whole year. Draw your friends or family near and count the blessings God has showered on you. Abundant life!

Teetering!

Matthew 18:18-20
Exodus 20:7

HAVE you selected your new spring shoes? Here's a word to the wise!

Can you believe that wearing high heels uses up energy? That's what my doctor told me when I complained of fatigue, backache, and a suspicion that I was becoming swaybacked.

"You're wearing yourself out doing a balancing act on these," he said tartly as he removed my high-heeled, platform-soled, strapless sandals.

"These place abnormal strain on the ankles, legs, and hips—and the danger of falling is acute."

Did the man realize that women's dress shoes come in four-inch heels? "I guess that I have no choice but to go barefoot," I said bleakly.

"Nonsense! Of course, you have a choice. Complain to the stores and manufacturers that you're getting hammer toes, debutante slouch, pelvic thrust, and bunions—besides using up too much oxygen. Demand that they put some sensible shoes on the market. Let them know that you won't be purchasing their product unless they clean up their act!"

I remembered the words of Dr. Jennings when I ran across a note from Kay Williams in *Guideposts* magazine. Kay wondered if readers were disturbed by misuse of God's name on TV. Who would be willing to help her circulate petitions of complaint?

I am. And I did. I'm willing to let the media know that I won't be listening to the programs or purchase any more of the products they advertise until they clean up their act.

To Think and Pray About: Freedom of speech? Violation of their rights? What about *ours*? There are other ways you and I can change things when we rally for Christ. Let's speak up for His cause before there's permanent damage. Teeter no more! Why risk a fall?

Oh, to Be a Firefly!

John 8:12

April 17

Matthew 5:14; 1 John 4:18

I REMEMBER a moonless evening long ago when the only lights seemed to be the incandescent flashing of fireflies against the stormy spring sky. Fascinated, I watched—my body pressed against the doorjamb in case something moved toward me from the shapeless dark of the back porch.

At first I thought I was alone, having escaped the adult world (but sticking close by, just in case!). But when the flow of conversation between aunts, uncles, and my parents slowed inside, I heard whispers nearby.

"Mankind! Lookit them lightnin' bugs," one of my Southern boy-cousins marveled softly.

"Yeah," his brother whispered back. "I wish *I* had a taillight that would shine like that!"

There was a pause. Then the first speaker said slowly, "Taillight? I dunno. But maybe we'd glow out there . . . but we're 'fraid of the dark."

It must run in families, I reasoned in my eight-year-old mind. So, then and there (not wishing to be a scaredy-cat), I would work on my fear. Who knew—maybe I could shine.

Unrealistic, of course. And now only a tender memory. But the thought carried a spiritual reminder. God has gifted us with His light. We can help Him dissipate the darkness—providing we conquer our fear of dark places in life.

To Think and Pray About: Are there unconquered fears in your life? What are you doing about them? Fear robs us of the mirth and joy we need to shine for others. Ah, but Jesus robs us of that fear! Talk to Him about your fears. He understands. There is nothing like a reformed "scaredy-cat" to light up this world for Him!

Discarded Bulbs—Nourished in Faith

John 4:14; 6:35; 8:12
                                                2 Timothy 4:6

SPRING was late. I was separating tulip bulbs one raw day when Bryce, my then four-year-old son, came to peek over my shoulder.

My back ached and my fingers were icicles. "Step back," I said a little crossly. "I don't want the bulbs mixed."

The words piqued his interest, bringing the inevitable "Why?"

"Because," I said. He deserved a better answer, so I explained that the fat, healthy bulbs might bloom, even this late.

"And the little ones won't?"

No, they would have to be discarded. I stood to support my back. "Let's go in where it's warm."

We did, but not before little Bryce stooped to rescue one of the puniest bulbs in the discard pile. No amount of coaxing convinced him it would not grow. God would help him, he said.

And He did. With a little advice, Bryce potted the under-developed bulb. He watered it. He fed it. And each night he ended his prayer with: "And God, let my flower bloom because of me!"

It's a tender story that touches my heart after all these years. Because, you see, I learned so much when his bulb bloomed. Oh, not about gardening. But about those "little bulb" people in my life whom I may have cast aside—even shunned—instead of helping them grow.

To Think and Pray About: Reread the suggested Scripture above. Who gives the water that satisfies all thirst; the bread that satisfies all hunger? And Who is the Light of the world? The world waits to hear our answer—and it waits to bloom! "Don't mix them up," I had said of the bulbs. I was wrong! *Give us faith, Lord, as we try to nourish others, mingling them all in Your kingdom of love—remembering the discarded bulb that bloomed.*

...At My Age?

Lamentations 3:18-25   April 19
Psalm 103:1-5

COMES THAT FATEFUL birthday (setting an age for it should be considered a felony!) and, having reached the top, it's time to slow down. Right? Wrong! That kind of thinking is against the laws of gravity. When you're "over the hill" (if you insist on that silly phrase), it's full speed ahead! So start pumping and get that pulse rate up. (And, younger women, beware... it *can* happen at any age.)

You can't budge? No way can you get the wheels rolling? Then maybe you are carrying an overload. Is it caring and giving or is it guilt and/or self-pity? Let's see what we can toss overboard. (A danger signal is your unwillingness to take this test.)

To Think and Pray About:
- Is your family no longer willing to accept your advice, no matter how sound it is? (Do they ask for it?)
- Is a friend's attitude toward you worsening despite what you consider to be your best efforts? (Have you talked this over?)
- No matter what you do for your church, it's never enough? (Who said?)
- Are you too exhausted and resentful to take good care of your body and personal grooming? (Join a group... take a class... have fun!)
- Are you lonely because your mate no longer finds you appealing—or because the opposite sex steers clear of "old maids" and "widows"? (Come now, could you have isolated yourself because of a conviction that your lady friends fear an "extra woman"?)
- Are you overindulging in anything (and that includes food), starving yourself, or scolding the butcher and kicking the cat?
- Are you heading in a no-win direction because you fear a collision course? (Learn to recognize *over*-stress. Be flexible.)

Trial By Fire

April 20

1 Corinthians 10:13
2 Corinthians 12:9; Psalm 26:1-3

UP FROM THE ASHES! This sign greets motorists entering a little seacoast town in southern Oregon. Visitors who tour the thriving outlets for the famous Bandon-by-the-Sea Dairy Products would never guess that once the entire community lay in ruins from a devastating fire.

Before the fire Bandon was a summer resort. Beaches were crowded, so concessions flourished. Guests sometimes stayed for the entire summer. Motels did a rushing business as did downtown restaurants and the glittering night spots. But when the hot winds blew in without warning, nobody was prepared. Flames swallowed everything for which the town was noted.

What happened once could happen again. Small wonder those suffering losses did not entertain the idea of building back. Instead, they studied their natural resources of adequate water supply, natural grasslands, and—determinedly erecting the slogan UP FROM THE ASHES on the outskirts of the charred little town—they made the most of what they had. What they came up with was something far more successful than mere summer trade ever could have afforded.

To Think and Pray About: Isn't that the way God works in our lives, too? "I've got it made!" we claim smugly. Then disaster strikes and our gains are swallowed up as if by tongues of flame. Maybe these are blessings in disguise—opportunities God provides to take stock of our inner strengths, bring them out, nourish them, and—with His guidance—see them grow beyond recognition of the former self. Is there a loss in your life today? God will never give us more than we can bear. And in our weakness, we are made strong. Those are the promises in today's reading. Shall we pray together? *Let us triumph, Lord, over every "trial by fire"!*

Stone Soup

"WELL, bless this mess!"
All day you've shopped. Now you have a double-strength headache and the pain in your arches is undoubtedly terminal. You set out the ice cream to thaw (instead of the steaks) and forgot to set the timer on the oven. Put micro-waved potatoes before your family and they go on a hunger strike. Family? Alas, they're due now. How many will help you survive? About the number of fowls that helped "The Little Red Hen." Father enters first—yes, with a scowl as he surveys the kitchen which holds no promise. You are wishing you had taken that course in self-defense, when unpremeditated tears fill your eyes. "Hard day, Mom?" There's a supporting arm around your shoulders and a call to arms.

"Hey, you kids get in here on the double—we're going to have stone soup!" And, knowing the tale, they giggle and pitch in. (You had forgotten that they knew how to do either!)

Stone soup? Well, there was this man whose only posses-sions were a stone, an appetite, and great resourcefulness. He built a fire in the center of the village and announced that he would make some stone soup for all—if he could borrow a big pot. There was an instant volunteer. And now some onions? Presto! Onions. Of course, a good stew needed potatoes . . . *Thank you, my good man* . . . parsnips . . . *Oh, bless you, madam* . . . And, of course, some meat would add flavor to the stone. The butcher waddled to his shop to oblige, *etc.* and *etc.* "Oh, never have we tasted such soup!" they declared.

Peelings fly onto the linoleum. The man of the house announces that hamburger will do in a stew. And then—*Oh no!*—goes to the rock garden in search of a stone! Your head and feet are no longer killing you. But you may die of laughter. The stone is lifted from the tomb. You are no longer a Good-Friday Christian. Christ has risen again!

To Think and Pray About: Share in all things. And yes, there is a "holy hilarity"!

The Egg and I

A COMMON THREAD of similarity of "Easter Around the World" is the egg. Oh, beautiful memories of Mama's painting eggs for Daddy to hide in a clump of purple iris. I never could wait until after breakfast (and neither could he!). And the next day we stuffed eggs and ourselves (never having heard of food poisoning, we were immune!). We had such fun: Mama, Daddy, the egg, and I!

As we dye eggs for the children's egg hunt or for the baked-ham-dinner centerpiece, let's all take a vicarious journey. First stop in England for sunrise services, hot cross buns, and a "spot of tea." There was a time when dated messages were written on eggs to establish family records. On to Italy, where families decorate special cakes with colored eggs. After feasting, people gather to pray that the Crusades were not in vain. Hear the beautiful sacred music in Switzerland? Adults, in their finery, are watching children tap their eggs together. Winners are those whose eggs survive without a crack. And it's eggs again in Norway, Sweden, and Denmark. Hard-boiled eggs are rolled in a downhill race. The winner's award is presented to a grandparent. In France, eggshells (with contents blown out) are filled with chocolate and offered to the priests or shared with the poor. Meantime, Germany and Belguim are ushering Easter in with mountaintop bonfires. Can't you almost see children weaving nests of moss which a mythical Easter hare will fill with splendid eggs? And so it goes, hopefully to inspire you.

To Think and Pray About: We have an idea—the egg and I. Wouldn't it be great to put these customs to work for the glory of Christ this Easter? Group projects draw family and friends together. We could study and better understand the history of our ancestors. We could print *He Lives!* on the Italian cake . . . write a Scripture reference on the "message eggs," etc. Then we could share the story and the *glory* of Easter with others who know about neither!

A Need to Be Needed

KAY WAS HAVING mother-in-law problems. Everybody felt sorry for her, but it was Faith who did something to help.

When Kay said, "She has taken over completely!" Faith answered with, "I want you to meet Berta."

Kay agreed quickly—thinking this Berta person had a solution. Anything was better than having her marriage split up over who was in charge. Lately her husband's mother scrubbed the tile daily, insisted on doing the laundry twice a week and ironing the sheets (which made Kay feel guilty).

What Kay found was anything but a solution. It was more of the same. "Sh-h-h! She's sleeping. If she wakes up, she'll need to go shopping again," Faith said, putting a warning finger to her lips.

"How old is she?" Kay whispered, thinking Berta was a baby.

"Old enough to know better," Faith giggled. "My mother-in-law makes 12 trips to the market daily. Sometimes she walks. Other times she has me drop her off when I pick the kids up from school. Berta needs mushrooms for Don's favorite casserole or needs a wee bit more cheese." Faith turned serious. "But now I understand why—"

At that moment the older lady came from the bedroom. "Why did you let me sleep so long, dear? I need some green onions—." Berta hesitated. "Oh, have you told your friend that I never had supermarts in my day? They're so friendly—and fill my time—"

She's lonely—lonely and needs to be needed. When the idea came Kay realized that she had both mothers-in-law in mind. "I was so ashamed," she confessed. But a new understanding was born in her heart.

To Think and Pray About: Find ways to let *all* family members use idle hours constructively. "Nothing to do" creates depression in older people and breeds mischief in children.

Spring Up—and Give Praise!

THE AIR was sweet with spring; but inside me was a winter heart—hurt, angry, and defeated. I tried to be a good wife and mother. Why then would my family (admitting that my idea was sound) reject it to the point of rejecting *me?* *It's no use. They won't budge,* something mean inside me whispered. *Why bother?*

Paying no attention to my surroundings, I crawled through a fence separating me from an untracked meadow and continued my lonely walk. A million songbirds chirped "Good morning!" but I did not hear. The scent of growing things rose up from the warming earth, but I did not smell them. The pink-clover carpet beneath my heavy feet went unseen and unappreciated until there was a call from a fairy-like creature who was hanging onto the fence just feet away.

"I'm watching the blooms rise up from your tracks," the little girl said with a look of awe and wonder on her pixie face.

"Oh?" I murmured and turned to look behind me. What I saw fascinated me. One by one the dewy blossoms rose from their knees and turned their pink faces to the heavens. Bruised of body and helpless, the mindless clovers possessed the miraculous capacity for springing up and trying again—crushed though they were. Why, it was almost as if they were praising the Lord!

Then the miracle of spring spoke to my soul. What the Creator had given to the least of these, He had given to me more abundantly! I lifted my face to Him and silently promised to try again. Why had I allowed my faith to go on vacation?

To Think and Pray About: What does God's Word tell us about faith? "If ye have faith as a grain of mustard seed . . ." you can remove mountains! The effectiveness, then, is *not* how much faith but the fact that it is present! My family was a mountain I could move—with God's helping hand. *Father, we would spring up like clover—not GIVE up!*

Spring Forward!

"SPRING FORWARD!"
The time (no pun intended) is near at hand when radio commentators will announce the setting forward of clocks at every station break. We live in an artificial environment, don't we, those of us whose lives are dominated by clocks, calendars, and schedules...workdays...weekends... a time to go to bed, get up, eat? Time orders our lives unless the clocks go on "strike." Let me share.

Two clocks in our house are the despair of my husband and the repairman. But to me they are faithful reminders that it is time to praise God!

The grandfather clock pulls rank no matter how far behind the Old Dutch clock on the dining room shelf. Proud of its set of Westminster chimes, the big clock announces quarter hours with great aplomb as if aware that the other timepiece can only strike the hour. As if that were not accomplishment enough, it rushes ahead at striking time no matter, it seems, where the hands are set.

Secretly, I have always wondered if Grandfather and I don't have a kind of understanding. Maybe the clock recognizes that I have a need for a special moment alone with God to start my day. You see, it is especially careful to strike a full minute ahead of the dining room clock at six A.M. How wonderful to awaken in the rosy freshness of another morning, stretch to my full length, and know that just as faithfully the second clock will echo the hour as a second reminder. For 30 full seconds I can say, "Thank You for another day, Lord, for the balm of slumber. Thank You for another day of life which I commit unto Your care. And thank You for another opportunity to praise Your name!"

To Think and Pray About: We arise, strap on a timepiece, and let it order us around. Find a way today to live from tide to tide, "springing forward" joyfully, praising Him whose love is timeless!

For Him the Bells Toll (No More)!

April 26   Mark 16:1-6
                                    John 14:19; 2 Timothy 1:10

DEATH. The mere word is frightening to most people. Yet it is as inevitable as nightfall—as undeniable as the dawn.

The bells are tolling somberly in the towers of several churches this Good Friday noon. Their mournful notes sound out-of-place, borne on the flower-sweet air. I pause and within me rises hope. Offices are closed and traffic is heavy—as if drivers are vainly attempting to escape the meaning of this day. True, it was not Pilate alone who allowed the crucifixion. We all did—with our sins. But should we feel guilty? Jesus went to the cross—willingly!—to erase our guilt and shame, I want to tell them. Yes, I too am sad—sad that they do not believe.

I am reminded this day of an incident related to me by an older gentleman who took a small niece to church with him. They were of different faiths and the little girl (taught to sit perfectly still in church) was rigid and there was a look of concern in her onyx eyes.

"Uncle," she said once they were outside, "Jesus was not on the cross in there. Does your church not believe His death?"

"My child," he replied, hoping she would understand, "all Christians believe Jesus was crucified; but we worship a living Lord."

That's the message! The world so desperately needs to know that the Savior Jesus Christ, our Redeemer, no longer hangs on the cross and that the chains of death could not restrain Him. His resurrection is the very core of our faith. Death, our final enemy to conquer, is to us the dark unknown. But it has no power over those of us who believe.

To Think and Pray About: Shake off your guilt, your fear, your shame. Walk among the lilies and transfuse the bleeding hearts around you from the most wondrous "blood bank" the world has ever known. Listen! The bells no longer toll!

Never Far Apart

M ARION MOVED AWAY the year she and I were
eight. I missed her with all my heart. But I was comforted, because I had her heart!

We played tag among the packing barrels as my parents
helped hers with last-minute details that day. We ran upstairs
and down, shivering deliciously at glimpses of imagined ghosts
in the empty rooms. Then we wrote in each other's memory
books again. Anything to postpone the awfulness of good-bye.

But the moment came. The moving vans loaded in the last
crate, and white-faced, we two best friends stood looking at
each other. Then, without a word, Marion darted to the
family car. There, in spite of her parents urging her to hurry,
she dug among her souvenirs in the shoebox in the backseat.

When Marion returned, I knew she had a treasure the way
she held both hands behind her back. But the last thing I
would have believed was the heart-shaped candy box we both
loved. Once the box had held plump chocolates—a fact that
appealed to neither of us as much as the beautiful box, edged
in gold and centered by a crimson velvet rose. The kind of
thing a little girl keeps forever.

Only Marion gave hers away! "You keep it," she sobbed.
"Then when I seem far away, you'll know you have my heart."

Sound familiar? Yes, that's what Jesus promised when He
left us behind. We have His heart "even unto the end of the
world."

To Think and Pray About: How do you stay in touch with
beloved friends? A letter removes our overcoats of daily care
and hangs them in the closet where we can forget them for
awhile. Write that "somebody" today. How do you stay in
touch with God? Practice a run-on prayer . . . *For, if we "pray
without ceasing," You never seem far away, Lord. We are in Your
heart and You are in ours.*

"Good-bye" Way of Life

April 28

John 21:15-23
1 Corinthians 3:8

YOU REMEMBER it well if you remember it at all...
Good-byes were a way of life with us World War II war brides. We endured packed buses, whimpering children, trampled feet, and stale lunch-box smells to be with the men we loved.

A sense of finality settled over me when my husband and I said our last good-bye when the Seventh Air Force was ordered overseas. The war had not ended on schedule. Maybe it would never end. Maybe this was Armageddon. And I was alone with a glacier for a heart.

When the men boarded the troop train I decided against staying to see them off. Instead, I ran blindly for the nearest exit only to be detained by a firm hand of another wife. "We have to be there," she said, towing me back to the platform.

"I can't face another farewell!"

"Don't make it a farewell. Just salute. He'll be back!"

A reassurance swept over me. The frozen sea within me melted into a thousand warm, new seas. Of course, he would be back. And meantime, I had a job to do on the home front.

Suddenly, I knew how the disciples must have felt when Jesus left them here. Until they remembered that He would be back. And they must have remembered, too, that until then they had a job to do.

To Think and Pray About: We live in a "good-bye world," don't we? Spring hands us a forever-world which winter snatches away. Children grow up (which seems to take forever), then they are gone (and it seems we had them no time at all). We build our lives around loved ones only to bid them good-bye— and a lamp goes out in our lives. Neighbors move... jobs change... we live in a shifting world. But life is made up of moments—opportunities to exercise faith in new ways and light the way for others. Ask God how your heart can in its sorrow rejoice. Spring will be back. So will the children. And so will Jesus. Salute Him and await His return!

My Prayer at Easter Dawning

Matthew 28   April 29
John 14:13

How lovely, Lord, the oceans, and silver ocean bars,
Reflecting Heaven's glory in dippers full of stars.
How lovely, Lord, the mountains that lean against the blue,
Resting in the rainbows of sunshine mixed with dew.
How lovely, Lord, the valleys like patchwork quilts below,
From primrose-spring through summer to autumn's afterglow,
Then starkly into winter when trees are trimmed with frost,
How lovely, Lord, this knowing their pulses are not lost
For You have set in motion with a flawless hand
The earth; and all within it responds to Your command...

                                                J.M.B.

DEAR LORD, each dawning is a poem—a poem Your infinite mind has painted which our mortal tongues cannot express. We listen to the orchestral music of the birds and hear the Voice of Heaven saying, "Rejoice and be exceedingly glad." Give us hearts filled with gladness, Lord, that we may offer acceptable praise to You, the Creator of the world's first dawn.

We know this dawn is special, Lord. How silently it came, how peacefully, unfolding Your promise, and wrapping Your garments of hope about us once more. Then came the wonderful sense of awakening to Your presence as the first rays of day touched the blossom-sweet hills. *It is Easter!*

Let us store the beauty, the tranquility, and the miracle of this moment to be unfolded again and again as our lives, like the forests, become so overgrown and shaded that our senses are numbed. Let us remember and our hearts leap up with gladness as our spirits walk with the Risen King.

The Five R's of Spring

April 30   Ephesians 1:7,8; 1 Corinthians 3:7-9
                     2 Corinthians 5:17-21; 4:15-18

P AUSE no matter what you are doing! Maybe you hadn't
noticed that since mid-December the days have length-
ened... that wee buds are greening... that the warming
earth whispers of tulips... and that the sweet incense of
flowering trees stirs in sudden jubilee. Maybe you've been
thinking "winter" and failed to heed the warning of "spring!"

The wind's taut chords have slackened. The palms of the
warming sun smooth snow from mountain peaks. Pussy willow
branches are strung with soft, gray "kittens" and the channels
of the swamp open ice-locks for the muskrat to use. A chip-
munk scurries past—a yellow streak like a child's crayon drawn
quickly across a page. The trill of a lark fills the air with
expectancy and hope. All the earth holds its breath for the
great awakening to the five R's of spring.

- *Redeemed.* Winter held the reins of the year in its icy grip.
  Now there is no malice, just sweet forgiveness. (How does
  this compare to our Christian redemption?)
- *Reconciled.* The ground, so long frozen and still, then wet
  and chill, suddenly surrenders sweetly to the life-giving rays
  of the sun.
- *Renewed.* The whole world is changed! God has sounded His
  golden trumpet in the daffodils and adorned the orchards in
  bridal white. (How are *we* changed when we invite the
  Creator into our lives?)
- *Rewarded.* Buds burst into leaves. Grass covers the hills.
  Migrating birds come home in swarms, guided by that inner
  instinct. (And to us to who our Father gave dominion, what
  rewards have we?)

To Think and Pray About: Did the great awakening come?
There will never be another spring exactly like this one.
Reveal your heart to Him.

Prayer for the Memories of May

L ORD, we are entering the month of memories. Perhaps on
Your great calendar You planned May's sweet interlude
between an uncertain—sometimes stormy—spring and the
wrath of summer's heat-to-come for us to pause and remember. . . .

We remember other springs, Lord: the clustering of leaves,
the gentle dawns and fiery sunsets, the misty morns and purple
dusks. Yes, age remembers the frail echoes of yesterday. Youth
harks to the haunting promise of tomorrow. But, Lord, let all
of us know that today is important. For what we say, what we
think, and what we do in Your Name will remain forever. So
let us take with us a scrap of May in our hearts all through the
year.

We listen to the hummings of May in every bush and tree,
Lord, and remember the silence of winter. Now we welcome
back the songbirds and the chirping crickets. And we ask Your
patience when the buzz of the flies and the whir of the
mosquitoes become too much. We know it is all a part of Your
balance of nature. So, let us watch for the glory of the sun
on the colored throats of hummingbirds and the graceful
sweep of butterfly wings and make them a part of next winter's
memories. Remind us to point out these strange paradoxes of
nature—appreciating, if not always understanding—to children. For them, the glory of May is a discovery—to be remembered with our help.

We remember, too, Lord, that May is the sobering month in
which we pay tribute to those brave men who have fought and
died for our nation's freedom. As the bugles blare, the flags
wave, and poppies bloom in our buttonholes, let us remember
with a mixture of pride and sorrow the bloodstained portrait of
brother-against-brother and pray that it was not in vain.
Memories are not always pleasant. But remember we must.

A Fairy Called "Faith"

May 2

1 John 5:4
Mark 11:22-24

AH, BEAUTIFUL MAY! Month of gentle sunshine and disgruntled rumble of retreating thunder, a reminding echo of April showers that brought the brilliant blossoms flooring the earth. May, beautiful May—the month of unpredictable magic . . . of miracles seen and faith unseen.

Do children still wind the maypole? Oh, I hope so! The lovely tradition (once frowned upon by the Puritans) came back in all its spring loveliness with the Restoration. The sky-high maypole with its colored streamers suspending to earth . . . the May queen and her court of little fairy princesses in gossamer dresses to match each streamer as they danced on tiptoe in and out, ever winding, until the pole looked much like an unbent rainbow.

How well I remember my blue, blue dress, the wreath of matching flowers on my nine-year-old head, and my name—Faith! Ah, yes, it was the name I remember most . . . for it was the "why" of the magic.

We held the *fete* outside that year with the maypole centering the green. I still wonder how the upper-grade boys managed to get the upright piano from the upstairs auditorium to the school yard below. A part of the magic, I guess, as was the indigo sky tufted with fleecy clouds. Jubilantly, we little girls dressed and waited for the music. Instead there was a clap of thunder. And the sky turned to gray wool as a brisk wind tied the streamers into knots of despair.

I ran into the hall to hide my tears and bumped into the principal who was carrying a ladder. "Oh, don't leave us, *Faith!*" *Faith* . . . was he saying my name or whispering a prayer? Either way, the thunder was applause . . . the handful of raindrops, the making of a rainbow whose streamers the boys were already unsnarling and securing with weights at each end. The little squall passed. And the rainbow turned from straight to arched miracle!

To Think and Pray About: Praise God for May and its colored miracles. Faith is the key.

"Fill It Up to Here"

I T WAS A GREAT DAY when my father brought home the hand-crank cream separator. I hadn't muscled out enough to man the crank, but I insisted on standing on a stool to ladle the milk into the enormous milk container. My mother cautioned me to be careful; but I was impatient with her instructions. Of course I could use a ladle.

Daddy brought the still-warm jersey milk from the barn and I had him set the galvanized pails near the new contraption and hurriedly began. It was such fun that I failed to see the "Fill it to here" line. In my enthusiasm, I filled the container to the top. The result was disastrous. The first turn of the crank sent milk splashing all over my checked apron, into Daddy's face, onto Mama's freshly done-up gingham curtains, and onto her spotless linoleum.

I never made the same mistake, of course. Little incidents such as this live in the minds of children. Many times I have thought of what happens to my day when I allow it to fill beyond the danger point with annoyances, petty thinking, and unworthy thoughts. Sooner or later they're going to slosh out all over those around me. I look back on the day and realize that there was something I could have done, after all. Difficult as it might have been, I could have siphoned out the excess with a turn of the spigot below. So I take a day gone ragged with care and let the sunshine and the bird song take over. How refreshing! How clean I feel! How ready to face the day! And all it takes is a little turn of the spigot of the mind.

But, of late, I have been thinking about a more positive side of the little cream-separator incident. Why not be daring? Why not go past the danger mark and overflow my heart— providing the thoughts are lovely? Why not let them splash onto everyone I meet?

To Think and Pray About: Memories are wonderful things. Love remembered is love shared from one generation to the next. Let's fill our hearts to brimming with love—building memories with family and friends!

The Therapy of a Hug

May 4   Hosea 14:4
1 Corinthians 16:20; Psalm 85:10-13

MY HUSBAND laid down the newspaper with a sly grin. "It says here that medical research has deemed hugging is good therapy. Want to test it?"

George gave me a big bear hug. And it worked!

Now some other doctors have come up with some reasons for hugging. Yesterday I received a note from a friend who included a little clipping from a women's magazine. It read:

> Hugs are not only nice, they're needed. Hugs can relieve pain and depression, make the most secure among us even more so. Hugging feels good ... overcomes fears ... eases tension ... provides exercise ... Hugging also does not upset the environment ... saves heat ... is portable ... requires no special equipment ... makes happy days happier ... makes impossible days possible.

Nice? I think so—except that there is an absence of what the warm show of affection will do for the sad, the lonely, the neglected, and the rejected. I have a feeling that an understanding arm around the shoulder of someone in need today will put an arm around our own shoulders. And the Lord's!

Ours has become a sort of touchless society. Sadly, we are conditioned to control our emotions to the point that we are ashamed to cry, hesitant to laugh, and afraid to touch. Have you noticed how subjects must be urged to stand close together in a group picture? But we have an advantage! Remember that people delight in the unexpected. Surprise triggers a laugh. And you know what laughter does!

To Think and Pray About: So give somebody an unexpected hug today. It could change a life—no, make that two, for one will be your own! *And here's a hug for You, Lord!*

Gratefully

Galatians 5:13   May 5
Psalm 100

A SHRILL RING of the telephone broke the tranquility of the afternoon. "I knew it!" Chris, the hostess, pressed a hand to her forehead as if nursing a headache in advance.

The Patch-and-Chatters looked at one another sympathetically. The get-togethers afforded the only time Chris had for some heart-to-heart talk with other women as they mended and sewed on buttons. She had five children and kept books for her husband's business.

"I don't know how she does it," Sue marveled softly.

Mavis, sitting beside her, bit off a thread. "Me either! Even with my two underfoot and Daddy Don telling me what time to pick him up at the train station, I sometimes wonder how to meet the day."

"*Gratefully*," a quiet voice from behind them said.

Nobody had heard Chris' merry-eyed mother enter. But she made a valuable contribution to me when I heard the story.

Now when I find myself irritated, maybe even a little self-pitying, when my feet burn with fatigue as if I had walked over a bed of hot coals because of demands of family, colleagues, or neighbors, and am ready to say, "I'm in over my head, Lord," I remember the wise lady's descriptive adverb. *Gratefully*. That's how God would have me serve—even though I still dislike sewing on buttons and tense up when my husband says, "I really *do* have a ring around the collar." I am needed—and loved.

I remember a day when my son's cowlick stood up like "Alfalfa's." When he asked if I would help with his hair, I said, "Gratefully." George looked puzzled then grinned. "Yeah, for someday it'll be gone!"

To Think and Pray About: Attitudes are contagious. God gave us women a special something nobody has identified. We set the mood in the home and in the workplace. Be grateful for that, too!

Time Should Be Spent

May 6

Psalm 90
Matthew 25:45

D O YOU BUDGET your time as well as your money? A time budget can spread your day, week, or life out efficiently and help avoid impulse items. But (warning!) it will leave you without change. That's the whole idea, learned from a dear lady many years ago.

We all wondered how Miss Katie, an aging music teacher, managed to do so much. "She's the only woman I know who can ride a horse all directions at once," my grandfather said of Miss Katie's church, civic, community, and personal involvements. I liked the "personal" part best. That meant delectable doughnuts, embroidered handkerchiefs on birthdays, and all the punch children could drink at the weekly piano recitals— even for those who didn't take lessons.

Asked how she managed to accomplish it, the quick-stepping little lady would poke at a loose strand of hair escaping the tight granny knot and say: "Well, you see, most folks worry about saving time. I figure the Good Lord gave me so much time on earth and meant that I should spend it—not hoard it up."

Those words gained more impact as the years passed and life began its demands. *Spend time*, I used to think when my young son came to me with some mystery-of-life question. *Spend time*, I thought again when my parents needed a margin of my day. *Spend time*, I still think when my husband unplugs my washing machine and invites me to ride with him on some errand in the country. *Spend time* . . . what a wonderful thought when the wild larkspur is in bloom and the sun warm on my back . . . when there's a sick friend in need of a word of cheer, a stranger in need of a smile, a stray cat in need of milk.

To Think and Pray About: Time is our most valuable commodity only when well-spent. Blessed are we who learn that hoarding is a cardinal sin.

Our "Beautiful" Days

M Y FRIEND Blanche and I used to have what we called our "beautiful days." The adjective had nothing to do with weather or smoothness of the day. It meant how we felt about ourselves.

On a *beautiful* day we could pass a geometry test, win the debate, or catch the eyes of the new boy. All things were possible.

Blanche was taking introductory psychology and decided to analyze one of my better days. There had to be an "underlying cause."

So one of those days when I could have broken into the movies without a hitch or swallowed fire in a circus act, I called her. "It's the blue dress," my friend decided. "Matches your eyes." But the next time I felt beautiful, I was wearing green. "Your hair?" she wondered. And when my hair refused to follow a pattern, we concluded that the secret had little to do with externals. "It just has to be how we feel inside that gives us confidence," she said.

Now, although my friend is no longer alive to share it, each time I have a beautiful day, I remember her and ask myself: *What makes it so?* Sometimes it's because I've brought a bit of excitement to another person, taken a prayer break, or read a devotional that sends me humming through my work. I feel good inside. I feel good about the world. And I move with confidence through the beautiful day I have allowed God to shape. (*Thank you, Blanche.*)

To Think and Pray About: Today's reading itself is a thing of beauty. Right? I think we women can identify with the singing words of the lovely metaphor to illustrate Christ's love for the church. Today, know that you are loved and that love makes a woman beautiful. In what ways can you make others feel good about themselves and the world?

And praise the Creator, who is the "underlying cause" of all things beautiful!

One Woman's Treasure

RECENTLY my mother called for me to come and see something she had bought for 50 cents at the city dump! This particular disposal site is unusual in that some entrepreneur has set up a collector's business in a swept-clean corner where he displays salvaged wares for sale.

My mother's newest purchase was a squatty, unimaginative-looking pot. "Exactly like the one Grandmother kept by the fireplace," she beamed.

"Maybe Mama, but—" I was about to say that I wouldn't retrieve the crown jewels from a *dump*. But my mother, who was rotating a polishing cloth gently over the painted surface of the cheap-looking pot, let out a squeal of delight. "See! You just never know what's underneath."

It was my turn to gasp. Why, the pot was copper. *Real copper!*

My mother, the wise philosopher! My attitude made a right turn. Maybe it was the shine of the copper, or maybe God flicked a switch inside me. At any rate, I was seeing life in a new light. All around me there are persons like that pot, I realized. Persons who, perhaps through no fault of their own, have been cast into the dump of despair. Once created in God's image, now they are layered with ugliness. And supposing them worthless, society has cast them aside. Now they need somebody like my mother who cares enough to look for their hidden beauty. To polish them and let them shine the way God intended.

And who is that person? You, me—*all* of us!

To Think and Pray About: Thomas Gray took seven years to "polish" his immortal poem "Elegy Written in a Country Churchyard." Time well-spent, for his poignant work so beautifully illustrates the value of searching. Let these lines speak to your heart: "Full many a flower is born to blush unseen, and waste its sweetness on the desert air." Unless we search out the treasure!

The Attic of the Heart

1 Thessalonians 2:7-11   May 9
Romans 10:13-18

WHOEVER said, "You can't take it all with you," should see the moving van when we change abodes. "Grapes of Wrath" would not capture the picture—except perhaps the driver's mood when he spots the tenth "just one box more." It would surprise him to know that I've stored up even more in my heart. You see, I am just a sentimental silly, packing around a collection of treasures that I thought nobody wanted to share until a very special book came from Bryce, my once-dumpling baby who has stretched out now into young manhood. But talk about sentimental! He screamed when I discarded a pesky hot-water bottle that had sprung a leak (his "heater" at four). He refused to let the old car go when we bought a new one even though it threw oil seven directions at once and puffed out smoke like a dragon—the kind of thing I thought he'd outgrown.

But the gift he gave me recently was chosen with care. Inside the cover Bryce had marked a passage from *An Old English Birthday Book*:

> SUNSHINE IN THE MORNING, moonlight at night, the fragrance of gardens, the deep silence of harvest fields, the musical rattle of teacups, the laughter of happy children, the familiar tread of loved and approaching feet, a beautiful thought, a pleasant dream, a letter, a kindly greeting, a worthwhile job to do, a joke, a song, a kindness received ... these are the things which cost us nothing, but enrich all beyond the telling.

Beyond the telling? Not quite. My son, *God bless him*, wrote in his left-hand scribble: "These are the things you taught me." I shall store this in the attic of my heart.

To Think and Pray About: Other than the disciplines, how do we prepare children for "the good life"? *By whatever means, Lord, let there be gentleness.*

Let Go and Let Grow

1 Samuel 12:2
Psalm 27

DEAR DAUGHTER: Once upon a time you were my baby. In my mind you still are. But I had to let go and let grow by granting your independence. The hurt was, in a sense, self-inflicted. Here's why.

It was I who taught you to curl baby fingers around buttons so you could dress yourself. It was I who taught you to lisp the words of "The Gingerbread Boy" which led to recognition of numbers so you could use the telephone. It was I who finally gave in to your cries of protest and let go of your hand so you could prove to the world that you could cross the street alone. Then came the realization that I must allow you to choose your own clothes and decide if you needed a sweater. The time had come for your ascension to the throne of maturity and taste the joys of being a woman. The time had come, too, for me to measure my own success . . . to wonder if I had interpreted the Proverb right and brought you up "in the way in which you should go." The Lord was my strength . . .

The years slipped by. And somewhere, somehow, in a way I am unable to understand, our roles began to change. In little subtle ways you became the mother. Ever the dutiful daughter, you began zipping my blouse in back when arthritis stiffened my thumbs and I fumbled. You looked up telephone numbers when I complained that the print got smaller in the directories each year. And then you took my elbow at intersections, saying, "The traffic is awful!"

When we lost Daddy I had to learn the arts of making out checks and living on a budget. I was lonely. And coping alone taxed my courage. But, like you, I grew. Now, I know your new-found freedom must have taken all the faith you could muster. But you made it . . . and so will I. You owe me nothing for your upbringing, darling—except respect, of which I have an abundance. What do I want for Mother's Day? Just what I have: your love and my independence!   J.M.B.

To Think and Pray About: Happy Mother's Day, dear wonderfully independent mom of mine.

The Three T's

Romans 12:19-21
1 Corinthians 13

May 11

A PROVOCATIVE QUESTION in a Bible study brought an even more provocative answer.

Question: "When and where do you think the Holy War will occur?"

Answer: "Today—right here in my heart!"

Startling? Yes—until you think about the daily battles. There are two selves inside us. Agreed? The human self and the spiritual self. The human self, in spite of good intentions is quick to anger, loses its patience, envies a bit now and then, and allows unworthy thoughts to creep through the crack in the door to the unsuspecting heart.

Aha! Those invaders do not get far. You see, the spiritual self is stronger because it is a soldier of our commander-in-chief, the Almighty God who has placed His guardian angels there in waiting for just such enemies. And good overcomes the evil forces—eventually. Another way of saying it is "in God's time." Daily victories are not enough. We "soldiers" are expected to separate the light from the darkness in our homes for a sometimes trying family and serve as an example to each member as well as to all others whom we encounter in our daily computerized rush.

Feel like you are driving downhill without any brakes? You are not holy, so how can you "be perfect"? None of us are! But, with Paul, we "press toward the mark." And it helps to remember the three T's of patience with yourself (*then* with others): Things Take Time!

To Think and Pray About: Ask God to help you with the small battles of the heart. He will help you win the war. Remember: *Things take time!*

A Child Is Given

Matthew 19:13,14
Proverbs 20:11; 22:6

THE ROOM, made ready in the waiting period, captured the glow of a firefly, borrowed dancing sunbeams from enchanted seas, and is freshened by a tropical breeze you found napping in your dreams...

Now the dream has come true. Forgotten is the waiting and the trauma. *Baby is home!*

Across the tiny face flits a repertoire of expressions. He is surprised, skeptical, delighted, absorbed, forgiving, trusting, puzzled, and amused. How mature can a week-old get? Why, this one yawns, stares, frowns, listens, and attempts a smile when you chuck the pink chin. Strong, too! He makes fat fists and bicycles plump, perfect legs. Awake, he is a wonder. Asleep, he is poetry.

And the parents are totally mesmerized; their strong hearts, jelly. Already this special child (who will write the greatest novel, paint the greatest picture, or inspire his country in its greatest hour of peril) is learning to respond. He recognizes sounds from the musical toys, bats at objects with open palms, and knows that a cry brings a bottle; a coo, a hug. He is aware that both Mother and Dad are pushovers and cuddles up to them like a blessing.

Once again life has renewed itself. Love, that indescribably beautiful interaction between man and woman, has wrought a miracle. And faith is renewed because:

> You believe in children—little ones, big ones, chubby and thin ones... for wherever you go you find yesterday's children who are nurtured in the things of Christ at work in the building of the Kingdom of God.
>
> (Author unknown)

To Think and Pray About: Praise God together for this incomparable gift. Point heavenward, climbing ever upward. Baby will follow.

The Joyful Mother of Children

Psalm 113   May 13

I N THE BEGINNING there was Eve, "mother of all living." We all have them in common—those wonderful
creatures who cook, clean, mend, dream, improvise, and make
things go twice as far—including love. Their offspring are
what they listen for, read to, watch over, worry with, and pray
for. Mothers do all this—and more—intuitively, because
their children come without instruction books.

Mothers, from the Arctic Circle to the equator, are prize-
winning cooks. The years pass. The children wander. But all
take with them a memory of Mom's apple pie or chicken and
dumplings.

Mothers have the patience of saints. Who else would have
scrubbed our faces, accompanied us to Sunday school, and
relearned the three R's with us in an effort to prepare the small
heathens for a civilized world?

Mothers are beautiful. Then care-laden decades introduce
a new man into their lives, Father Time. At first, he is
invisible, and she goes on shuttling her family here and there,
assuring them that all will turn out well. So good is her act that
the growing-up children fail to notice that her smile is a bit
tired, that she carries the grocery bags less jauntily than when
they skipped by her side.

Mothers are most always right. When the sad day comes
that they look into their mirrors and Father Time looks back to
taunt, they are *wrong* this time. "I am no longer pretty," they
sigh. Not pretty? Maybe they are right, after all. Not pretty—
beautiful. Their beauty is as indestructible as hope, faith, and
charity because they *are* these things—demonstrated in their
sacrifices to be "the joyful mother of children."

To Think and Pray About: If you are a mother, wear the
crown God gave you with pride. If not, those who are giving
your time, energy, and gifts to social service, we salute you,
too. Your contribution is unique—one which only women,
with their capacity for love, could have given. God bless you.

The Thornbush and the Willow

THE THIRD-GRADE rehearsal for the maypole dance came to a climax when Annie tripped Ellen Sue. Ellen Sue had the part Annie wanted with all her eight-year-old heart. But in the final audition (in which Annie was runner-up), wasn't it just like Ellen Sue to come with her hair all in curls and get the part? Being "second-best" wasn't enough. Who wanted to be a stand-in? Of course, if something "accidently" happened to her . . .

Ellen Sue wasn't hurt in the fall, but she cried. She knew Annie tripped her purposely. Annie's face was filled with remorse, too, so she cried right along with her previous friend.

It was then that an understanding teacher took the two little girls aside and told them the story of the thornbush and the willow.

"Why is it," asked the willow, "that you're so envious of the clothing of others when you cannot possibly wear the garments?"

"I don't wish to wear them," said the thornbush sharply. "I want to tear them!"

The story made its point. But something else the teacher said made it more meaningful in years to come. "Envy has no quality but that of detracting from one's own virtue."

Teachers out there—you are a great influence on the lives of your charges. How wise you are when you encourage youth with your "lessons" within lessons! Maybe all of us would be the proverbial "thorns in the flesh" had we not known you.

To Think and Pray About: It is so easy, isn't it, to resort to little criticisms "accidently" when others achieve? Today encourage one another (for we are all teachers!) to forego a grudge, forgive a wrong, apologize if you are wrong, accept an apology if offered, avoid envy, and laugh a little over small defeats—and, most of all, express love, both to God and those around you.

A Hatful of Religion

Proverbs 23:7   May 15
Psalm 62

"OLD SALT," a retired sea captain, had what he called a "hatful of religion." Here are the words he pasted onto the sweatband of his hat:

> Now, you look backwards and you're sure to plow a crooked furrow. Look sideways and you're apt to trip over the stumps and rocks. Look down and you're bound to lose your bearings. But to look ahead makes a perfect furrow. And to look up guarantees a righteous life because you'll meet the eyes of Him who created the field and said: "Make the rows straight!"

Now, maybe the words would have served no purpose pasted into the hat and forgotten. But Old Salt didn't forget. And neither did he allow others to forget. He would grab that dusty, old fedora every time he felt he had been snubbed, short-changed, pushed aside, and even before getting into a dental chair. Then, with a lopsided grin, he'd meet the problem head-on.

Once when there was a disagreement at a church meeting, the old gent stood up and said, "Well, mates, I guess we'd best be passin' th' hat!" And everybody knew it wasn't for taking a collection. It was for whittling everybody down to size in a language the farmers could understand. And the spirit of the meeting changed. Not a bad idea—having "a hatful of religion." It's just one more reminder of the "straight and narrow" of our focus. And that's one of the few things in life, as Old Salt saw it, in which we need show no moderation.

To Think and Pray About: Imagine yourself preparing a garden for planting. There must be a beginning and an end and rows should be straight. Keep working toward that straight path that leads upward until you plow past *fair, average,* and *good* to *excellent.* That's a hatful!

Remember the Sabbath

May 16   Genesis 2:3; Exodus 3:14
                          Deuteronomy 5:15; Luke 6:5-10

God fashioned lovely butterflies and put them on the wing.
He feathered all the baby birds and gave them songs to sing.
He painted blue the arching skies as backdrops for the trees
Which He dressed with leafy skirts and ruffled them with breeze.
God built a colored rainbow bridge and swung it in the clouds,
Made perfect daisy-patterns, then planted them in crowds.
He fashioned us much like Himself then rested for a day—
In hopes, I think, we too would pause and see His work this way.
                                                    J.M.B.

SO THE WEEK has been overwhelming? You want a sanitized house. Your family deserves nutritious meals. Your job is demanding (whether you are an office slave or a household servant!). You would like to take an art course, write a poem, create a garden, maybe take a trip...

"I can't do it all!" you screamed above the hiss of the shower over and over when you were alone half a blissful moment.

Of course, you can't. Don't you think God knew that? That's why He created Sundays. Now the helter-skelter existence will commence anew on Monday. But maybe you can face life a day at a time if you use today wisely—breathing in God in big, big doses.

Normally, when the channels get clogged, you have to kneel in a wee chapel inside your heart. But in today's reading, you found the sabbath referred to as: 1. a blessed and holy rest day (meaning *happy* and *set apart*); 2. a day of deliverance (you need it!); 3. a day of delight (haven't you escaped bondage?); and 4. a day made for us. Christ is Lord of the sabbath. He wants it restful, peaceful, and *healing*.

To Think and Pray About: There! See the violets thrusting purple bonnets through the unkept corner of the garden? God can bring good from those "impossible days." Rejoice!

Little Promises—and Great Ones

2 Thessalonians 2:13-17; 3:13   May 17
2 Peter 1:4

SPRING IS a time of promises—and promises fulfilled. And yet I broke a promise today. . . .

The telephone rang just as I sat down to type the recipes for the church cookbook. The Mercantile was having an unannounced clearance sale on women's dresses. Wouldn't I like to come down while there was a wide choice, my clerking friend wondered. Of course, I would, but here were the recipes to do. "Maybe I should wait until tomorrow—" I began (secretly hoping, I think, that Greta would say just what she said):

"There won't be as much selection." So I hurried down at the speed of light, almost flattening a pedestrian in my haste. Inside, I was near-trampled myself. Unannounced to whom, I wondered, grabbing all the "possibles" I could sort from a rack. By the time I stood in line to try them on, the morning was gone. So was my opportunity to fulfill a promise. And my recipes, I realized with belated remorse, would have completed the church cookbook that Mrs. Michaels was coordinating.

Later, as I took my son to a Cub Scout meeting, I stopped by the retired schoolteacher's home to explain. "I do hope you'll understand, Mrs. Michaels," I finished, "and forgive the delay."

The older lady was silent for what seemed a long time. And then she answered. "Of course, I understand," she said kindly. "It is so much easier to ask forgiveness for the things we leave undone than to *do* them."

Ouch! That smarted, but it's true, isn't it? True about the little promises we make to others and true about the promises we make to God. I know that He will understand each time I explain how I omitted an assignment. But He deserves better than that!

To Think and Pray About: The Bible is a book of promises— *great* promises about life here and hereafter. A promise is a sacred thing. How can we arrange time for keeping each one?

Beauty Treatments with a Guarantee

May 18

Isaiah 61:10; 1 Corinthians 1:20
Colossians 3:1,2,9,10

POOR POLLY. She's seeking the fountain of perpetual youth. There, look at her purchases at the drugstore: grapefruit astringent, corn soap, Black Hills mud pack, aloe moisturizer... sponges... brushes... tubes and sticks. Now, she rushes to the cosmetic department as if another year were in hot pursuit. Ah yes, the lady-in-waiting (with a gleam in her eye) tells Polly her coloring is just right for over-ripe boysenberry blush... underwater green mascara, and a lipstick to match each dress and blouse in her wardrobe.

Poor Polly. Don't you feel a bit sorry for her? Then, let's help her out. Help me add to this treatise on tricks guaranteed to keep you young at heart!

- Hold fast to faith in people. It is amazing how few prove unworthy of your trust.
- Master new skills, then teach them to others. Watch the joy!
- Laugh in the theaters until it hurts (clapping when the good guys win). It's a myth that anybody ever died from laughing!
- Look at your Christmas tree ornaments on a rainy day and remember how lovely the holidays were.
- Bring in the rarest flowers from your garden.
- Cry at a sunset. Laughing is the "mirth" response; weeping is the "weep" response. Psychologists now tell us that both are youthful responses to life.
- Become so engrossed in other people's joys and sorrows that they literally become yours.
- Fill your arms with so many books that you stagger home from the library (weight lifting builds firm muscles!). Begin with the Bible. End with it.

To Think and Pray About: There—the only wrinkles that remain are from laughing. Your name was omitted from the obituaries. So praise God for a new day—and a new *you!*

How May I Serve You?

Galatians 5:7-14   May 19

I WAS IN NEED of a summer job when I was in school a good many years ago. Somebody told me there was an opening as a salesperson in a local store. I applied but admitted that I had had no experience in selling.

The manager was most understanding and gave me a piece of advice that I have been able to apply to a number of life situations. See if it helps you.

"Your job is to sell, you know. And nobody ever sold much by approaching a prospective buyer and asking weakly, 'May I help you?' I prefer, 'How may I serve you?'"

The manager's assumption was that everybody who entered the store was in need of service. It was my duty to find out what that need was and how I could fill it. It sold the merchandise, I might add, for the benefit of those of you who sell. The "lookers" became "buyers."

I remember that little pointer when I find myself on the verge of asking a friend who I know is in need of help. Of course I can help! The question is how? "How can I help you?" to the person who's trying to find a spot on a map is sure to encourage a weary driver to roll down the car window and let me serve. The new person in the community will respond to a neighbor who rings the doorbell and asks, "How . . . ?" And we know that words are poor tools in the face of tragedy. It's so much better to ask for one small assignment than to say vaguely, "Now, if there's anything I can do—"

To Think and Pray About: It matters not to me his creed; he was a friend who saw my need.
I stood alone—no way to turn—he, naught expecting in return
Addressed me in unstudied phrase that touched me in its friendly ways.
I never saw my friend again; but he left me a better man . . .
My life's a service now, it's true, because of one I hardly knew.

J.M.B.

Lasting Link

I T IS just a legend. But it is lovely enough to share with your mother, your family, a friend, or a someone who is lonely and in need of being needed. For all have loved. . . .

One bright, cloudless day, just right for angel-flying, one of the shining creatures descended to this dark earth on a heavenly mission. Just as the sun turned the western sky to spun gold, he spread his silver wings and said softly:

"My visit is ended. But before I return to the World of Light, I must gather some mementos of my visit."

The angel looked into a beautiful flower garden and said, "How lovely and fragrant these blossoms!" He plucked the rarest roses and made a bouquet and said, "I see nothing more precious, so I shall take them with me."

But he looked a little further and saw a bright-eyed, rosy-cheeked baby, smiling into its mother's face. And he said, "Oh, that baby's smile is prettier than this bouquet. I will take that, too."

Then he looked just beyond the cradle and there was a mother's love pouring out like the silver rush of a river. And he said, "Oh, that mother's love is the prettiest thing I have seen. Although it will darken the earth some more, I must take it, too."

So, with the three treasures, he winged his way heavenward. And, pausing at the pearly gates, he said, "Before I enter, I shall examine my treasures." He looked; but the flowers had withered and the baby's smile had faded. Only the mother's love retained its pristine beauty. He sighed, tossed away all else and said, "This is the only lasting line between heaven and earth—*love!*"

To Think and Pray About: Would you leave footprints on the sands of time? Then wear work shoes—and work with children! We women have an advantage. Love is our "sole existence." (Substitute *soul.*)

Grapevines

1 John 2:8-11   May 21
John 15:1-9

"NOW YOU can see the sky!" my father called through the kitchen window (afraid, I think, to come any closer).

At first my mother refused to look. She had made no secret of her objections to Daddy's pruning the lush grapevine. The enormous leaves and Promised-Land-size clusters of fruit made the dining nook cool, shady, and inviting. But the vine also robbed the window of the right to do what a window is supposed to do: let the light shine through.

What my mother saw when at last she looked made her gasp. "I had forgotten how bright that window was before the vine took over," she admitted. Sure enough, there was a great arch of blue where the vine had been and shafts of golden sunlight danced across the floor as if in praise for their release.

There are "grapevines" in the lives of us all, I suppose. Those creeping little activities, interests, or thoughts which— given too much freedom—very quickly shut out the light. The problems are much like Mama's grapevine. They grow rapidly when watered and fed. They are too lovely to prune back, we say. Then suddenly the tentacles of darkness surround us. And the "Light of the World!" dims.

To Think and Pray About: What is your itinerary for today? Do you belong to too many organizations to help your neighbor search for a lost kitten (the only thing that brightens her life)? Do your hobbies or the play-off game keep you from church? Are your thoughts elsewhere during prayer because you're carrying an overload? See what you can prune away. Sometimes it is good to have a family caucus, too. A car wash (with tape decks turned loudly to rock) may need a pruning. Yes, the band needs new uniforms. But if the youngsters have to sacrifice their Sunday-night "sings" at the rest home, you will know what to say. God will light the way.

S-T-R-E-T-C-H

Matthew 9:20-22
2 Corinthians 10:12-17

ALMOST EVERYONE these days seems to belong to a stretch club. Do you shy away because of a childhood hang-up? Remember Mother's advice to stretch and grow tall? I obeyed which made me the "good daughter" but also caused me to outgrow my junior-high admirer! I am still afraid to join the group, although George is taller and surely I am past the growing stage. Or am I?

I saw some stretching in progress recently which caused me to reevaluate. Maybe none of us are finished growing—*ever*.

An elderly gentleman dropped a dime by the checkout stand in the supermart as he paid his bill. Immediately a tiny tot pushed ahead in line, dropped to his chubby knees, and recovered the coin.

"I found it, mister, but I dunno if I can reach you," the child said, standing on tiptoe, "unless I stretch."

"Sonny," the grandfatherly man smiled, "I think it'll take both of us stretchin'." And, with an effort, he stooped down.

And there, in that mutual "stretched-out" position, the man pressed his crinkled cheek to the ruddy cheek of the little boy. I was touched by *their* touching—all because of a stretch.

Come to think of it, maybe I do want to stretch and "grow tall" (or stoop, whichever the case may be). Out with the hang-ups. Out with the taboos. Let's design our own commercial: "*Stretch* down (or up) and touch someone—in His name." We'll come alive with growth.

To Think and Pray About: How can you stretch your day to include all that needs doing—and then some? (Hint: It *does* feel good to stretch. I just tried it . . . and our doctors will approve!) With hands uplifted, you are in a perfect posture to lift your face Godward and pray. You can almost touch His garment and, knowing you are healed in spirit, you will find a way to get those jobs done. For like the woman in today's reading, God has made you whole. Ready? S-T-R-E-T-C-H!

Unfinished Symphony

The gem cannot be polished without friction, nor man perfected without trials.

Confucius

AN ORCHESTRA, to be worthy of its name, is like love. It demands *doing* as well as *feeling*. And it *takes practice, practice, PRACTICE*. Its members may not feel like correcting the mistakes, but they do—until the problem is resolved. They may not feel that they can endure going over and over the areas in which they continue to make mistakes, but they do—until they can communicate, share, and encourage the other members in spite of the difficulties. Only then can they become a "whole." Otherwise, the symphony will be unheard.

Each instrument occupies a special "chair." Each adds a unique movement. Yet each must retain its individual beauty. And oh, how fine-tuned each instrument must be!

The metaphor holds a lesson for us all. For we form an orchestra, too. Each of us is an integral part of the whole with our families, coworkers, friends, and—yes—the stranger on the street. Until we learn this, our differences will continue to produce discord instead of music, chaos instead of God's central theme, and we will lack the harmony of peace. The beginnings of a melody are lost when even the "littlest instrument" breaks a string of communication.

To create a symphony, we must keep our ears tuned to one another, our eyes focused on the director—careful lest one section drown out another. For all must be heard. To be great, we must refuse to indulge in indifference, become uncooperative or blame others for our failures.

To Think and Pray About: Can we meet the requirements? Then the Author of love is preparing a perfect score. Our music will be majestic. The world will be a listening audience for a movement they have yet to hear.

How Long Has It Been...?

HOW LONG has it been since you:
1. Read a good book... wrote a poem... sang aloud?
2. Massaged your husband's neck... drew your children close and said, "I love you," for no reason... called a friend over for coffee, saying, "Just come as you are"?
3. Spent an hour in the hammock making the clouds into circus animals... walked alone in the woods or barefoot in the sand?
4. Took painting lessons or played the piano?
5. Walked instead of drove to work, taking a new direction... stopped at a roadside stand, bought an apple, polished it with the palm of your hand, and ate it right there?
6. Said "No" to a for-business social gathering to spend a quiet evening with your family or a few friends... baked gingerbread from scratch for them?
7. Removed the phone from the hook, filled the tub to brimming with bubble bath, and "soaked in" some of your favorite psalms of praise until the water cooled?
8. Greeted a stranger with a smile... praised a child for walking a bike across the street... let another driver go first... gave your place, after a long wait in line, to the person behind you with fewer items... stroked a kitten... hugged your dog?
9. Spotted a pesky dandelion in your yard and saved your back for picking daisies... telephoned your mother... laughed deep and long just for the sheer joy of it?
10. Made up an absolutely nutty bedtime story for a child then said, "Can't you almost hear God laughing with us?"

To Think and Pray About: *How long, then, has it been since you felt that God was in control?* He wants joy to invade our hearts and take over completely.

Home Free!

Matthew 18:10-14   May 25
Proverbs 15:23

"ONE, TWO, THREE for me! And I'm home free!" What a thrill to have slipped past all the "catchers" in that childhood game and be at home base! Remember?

Those who played "Lead Them Home" in years past will recall the rules. There was only one catcher to start the game. Then those the catcher caught trying to make it to some designated spot became catcher's-helpers.

Not getting caught was the victory. But responsibility did not end there. Once players were home, they must make every effort to find hiding places of the other players, run and rescue them—leading them by the hand past the dangers between them and home.

Of course, there was an element of risk involved. Both players might be caught. But we never thought about that. You see, we were the victors. The very thought of that strengthened our legs.

I was thinking of the little game the other day when I heard an old hymn—one as old as the game, I guess. I suppose its "ratings" have dropped as hymnals seem to have dumped it. But it sums up spiritually what "Lead Them Home" communicates. The words go like this: "Bring them in, bring them in, bring them in from the fields of sin, bring the wandering ones to Jesus . . ."

If you have accepted Jesus, you are home free! But wait—there is more. You and I must help others slip past all the dark catchers that lie in waiting. Then all of us can say victoriously, "One, two, three for me! I'm home free!" Our side has won the game.

To Think and Pray About: In what ways can you lead others to the Lord? Each of us has a gift, a skill, a "something" we can put to use without standing on the rooftops and shouting. The very taking of another's hand is the first step. God will lead you as you lead another. *Home*, a lovely word.

Let Us "Be"

"LET'S PAUSE a minute and enjoy the view," the guide said as the hikers stopped for breath on a nature walk at the Grand Canyon.

Everyone gasped in awe at the splendor spread below. The *huff-puff* of the steep mountain trail robbed the procession of a chance to see the cathedral-like monuments—some magnificent, some grotesque—time had carved along the way.

"Were those formations there when we passed?" one of the tourists teased.

The guide nodded seriously. "They were. But in our struggle to reach the top, we missed the view."

Guilty as charged. And I had been one of those hurriers. Well, no more. Then and there I let every nerve ending uncoil. I basked in the warm glow of the eternal sun overhead and watched it change the mood of the glorious feast spread below. "I have this minute, Lord," I whispered. "I have this day."

The short vacation ended as vacations must. But I brought home something more precious than a camera could have captured. I had zoomed in on one precious moment and made it mine. What's more, all can apply the guide's comments to our daily lives. Are we in such a rush to climb the ladder of success that we never look over our shoulders? So we reach the top . . . so we bump our heads on the very ceiling of achievement? How sad to realize one day that the rush to a destination robbed us of the joy of traveling. It's been said many ways. But I like the words of Edward A. Gloeggler: "In the race to be better or best, miss not the joy of being."

To Think and Pray About: Wherever you are today, it is my prayer that you will stop, look, and *be*. There's a beautiful view from here. Praise the Lord for this day. And may you see . . . may you BE!

After the Dark

Mark 9:41-50   May 27
1 Corinthians 13:8-10

Between the dusk and the dawning comes the grip of
the long, dark night—
Hours that pray with deep longing for rays of the first
morning light.
Then when the earth-dark has ended and shadows are
lifted away,
The hand that folded the darkness will bring of
immortal day.
Then there will be no more sadness; then there will be
no more tears—
Walking and talking 'mid roses God has been growing
for years.
May this be your strength and comfort, His promises
be your stay,
That He'll dry your tears with His sunshine and
darkness will vanish away.
                                                    J.M.B.

IWEPT as I prepared the lines of the poem for the memorial service, for I had grown to love the man who was kind to animals but looked with disdain on the human race. I don't remember ever seeing the 85-year-old man smile. "*You're always smiling,*" he said to me once. "Most Christians look like they're going to a funeral!"

Tomorrow is Lloyd's own funeral—without my finding a way to share the Source of my joy. More reference to my faith than he had made would have cut him off. I can only find comfort in prayer that the little things I did found a home in his heart.

My husband and I knew little about him except that he forgave us for being Christians—actually took a liking to us! George won him over first by pruning his roses (a task he deplores). I prayed for him and put his name on my prayer chain the sad day that I learned he was a victim of cancer.

To Think and Pray About: It is up to God to weigh and measure. How has He used you to minister to persons who reject a strong approach? If we can't say it, we can *pray* it!

Halfway Home

Philippians 3:14-19
                                                          John 15:14,15

ONE OF THE VERY SPECIAL things about the Sundays of my girlhood was the all-day visit (after church) with a special friend. Margaret and I alternated Sundays for years—one Sunday at her house, the next at mine—running home as fast as possible, unwilling to lose a single minute of play. And even then there was never enough time to get all our talking done.

"Come halfway home with me," Margaret begged one Sunday.

The little bonus-visit, a stolen sweet, was such fun that the next Sunday we extended it a bit. When my friend walked halfway home with me, I in turn walked back part of the way with her—a little transgression my mother overlooked for a while.

Eventually, a problem developed. The back-and-forth trips went on and on, neither of us any closer to home than when we had reached the halfway mark the first time. It was sundown, my deadline, and I knew that the halfway-home practice would be no suitable explanation. And I was right.

"You realize, don't you, that loitering is wrong when I call?" Mama said. Then, "Half the way home will never get you there!"

I lettered a little sign which helped me to overcome dilly-dallying—even with the more pleasant things in life. *Half the way home will never get you there,* it says.

To Think and Pray About: Procrastination is a thief of time. How can we avoid putting off that which needs doing? Has anybody ever served God or others by doing things *tomorrow*? It is what we do today that counts—even small things— because *if we do one small thing for someone somewhere, we help everyone everywhere!* Cervantes said: "By the streets of 'by and by,' one arrives at the house of 'never.' " Is God calling? Go all the way on the street of "Today"!

Alice in Blunderland

Proverbs 20:11; 22:6   May 29
1 Corinthians 13:11

I T BEGAN in the supermart—and ended in chaos, then understanding. My bill totaled to something resembling the national debt. While I figured which items to eliminate, my four-year-old played happily—unless you count the displays of canned goods he upset and the time he followed the butcher into the freezer. My patience, though thinning, lasted until I dropped my purse. Bryce helped by retrieving the loose change—then darted out to feed parking meters.

He and I talked privately. I reviewed the rules. Bryce listened, then said he was hungry. Fed and energized, he began a one-man game of hide-and-seek at the next stop, a fabric shop. I ignored it until he alerted bystanders by singing lustily: "Round and round the mulberry bush, the monkey chased the weasel..." and "bushes" of yardage collapsed.

I (the weasel) joined the chase—and won. One swat, properly placed, would do it. The minister chose that moment to appear as a witness from behind a bolt of goods. He wore a dark look. Why not? Hadn't he advised young parents to turn their children over to the Lord? And I had turned this one over my knee instead.

But blunders can turn to wonders. "I'm sorry," Bryce said, reaching up for a hug. I obliged just as the Memorial Weekend Street Band appropriately struck up "Stars and Stripes." I laughed through a tear. And my wonderful son laughed with me. We've always understood each other.

Ah, the flag—symbol of unity—floated past... and I looked down with pride on my future Jefferson, Franklin, and Nathan Hale rolled into one.

Bryce? He's a school administrator now—firm but gentle, a young church deacon, too. But his parents remember him as "such a good boy."

To Think and Pray About: How do you differentiate between embarrassment and a real blunder? Talk to God about your methods (they differ with each child). Do laugh together.

Everyone Loves a Parade!

I F YOU GREW UP in rural (or small-town) America, you remember Memorial Day parades. Sunrise found the waiting crowds—children claiming the vantage points, oldsters claiming the shade.

The sun rises higher and so does the excitement, for parades are never on time. Neither is the band quite in step or on key. Players drop all the flats along with their music. But nobody minds.

Ah, here come the floats . . . the VFW bearing the flag . . . the mayor and the beauty queen. But their moment of glory is stolen when 32 clowns jump from a car built to accommodate two, each throwing a lollipop. Good timing—just before the car backfires and clowns are compelled to go into a tumbling act to extinguish the fire in the seat of their pants! Remember how good it felt to laugh together?

Other recollections parade across the field of the mind today. Cemeteries bloom with flowers placed there by loving hands in memory of those who have journeyed on. Veterans' graves bloom with flags whose colors required the sacrifice supreme. All of them were the weavers of history. Let us not forget that God designed the pattern. He knew from the beginning that ours, the New World, would be shaped by the sacrificial devotion and zeal of those who caught the vision of a worthy dream.

On this Memorial Day pause wherever you are and remember a loved one you have lost. What did you admire most in that person? Hold it close to your heart—and incorporate it into your life! What greater tribute is there?

To Think and Pray About: Let us renew our sense of destiny, those things which make us grandly human and nobly divine. Isn't the continuing of the Great American Dream fulfilling God's purpose? Lift high your banner of tribute. Everyone loves a parade!

Bowing Out

Psalm 8   May 31
Matthew 11:28

YOU KNOW May is bowing out. Days are more balmy and twilight is extended. Male birds have shortened their serenades and joined the work force scratching for worms to nourish the young. Even with your eyes closed, you know that the exodus has come. June, standing just a turn-of-the-calendar away, blows warm, clover-scented breath across the meadows to tell you. Children have shed their shoes and stars have shifted in the heavens making way for a galaxy of fireflies. Everywhere there are the subtle signs of early summer.

While the children do the countdown until the last school bell rings until September, savor the moment, moms. For, as their vacation begins, yours ends! It is time for gardening... preserving... and surrendering your privacy. Not to mention endless shopping. Aside from the Christmas season, this may be the most loved by retailers and the most dreaded by parents. It is time to shop for vacation togs. Ah yes, local shops and malls have become the testing ground for family patience and love. How it can take so long for giggling girls to select "casual cool" and slouching boys to choose "killer clothes" defies scientific research. Last year's denim will never do. You see, this year's girls have rediscovered the flounce and the mini just as boys have gone back to gel and jeans that are "uneven bleached."

Things were so different a good many Junes ago, you say? Yes, and they will be different in Junes to come. Time has no resting place. So, with a small smile that suddenly turns radiant, you begin to stock the camper. You are a child again ... no, better! a child-turned-woman... remembering, as you will help this generation to remember.

To Think and Pray About: Summer is briefly yours. A time for you and yours to escape the mob, head for the seashore, mountains, wooded hills, and lakes, and to rediscover God's greatness in the changing tides, the eternal hills.

Prayer for Our June Traditions

L ORD, lead us gently over the threshold dividing spring and summer. This is such a special month, Lord—so filled with beautiful traditions. Let us observe them with merry hearts, brimming with thanksgiving for the hospitable earth You have created. But let us pause often to meditate and to pray. For we must guard and cherish our environment, our country, and our world in order to live in peace as You intended. Let us know, truly *know,* the essentials of a loving existence in harmony with You and Your other children.

Let us slacken our pace, Lord, as this season bids. May we be reminded as we look at the ancient hills—now shimmering with tender grasses—that they do their job well without calendars and clocks. Turn our eyes toward the new green crowns in the treetops and make us aware that this they achieved without hurrying. But let us remember, Lord, that no season—however ideal—lasts forever. We treasure this day, accepting it as Your gift. We measure it by how we spend it for You.

We thank You, Lord, for the beauty of each dewy rose—ever aware of Your timeliness. For this is the month of weddings, a holy state created by You and blessed by love. So inspire each Christian couple that they will challenge themselves and change the world—for You.

You have made the world beautiful for this vacation month—truly a time for refreshment. Let us escape ourselves in search of You.

We thank You, Lord, for the red, white, and blue which decorates the sky on Flag Day. May we guard that symbol while praying passionately that its protection requires no further bloodshed. Make us Christian patriots, too, Lord—embracing the world according to Your will and withdrawing from it according to Your bidding. Make us content with all You have provided and discontent with our misuse. Lead us in Your blessed tradition.

Reaching the "True Ideal"

Love is a friendly silence that travels here and there;
It shows its face in every place where people seem to care.
Love does not boast or vaunt itself, is patient, suffers long;
Then surfaces with one soft word or in a sudden song.
Great love is ever humble, forgiving, and is kind,
And when rebuffed or criticized love does not seem to mind.
Sometimes it has no voice at all, so silent is its prayer,
Then friendly hands reach out to help and tell us God is there.

J.M.B.

ARE YOU a businesswoman? A homemaker? A student? All of these? Whatever your station in life, there are periods of time when you feel pressured to "keep up with the Joneses." Maybe we should examine our goals and strive instead to get ahead of ourselves. To outstrip our yesterdays by our todays. To bear our trials more beautifully than we ever dreamed we could. To whip temptation inside and out as we never whipped it before! To give as we have never given of ourselves. To do our work with more force and finer finish than ever. Then we will have gone beyond ourselves. We will have reached God's true ideal. And, praising Him for our success, we will want to reach out and help others reach their goals. Then we will have tasted the sweet joys of success.

To Think and Pray About: Home, the smallest social unit, is where it all begins. "Here," wrote Madame Schuman-Heink, "is the roof to keep out the rain . . . four walls to keep out the wind . . . floors to keep out the cold . . . and more. Home is a baby's laugh, a mother's song, a father's strength. It is filled with loving hearts, kindness, loyalty, and comradeship. It is where joy is shared and sorrow eased. It is where money is not as important as happiness—which even the kettle sings of. Home is the first church, the first school. God bless it!" And, yes, we can take a pocketful of that ideal into the outside world with us . . . if only in a friendly silence.

A Broken Rainbow

Psalm 19:6-8   June 3
1 Corinthians 4:1-5

THE FIRST WEEK OF JUNE is "America the Beautiful Week." We recall the lyrics of Katharine Lee Bates' song with its vibrant, patriotic reminders. And I remember the week for its broken rainbow . . .

Rain was coming down in solid waves against the windows. Even the fluorescent lights in the classroom looked dismal. "Rainy day schedule," the principal told us needlessly over the crackling intercom.

Great! Another day in a fishbowl, surrounded by 32 restless children and the smell of rubber boots, wet wool, and lunch pails. Rainy-day schedule means "Stick with your post; keep the children with you throughout the day; walk them to the restrooms; see that their feet stay dry." There had been a week's downpour. Clouds were black and getting blacker. So was my mood.

"I wanta share something." That was Chester.

"Go ahead," I said, unable to put any enthusiasm in my voice.

"You first," he said, trotting up to my desk to place a cardboard cylinder in my hands. "It's a kaleidoscope. See?" Chester snatched it back and held it against one eye, twisting and turning it like a periscope which we might be needing if the rain kept up.

Then I had the child's treasure to my eye and found myself gasping. Inside the cheap cardboard tube lay a bright and shining world—breathlessly beautiful. The slightest motion rearranged the position of the fragments of colored glass into a new pattern—symmetrical and varicolored.

"It's like a broken rainbow," Chester said. "The mirrors inside put it together again—but there's gotta be light."

To Think and Pray About: Be a kaleidoscope! Whose world can you light up today? Make America beautiful with God's love! Mend a broken rainbow.

A Frog Can Croak

A LINE from Liza Minelli's life story caught my eye. "I would rather present a first-rate version of myself than a second-rate version of Mama." Judy Garland's daughter was accepting that she was unable to sing her mother's songs or make her audience cry. But she can sing her own songs and make her audience laugh.

The comment stirred the ashes of a memory. Teacher was assigning parts for a dramatization of a fairy story the class was to present to parents. One little girl was more than "poor in spirit." She was downright impoverished. "I wanted to be the princess—not an ugly *frog*!" Elaine sobbed. "Ugh!"

"What a good croak!" Lynda, her third-grade playmate said in a truly awed tone. "That's why you got that part. You're the best croaker in the class!"

Well, the story had a happy ending. The frog stole the show with bellows that rivaled those of an alligator. In fact, the frog came to feel sorry for the squeaky-voiced princess. A first-rate frog, for sure—instead of the second-rate princess she would have been.

Occasionally, I chafe at my limitations. (Shame on me!) Are you aware that the greatest achievements have come from the deprived and/or those who, because of some handicap, have risen above it to compensate? Use of the phrase "over-achiever" in the academic field always bothered me. If a child is performing at a high level, he or she obviously can do the job. So out with restrictive tests. (Can you imagine God saying, "Stop 'overachieving for Me' "?)

And out with self-imposed restrictions because of limitations we have placed on ourselves. So you can't bake a 12-egg angelfood cake like Mother's? Buy a mix. It is so much faster you can bake several—and share! You may not write the world's bestselling book, but you can write a letter. "Croak" in your own way!

To Think and Pray About: *We offer You our gifts, Lord, whatever they are!*

The "Why" of Things

S TRANGE, isn't it, how a chance remark can transport us back to memories and the "why" of things?

"I see no reason for poring over the forgotten days of the past," one of my junior-high history students complained.

Remember how we wondered the same thing? I put up some pretty good arguments—especially about math.

"Why do I need to figure how much a gross of pencils costs?" I asked in fourth grade. "Why is *pi* necessary in solving an algebraic equation?" I asked in seventh. And in high school I was rebelling against any study of plane geometry.

To this day, I've never purchased a gross of anything. And who uses 3.1416 in figuring a grocery bill? I doubt that even carpenters worry about Angle A being equal to Angle B. But all of us, in one form or another, are putting some of the answers together.

Education, we learned, was to teach us *how* to think, not *what* to think. And somehow we understood. At least, that is about all I gleaned from my math assignments. As we waded through the *why* of things and pawed at the books for answers, we began to grow. We came to understand manners and morals, the value of money, the importance of neighborliness, family ties, and little social graces. Something good came from it all— something like the logic of mathematics which helps us resolve problematic situations. Early teachings *do* remain. Today's reading makes that clear.

"We study history," I told the young student, "so there will *be* no forgotten days."

To Think and Pray About: We are a diverse people in our land. It is important that we know how to think lest we be "blown about" by false doctrines. Read God's Word. Meditate. Ask for guidance from the Holy Spirit. Then you are armed with answers to the *why* of things. Let no day be forgotten. Find gladness in its difficulty and share its gifts.

Children of the Universe

NO MATTER WHAT THE WEATHER, Aunt Becky used to look out the window and say, "What a wonderful world!"

Until her visits, I had never given much thought to the beauty of our old house or its surroundings. Mostly the trees were scrub oaks and the grass was wild bermuda which turned brown with the winter frost or the summer sun. But Aunt Becky pointed out the intricacy of each acorn cup and blade of grass. And she said the house had "character" because it had been lived in and beckoned others.

As I grew older, I began to see the world was lovely because this grand aunt saw it through loving eyes. And she saw people the same way. They were all "children of the universe" she declared, and each had as much right to be here as the oak trees and the bermuda grass. We must be gentle with them and look for the hidden beauty as she had looked for it in the acorn cups and the blades of grass. We could not be selective. Love embraced *all*.

Aunt Becky has been gone for many years, but her teachings linger. With all the rumbling and rushing, with all the fears, complaints, and peculiarities, the world is peopled with wonderful "children of the universe." The world and all that is in it belong to God. I must never lose sight of His having created it and saying, "It is good," remembering always that this includes all people. It is easy to love the lovely. The difficulty comes with loving the *un*lovely—until I see them through His eyes. The non-Christian? *Especially* so!

To Think and Pray About: Look about you today. Find someone who is less lovely than those whom you usually encounter—an "untouchable" or a person whose code, creed, or color does not match your own. And reach out to that child of the universe. "Whether or not it is clear to you, rest assured that the universe is unfolding as it should"—Anonymous. And let us add "in God's way."

When Words Aren't Enough

Psalm 50:14   June 7
Galatians 5:13,14; 6:9,10

HOW CAN YOU thank those salt-of-the-earth people who gladden your days? The neighbor who picks up the mail when you're gone . . . the dependable girl who does more than baby-sit—she cares . . . the boy who mows your lawn when you've pulled something out of place . . . the friend who *loves* boarding "Rover" while you vacation . . . and another who just happens to be going your way when your car won't start?

There are warm and wonderful ways to say thank you! when words aren't enough—ways that are personalized, easy on the budget, and carry a bit of yourself. And you will have the joy of giving as well as receiving. You will let yourself shine through.

- *The homemaker who waters your plants* might welcome: a cutting from a favorite potted plant . . . a made-ahead casserole in a foil, no-need-to-return pan.
- *The boy who mows the lawn* would go for an item to add to his collection (stamp, rock, etc.) . . . a birthday cake with his name spelled right.
- *The faithful sitter* would enjoy your Book-of-the-Month Club books (if she reads for pleasure) . . . scraps of material or dried flowers (if she makes doll clothing or winter bouquets) . . . *your* service if a big event is coming in her life (wedding, graduation, etc.).
- *The person who has everything and will accept nothing for services rendered?* There is always some holiday just around the corner—so try a sprouting daffodil bulb in spring . . . a jar of homemade apple butter at Thanksgiving . . . a container of gaily-colored pickled eggs at Easter.

To Think and Pray About: This little exercise will pack a real bonus. You will come to know the receiver's tastes, interests, and life-styles. And you are thanking God already by giving of yourself to others!

In the Midst of a Sinister Garden

THE GRACEFUL COLLECTION of lantana, bird-of-paradise, and wisteria (the list goes on) on a local hospital's grounds looks deceptively innocent. Until you read the signs!

Every plant in this "sinister garden" bears a warning: "Toxic, entire plant" or "Toxic, fruit and seeds."

The message is clear: *Do Not Eat!* And yet the guide tells guests, "An alarming number scoff at warnings, saying that everything here is *natural*, therefore harmless. Natural, yes, but it's possible to die a 'natural death' by sampling!"

I gasped. "Surely nobody would dare," I whispered to my friend Millie as we shepherded the children back to school after a study trip. Millie looked at me darkly. "I'd have said the same about Adam and Eve," she replied.

I winced—feeling somewhat like I was aboard a plane zooming down the runway when a wing falls off. I was so confident—but now?

Well, I might as well face it. I had given voice to what I *wanted* to believe. Too, I was denying a little voice inside me the right to a hearing. But the voice would not go away: "Aren't you a little guilty, too? Not overindulging, mind you, just nibbling a bit here and there? A berry to garnish the gossip you heard? A leaf of criticism . . . a seed of self-pity . . ."

Maybe I learned more than the children that day. We don't sin a little and get by with it, do we? It poisons us. And it harms others as well. I guess claiming that it is "natural" is the greatest evil of all. Only with God's help can we avoid that "sinister garden." We need something called self-denial (not denying the self, but denying the self to indulge in wrongdoing).

To Think and Pray About: Choose the good and live. Be long on self-denial in other ways, too.

Stoke the Furnace

Psalm 21   June 9
Psalm 34; Ephesians 6:11-18

A LETTER came from my friend Lila today. Her P.S. said: "Stoke the furnace!" In June? It's a war-surplus phrase we use.

Houses were heated by roaring monsters somebody called furnaces during World War II. They must have been rigged to test the patience and I.Q. of anybody who tried to stoke the hungry things in an effort to bribe them into giving out heat. Feeding the monsters was "man's work" in those days. That arrangement worked—until the war. It was then that all men able-bodied enough to stoke a furnace marched away. And we girls were left to do our men's job or freeze.

The night Lila's husband left, the temperature dropped to eight degrees below zero. Lila looked at the long list of things she must do in Bill's absence and called me. "Would you believe I must rotate the tires . . . surrender the extra gasoline rationing book . . . and *stoke the furnace?*" STOKE THE FURNACE! Even as Lila read, I heard the savage beast rumble hungrily in my own basement. Yes, I would believe. And yes, I was qualified by experience to lend a hand.

"I know if we don't go down, Old Ironsides will konk out—and who would be around to pull the levers and gadgets to get it going?" Lila made her way down a few steps with me behind her in the darkness.

"I've got to be brave," Lila said. "It's so small a job. But I'm so scared. Bill can wipe out a platoon. Me—I can't stoke a furnace."

"He's scared, too," I told her. "But we can maintain our cool under fire—if we pray."

Together we pried the door open and backed away from the roaring heat. I held the door. Lila shoveled. And then we saw Bill's note: *Good Girls.*

To Think and Pray About: "Fear knocked at the door. Faith answered. No one was there"—Old English legend. Pray for courage. It will come. "Stoke the furnace" you are afraid of.

Where Are the Lamps?

June 10

Romans 2:19-21
2 Peter 2:17-19

IN A CERTAIN mountain village in Europe several centuries ago (so the story goes), a nobleman wondered what legacy to leave his townspeople. At last he decided to build them a church.

Nobody saw the complete plans until the church was finished. When the people gathered, they marveled at its beauty. But one noticed an incompleteness. "Where are the lamps?" he asked. "How will the church be lighted?"

The nobleman smiled. Then he gave each family a lamp. "Each time you are here, the area in which you sit will be lighted. But when you are not here, some part of God's house will be dark."

Today we live in a world of darkness, a darkness in which even our secular problem-solvers are beginning to stumble. In spite of our "social conscience," all around us is evidence of ignorance, illiteracy, and dark imaginings. Today's reading tells us that we, as Christians, are "a light of them which are in darkness."

But the world is so big. And our lamp is so small. Yes, but we can light some small part each day. Look to the star-struck heavens. How small each star looks in the distance. Yet, put together, those tiny jewels can light the darkest night. Not one of those little lamps of heaven is ever missing—else the heavens would be less bright. Each of us is a star (or a lamp, if you will). And yes, we can make this world a brighter place. It all begins with the desire expressed in Michelangelo's prayer: "God, grant me the desire *always* to desire to be more than I can ever accomplish."

To Think and Pray About: Light your lamps. Let God send you in a new direction today. Meet someone at the crossroads of his or her life. Put on a bright face whether you feel like it or not. Gladness will come.

Resting Up or Tensing Up?

Psalm 55:6-9   June 11
Matthew 11:27-30; Mark 6:30-32

HAVE YOU had your vacation yet? You don't need one? There are some (so I read) who are "vacation neurotics"—you know: up at six, jog at seven, and so on through the day. They are afflicted with the "compulsive should" syndrome. Some go so far as to think a vacation is sin. What about you? Do you find yourself saying:

- "I need less leisure than most."
- "I am impatient with the world's slow motion."
- "I should speed up to beat that light."
- "I am lost—I forgot my watch."
- "I have nothing to do with spare time."
- "I thrive on activity and give it my undivided attention."
- "I enjoy my work better than playing."

Did you score high? Take heart—you are not alone! Recently I read a book (No, it was not a waste of time!) by Donald Demaray in which he referred to *Superwoman*. The lady, as the name implies, is one who feels she must be *super* in everything. She can smell like a flower garden 24 hours a day, rear children without emotional hang-ups, keep her husband happy, work 50 hours a week (or more), and maintain her physical, emotional, and spiritual equilibrium through it all. The good news is that a newsletter entitled *Superwoman* refuted all that. It's okay to take that guilt out of your luggage, leave some things undone, and get going on that vacation you "don't need!" Your doctor will say that your body chemistry has improved afterward. Your friends will say you look ten years younger. And God—well, He will be going with you!

To Think and Pray About: Now you *are* a superwoman, after a prayerful prelude. The world will still be here when you return—even if others are running the show imperfectly. Happy vacation!

Why Substitute?

June 12

Deuteronomy 4:2
John 1:1-17; Matthew 24:35,45,46

DO YOU FOLLOW recipes, no substitutions? I learned that is best a long time ago.

It began with an applesauce cake my husband's mother made so well. The recipe called for cinnamon and, having none on hand, I used a pinch of nutmeg. The cake had no zip.

My husband was philosophical. This wasn't the first blunder I had made in the kitchen and it wouldn't be my last (Oh, great!).

"What I mean is, we have to follow rules. Take my jobs around the house. They would be disastrous if I took liberties. Do I make sense?"

Yes, a whole lot. A nail when the job called for glue? A piece of string for wire? Putty in place of a washer? No way would our household hum so happily.

I am a *thinkaholic*—letting my thinking go out of control; but the practice pays better dividends than experimenting with recipes. I began wondering just how many liberties I take with God's Word. Aren't there times when I read into a passage what I want to find there? It is something I need to think about daily. Substituting meanings to please my own palate could be far more disastrous than using nutmeg instead of cinnamon. Maybe you'll want to think about that as you read today's suggested Scriptures.

To Think and Pray About: Why should we veer from the story line of the planet Earth, from Adam to Armageddon? It's all there. As Billy Graham says of the Bible: "No other book is so bold yet discreet, terrifying but reassuring, graphic while veiled in mystery, stern and still gracious. It is love and murder, heroes and villains, saints and tyrants, angels and demons, heaven and hell." And it has a happy ending! God searches and finds those of us who desire His eternal pleasures. Who can substitute?

Gaining Altitude

THE FLEDGLING—a wren, I think—was so tiny I marveled that it could fly. Its frail wings could scarcely hold the oversized body aloft more than a few flaps and then down to earth the little bird sank. Surely it would crash and never fly again, I thought.

Only, Mother Bird wasn't going to let this happen. Each time her baby would start to fall, she would fly beneath and—to my amazement—catch the small, fuzzy creature on her back, steady the feeble wings, and then fly from beneath to give it another try.

Baby Bird looked exhausted. Now and then it let out a pitiful little chirp of despair. But Mother would look all the more determined then, and I was sure I could hear love in her soft, twittering notes of response as, once again, she balanced the little fellow on her back.

At last, the parent bird flew skyward. Up, up, and up. Then, tilting her wings—as a plane might do—she slid from underneath her offspring. The little bird faltered. Then slowly it gained altitude and followed the mother out of sight. Confident. Triumphant. And singing a note of joy.

Watching gave me an opportunity to meditate on the many, many times I've ventured out on unsure wings, how I've faltered, lost altitude, and come dangerously close to crashing.

But each time my heavenly Father hears my chirp of despair, sees the fragility of my wings, and bears me up. Then I, like the tiny wren, am confident. Triumphant. And singing a note of joy.

To Think and Pray About: We all have those days when we can't gain altitude. A term paper's due and you sprain a wrist. Company's coming, so you vacuum with one hand—and *break* the wrist you twisted! How can you "fly" like that? You can't—alone. But God will sweep you up. In quietness and trust your strength will come. God's wings are sure!

Our Most Powerful Resource

*"I pledge allegiance to the Flag of the United
States of America and to the Republic for which it
stands, one nation under God, indivisible, with
liberty and justice for all."*

FLAG DAY. What is its origin? It dates back to June 14,
1959. On that day President Dwight D. Eisenhower signed
the bill inserting the phrase "under God" into the Pledge of
Allegiance. Today, may the words be a reminder that spiritual
weapons will forever be our country's most powerful resource.
That we must never rely solely upon laws and treaties, rockets
and bombs—but on God, the Father of the world. For:

In the beginning God builded a continent of glory. He filled
it with sweet-flowing fountains and traced it with long-wind-
ing streams. He carpeted it with soft-rolling prairies and
columned it with thundering mountains. He graced it with
deep-shadowed forests and filled them all with song.

Then He called unto a thousand peoples and summoned the
bravest among them. They came from the ends of the earth,
each bearing a gift and a hope. The glow of adventure was in
their eyes and the glory of hope was in their hearts.

And out of the bounty of earth and the labor of men; out of
the longing of hearts, and the prayer of souls; out of the
memory of ages and the hopes of the world, God fashioned a
nation of love and blessed it with a purpose sublime.

And He said, "What shall we call this land?"

And all the people said: "America—one Nation under
God."

—Adapted

To Think and Pray About: "I pledge allegiance to Thee,
Lord, and to the heavenly places in which You stand, one
family under Thee, indivisible, with hope, faith, charity, and
eternal salvation for all"—J.M.B.

Tell It to the Judge

THE SUBSTITUTE TEACHER lost control of the class when she went to the door to speak with a parent—and closed it behind her. "It's worse than a hurricane," she franticly reported to the principal. "There's no eye of calm in the center!"

When the regular teacher returned, on his desk lay a list of explanations as to the involvement of each student. These single-sentence (highly fanciful) excuses by third-graders are unedited:

"All I done was throw away a ball of used up paper I was spelling on and I didn't know the trash basket I aimed at was on Jack's head, honest."

"I plain dont no if anything happen causwe I run out the back way."

"I caint tell why Mike run into my fist and it hurt, so thats where the blood come from."

"I did'nt see nothing without my glasses."

"I gues it musta been his falt when he tole me he got hit befor."

"I bumped heads with somebody when he was a comin and I was a goin so the furst bump I put ther was a axadent."

"I couldna wrote it on the bored cause I spell bad and I never put that part on the stick figger somebody drawed neither."

"I never saw the princil cum in when I throwed the apple core, so Im sory he got hit on the spot."

"He said a bad word wich I made hem take back and I don't know wat it meens."

"Us grils tot it was horyble so we run to the grils room til we was threw."

And in summary: "What happened? I'm missing a pencil I never had."

To Think and Pray About: Well . . . what's my excuse? And yours? Let's tell it like it is to ourselves and make it right. That way we will never need "spell it out" when we give account.

Forgive . . . Forget . . . or Both?

June 16   **Isaiah 65:16-19; 1:16-18**

DO YOU SUPPOSE Eve ever forgave herself for her transgression in the garden? *Should* she have? If so, did she forget? If she did, the First Lady of Eden might have committed a similar sin of being disobedient.

I have to take a quiet moment and ponder that when I read articles in which writers use old words in a new way like our grandmothers used to rewind used yarn, mixing the colors until they lost their identity in the rolling. Today the item had to do with forgetting the past (on purpose, mind you). We were to forget our failures (the Christian article said). Psychologists would agree. Once we have opened the black umbrella of despair and walked beneath it briefly, we are to close it again and walk in the sunshine of self-discovery. We were to forget our hurts (which I took to mean forgive those who inflicted the wound, real or imagined). You see, I use the words *forgive* and *forget* interchangeably. So it was only natural that I should bog down when I learned that I was to forget my achievements, my pleasures, and my kindnesses (small though the latter appear in my eyes). Yet I *need* to remember those. Here I had to stop and ask: *Am I winding the yarn wrong?* Let's rearrange the words to put *forgiving* before *forgetting*.

To Think and Pray About: Have you judged yourself instead of leaving that to God? Warning: You'll come up guilty every time. So pluck the mote from your eye and set about forgiving yourself. Face whatever you have done (one issue at a time, please). "I exaggerate all the time" is more than you can swallow in a lifetime. "I embellished the truth yesterday" is bite-size—something you can chew, digest, and eliminate (after God's forgiveness). Now you are forgiven by God and self so why not rejoice in your achievement? Forget? Yes, forget that incident (God has!) but be on guard for another, knowing you *can* overcome. But we must remember, you and I, that our flaws do not disappear immediately; rather, they ebb out slowly like a brackish tide. God will remove the tracks!

Silence, P-L-E-A-S-E!

John 10:14   June 17
Ephesians 2:13-18

NO PRAYER, writers suggest, is complete without silence reserved for God's answer. But how can I hear Him . . . or, for that matter, how can He hear *me* when, by nature, I do all the talking? You see, a sound barrier separates us. Even when I am quiet, there is static.

Please harbor no idea that I fancy myself a better person than my rock-music-loving acquaintances. But do those young people doing car washes need to turn radios to high-decibel rock? And why do drivers who prefer noise to music always roll their car windows down in another form of highway assault? I can leave restaurants which have provocative menus and provocative prices—but *un*provocative blares. And I can hang up when somebody puts my call on "hold" and jars my ear with a practice session of "Rock, Rock, Rock!" And what does one do when the shopping malls play rock music?

Eventually came the day when I had to face rock music in one of the places I feared the most—an elevator. I had no choice except to take the elevator, and if ever I needed to pray for courage, it was then. The death trap was as packed with future corpses like me as peanuts in a vacuum-sealed jar. And the accident waiting to happen did! Power failed and I was between floors in that dark cube of confinement. Hysteria gripped my throat. Rock music blared through the elevator speaker and I was doomed to be bombarded throughout the rescue mission. Mercifully, the rock music died soon after the power failure.

Okay! Next step: *elevators, fear of.* A sudden theory was born. Maybe I could find a thin slice of peace now that God could hear my prayer. I tested the theory. And it worked! It was as if a mighty voice said: "I am with you on the mountaintops and in the dark valleys. Why not in this small box?"

To Think and Pray About: Would that the electronically entranced used earphones. *Lord, now I know that You speak to the heart and by an act of the will I can hear You in tight places.*

Cleaning Out a Handbag

MY PURSE AND I—like my body and me—have never been separated since, well, whenever it was that I first started carrying one. I have no plan of parting with it any more than I plan to let go of my other parts. It would take a surgeon to remove it—and then under protest. Women are to handbags as men are to motors—or something like that.

However, after a recent short trip, I reached a painful decision. I came home with a crooked spine from adding "just one thing more" to the address books, stationery, aspirin tablets, and an extra pair of shoes (in case high heels became too much).

"Do you mean you're discarding this felt pen?" my son asked.

"There's no cap and the ink dried up," I told him.

"And the coffee coupons?" Bryce persisted.

"Expired—two years ago."

"But the keys—hey, what do they open?"

"A trunk I owned in college."

He watched wordlessly from that point as I pulled out unwrapped gum, used tissues, and a broken mirror—finally touching bottom. And that's where I found the tiny Bible I had dropped into the purse about the time I bought it. The little book was yellow with age, rumpled, and dog-eared. But not from use. No, its sad state was due to neglect. All too often I just skim off the top between uses, picking up essentials like my reading glasses—never getting to the bottom of things.

Essentials, did I say? What could be more essential than God's Word? Yes, I read the Bible at home. And yes, I read the Gideons' copies in motels. But it was time I put my purse in the kind of order that would not embarrass me if someone else peeked inside for my I.D.

To Think and Pray About: How can we put our hearts in order so that we are not ashamed when Jesus Himself looks inside? Is His Word on top?

"Daddy Do!"

Ephesians 6:1-10   June 19
Psalm 103:13

WHEN our son, Bryce, was about three, he decided
there was nothing my husband was unable to do. No
matter what the problem, inevitably our little boy said,
"Daddy do."

It became a household password. When my vacuum sweeper
developed a wheeze, "Daddy do," I would say. If the sink
stopped up, our Bryce would pass the word before I had an
opportunity.

And then came the dreadful accident in which our child was
injured and in need of immediate medical attention. "No, no!
Daddy do!" Bryce screamed in a way that wrenched our hearts.

My husband looked at me helplessly. Then he did all there
was to do. He simply scooped the child up gently, said a few
reassuring words, and—holding him close—rushed into the
doctor's office.

That was enough. Daddy had been there. Daddy (not the
doctor) had put our little Humpty-Dumpty together again.

What a wonderful thought that we can trust our heavenly
Father as children trust their earthly fathers. There is nothing
in this world or in the world-to-come that He cannot do— *if*
we trust Him. Those of us who have tried Him know that
already. And we urge the rest of you readers to put Him to the
test. Whatever your problem, "God do!"

To Think and Pray About: *Mother's checklist*—How can you
build a positive image of your husband in your children's eyes?
Do you send them to their father for discipline more often
than for love? *Father's checklist*—Do you *demand* the best or
command it? How do you serve as a role model for your offspring? (You are ten feet high to them!) *Children's checklist*—
Have you hugged your parents today? Say, "I love you." *Everybody's checklist*—Consider the commandment to love God
with all your heart. How does this make all else fall into place?
Happy Father's Day, Lord!

"Honor Thy Father"

June 20   Exodus 20:12
                                                     Proverbs 22:6

DADDY, I wish you were here today. I am baking a ham for dinner. Mama always said that I overindulged you. But it was not your favorite foods that took you from us. It was time . . .

I was always my father's daughter, you know. I looked like you. I talked like you. And remember how we laughed together? You took away some of the laughter when you departed. But you left me with the "Master's smile" . . . and a map to heaven.

We continue to honor your memory, Daddy. You are still the "head of the table" in our hearts. Your decision was always the ruling one (though we smiled when Mama turned her back) . . . and I guess that is the way I have brought up my son. I never minded your being the governor (therefore, the disciplinarian) because I always gave you credit for being wiser than the rest of us.

I wish you could see some of the new TV shows in which the father steps down from his pedestal and becomes a friend. He makes mistakes. But he is no less revered than when you were here. He's just a little more approachable . . . a little *closer* . . . but, then, *you* always were. Thank you for the memories, Daddy. And thank you for the training. Tell God I will never let you down . . . J.M.B.

To Think and Pray About: Fathers, yours is the most gigantic of all earthly assignments. You're asked to give love when you need loving yourself. And you give it. You're asked questions when you are seeking answers. But you answer. You're expected to be strong while you are praying away your weakness. But you share strength. You're asked to hold us all up when you feel yourself falling. But you let us lean. What thanks do you get? Just knowing that there is nobody else who could take your place . . . that we adore you . . . and that God knew what He was doing when He put you in charge. For that we thank Him.

My Birthday Questionnaire

WITH THE SAME REGULARITY of the summer solstice, my birthday arrives on June 21. And, with equal regularity, I receive more attention than my simple tastes require. *Because of love.* So why should I ski down the bunny slopes when I can reach a mountaintop?

This year, I shall be a gracious receiver. David sang his psalms to the towering hills, focusing on Him whose fingers shaped them. Instead of a song, I shall prepare a questionnaire to rate my appreciation.

- Am I as open, as honest, with my husband as I am with my doctor?
- Am I as enthusiastic over his gift as when one of my new books arrives?
- Am I as careful with my grooming as if I were applying for a job?
- Am I absolutely sure my husband knows he places second only to God?
- Do I laugh at my mother's stories as I did when she read the "funnies" to me as a child?
- Do I still seek her advice, listening as if she were my lawyer?
- Do I tell her over and over how lovely she grows?
- Do I make it plain that her greatest gift was teaching me of Jesus?
- Have I cut the umbilical cord and allowed my son to become my closest pal, treating him with the respect he and his wife deserve?
- Have I continued to show compassion with his emotional pain that I once reserved for his trip to the dentist?
- Have I always, *always*, let him know that the gift of his presence saves my day—when I am the peg and the world is a mallet?

To Think and Pray About: To those who share my anniversary, *Happy Birthday!* Lock these ideas in the safety-deposit box of your heart, sharing them in your own way.

Joshua's Day

SOME CALL IT "Joshua's Day." Others call it the "Summer Solstice." By whatever name, the day is another marker in the endless cord of time, the day holding a single moment in the hollow of its hand in which the sun stands still (according to ancient scholars).

Ah, that it could be so. Would that the lush, warm days of green achievement and blossom-sweet rest could go on interminably. Here we would linger, at the year's meridian, and know the luxury of time without a swinging pendulum.

But the sun, like our lives, is in perpetual motion. Having achieved its zenith, it now turns back. Or, so it seems. Actually, of course, it is the earth—suspended by the sun's power—that pulls away, shortening the daylight hours, and moving slowly but surely toward autumn's color and winter's dark as the earth tilts on its axis.

But for now, we give no thought to summer's end. Doesn't the solstice mark its beginning? So we languish in the beauty of bee-drone days and firefly-lit nights. We inhale the mixed fragrances of June's roses and new-mown hay. We sweeten our tongues with the ripening berries—too comforted to think of preserving anything but the moment. Even the rivers slow down, having forgotten the floods of March-gone-past and icy fingers of November-to-come. Summer is forever.

And in a very real sense, they are right. God assures us that there will be another summer; hence, another flowering June, painted with silver-misted mornings and long, purple twilights. Year after year, God will turn His Great Calendar from spring's urgent growing to the tranquility of this month. But every meadow and field will remind us that it is a time of quiet abundance—that the long night is coming and we must store away what the sun has nourished. Already time is fleet of foot. June waits . . . reluctant to go, but fading . . .

To Think and Pray About: How is a season like our lives?

Use of That Good Right Arm

Psalm 89:13
Luke 11:4-10

June 23

There are few situations hopeless if love and faith enter into them. Anonymous

TANYA AND TOM quarreled bitterly and separated. Their friends doubted if the couple would get back together. The hostility was too deep and both were much too stubborn to make the first move.

Mrs. Barnhart, who had known Tanya since she was born, was bolder than the others. She approached the unhappy girl first.

"Still trust him?" Tanya did, but . . .

The practical lady marched out and over to the apartment Tom had taken temporarily. "Still love her?"

"I'd give my right arm to have her back, but . . ."

"Malarkey! You don't have to *give* it. Just put it around her!"

Why is it hard for us to reach out and touch those we love when words won't come? A touch can mean so much and say what words will not.

I've never needed to apply Mrs. Barnhart's approach in my marital situation. But I've found that it's a balm when it comes to apologizing to persons I have hurt. Words of apology come hard for me. I say too much or too little. I feel guilty and end up making the other person feel guilty, too.

There are times when I would "give my right arm" to take back a thoughtless word. But once a word is said, it can never be *unsaid*. It is then that I remember that I don't have to sacrifice an arm, after all. Just use it as a gesture of affection!

To Think and Pray About: So how's your good right arm today? Feel like laying it across the shoulders of the person at the water cooler you scolded for failing to return the pen borrowed from your desk? Feel like hugging the offspring who only wet his toothbrush when you told him to brush his teeth? Praise God for the arm He gave you—not to sacrifice on His altar, but to lay across the shoulders of someone who hurts.

Landscaping Our Lives

THE LANDSCAPE GARDENER looked surprised. "Will you say that again, ma'am?"

The lady-of-the-house waved a hand to include the several-acre woodland she was having landscaped. "I want a picture of how it will all look when it's finished—fish pond and rose garden included. Could it look like this sketch in *Better Homes and Gardens?*"

"Hard to say, you know," the man said after a pause. "Most folks get a notion that land's like cloth. You can cut it out, stitch it up, and forget about it. But we're dealing here with living things. I can show you a pattern, I guess, but these things grow. Okay? So you're going to have to keep on planting, cultivating, and trimming. Who's to say what it will look like some day? It's just never going to get finished growing!"

My friend and I smiled at each other as the man's experienced hands went back to their work.

"I had no idea I was hiring a philosopher," Marilyn said over coffee. "But that little speech reminded me that growth doesn't stop when we reach our full height."

No, not even in a physical sense. We have to flesh out or trim off our "baby fat." We have to observe the basic health rules to maintain that "picture" we want of ourselves. But isn't growth in our spiritual life even more pronounced? We, too, are "living things." So we must keep planting in faith, cultivating with prayer, and pruning out that which is unholy. For it is God's plan that "we never get finished growing."

To Think and Pray About: How will you grow today? Help someone across a busy street. Yield at an intersection. Read an extra verse in the Bible. Praise God for the sun-dappled shade in the heat of the day. *And . . . ?*

Trapped

RECENTLY I visited a perfect place where the not-so-perfect are locked away. "Homes" they are called—a sad misnomer.

From the outside Sunshine Cottage, which housed mentally handicapped children, looked inviting. And it was a fantastic day! The June sky was tile-blue, a refreshing backdrop for small pines holding their heads up high, as if auditioning for Christmas trees. But behind the landscaping were the "unteachables" (actually "un*touch*ables").

Nurses moved about efficiently adjusting straps, braces, bars, and computerized monitors. They spoke in the starched tones of those who are skilled in their profession but know little of love.

The meal looked appetizing enough, but few children could feed themselves and stared blankly at the walls with unfocused eyes as they accepted spoonfuls from attendants. Didn't parents ever come? "Not to feed them," I was told. "Parents are busy—far away—embarrassed—"

"There's little we can do," the woman told me tiredly. And I guess she is right—in a sense. But just one gesture of love—who knows where it can lead? Who knows what the "handicapped" understand?

I looked at a little boy with a skeleton-frame and an oversized head. *What would Jesus have done?* Without further hesitation I walked to him and pulled the enlarged head against my body. And for one holy moment he held my gaze, this wee soul who, by a trick of chromosomes, is trapped inside a body that is imperfect, neglected, and lonely.

To Think and Pray About: We are a strange society. We talk to babies, never knowing if they understand. We talk to animals like they are Harvard graduates. Yet, we turn our backs on these special children. If you know of an institution in need, be a volunteer for Jesus!

What I Like About You!

THE PERT LITTLE HAIRDRESSER had a certain flair. It showed in the way she listened attentively while her patrons complained about former operators or told her why they didn't like last week's "do." It showed even more as her deft fingers lifted, fluffed, or parted strands of hair, somehow managing to make the skimpiest hair look like Rapunzel's— her "crowning glory," indeed.

"Yes, a neckline like this looks chic with an upsweep," she would say. Or, "Look—a widow's peak! Let's show it off."

"Will most of them be back?" I asked when it was my turn for a trim.

"Oh, yes!" the young lady operator said confidently. "Most of the time it's not the styles they're looking for. It's something to like about themselves. I look for it and help them to make the most of their strong points."

Wouldn't we have a congregation of working worshipers in our churches if we made a concentrated effort to point up in some way the good in each member? You can begin the movement right where you are. (It will work with colleagues and neighbors as well.)

I am thinking of my own group. Now, Ellen makes the lightest pastry . . . Gladys has a way with children. Nobody's smile warms my heart like Jo's. But have I told them what I've discovered? And there are other areas of concern, too—areas I am unable to handle but which I must recognize. There's Mary who needs to make another appointment with God. He can restore her former glory. I must pray for her.

To Think and Pray About: Try a "What I Like About You" game in any group of people close to you. Concentrate on the person to your right (lest someone be left out). Find something you admire and say so! Now, sometimes it is hard (all the more challenging!). My husband has a cure for that. "I don't like that man," he's apt to say. "I must get to know him."

Happy Birthday to My Husband

Proverbs 12:4   June 27
Colossians 3:17-19

HAPPY BIRTHDAY, George! "In sickness and in health . . ." We said it so glibly at the altar. I remember that your voice, although it quavered, was louder than mine as we took our vows.

I always knew we had a good marriage—that you never played games with the most precious, fragile, and sacred relationship God has created. But I am afraid that I took it for granted, living in the security of the assertive manner in which you said "I do!" That is, until the last three years when the "sickness and health" clause became a reality. I have walked through the literal "valley of shadow," but you—along with God—have walked with me.

I thank you for all you have done, all you have been, and all you put up with. I deem it more incredible that *you* reached another birthday than my own reaching a milestone, for you had to kick off on every play. Me? I was the "wide receiver." You made life bearable. I was the *bear*!

You were housebound—a male nurse, chef, housekeeper (and yes, you do windows), plus all the other things from which women cry for liberation. While I, except for the pain, reigned like a bedridden queen. And never once would you allow a "changing of the guard." So thank you for:

- Paying my pain more attention than Quarterback Dan Fouts' standing.
- Monitoring my blood pressure, feeding me on schedule, and holding my hand until I fell asleep—or you did.
- Listening to my mechanical failures as intently as you listen to the auto mechanic.
- Pampering me more than the lawn.
- Putting your business on "hold."
- Saying "This gives me a chance to show my love!"

To Think and Pray About: Draw closer to a loved one. Pray for the "world family."

Needed: A Spiritual Glow

Matthew 5:13-16
1 Thessalonians 5:5-8

JUNE is the traditional month for schools to recess for the summer. And for retiring teachers, the long recess has come. It is a time for reflection. Yes, that is just the word. Here's why.

Recently I attended a brief but impressive retirement ceremony. High school coaches retire every year, I know. But this man was special. The students recognized that with just the right words.

"Cy here's more than a coach to his men," said the captain of the football team. "He was the best example in leadership we've ever had. Something made him glow—but that's not all! This man found a switch inside each of us, flipped it on, and made us glow right along with him!"

Yes, the ceremony was brief. What more is there to say of such a person? There was hardly a dry eye in the packed auditorium and my prayer is that each person went away as inspired as I. Not to be a coach necessarily. Or to be lauded at a retirement party. But to glow with that inner light that God's love offers . . . to look for and find the switch that turns that light on for others. He needs you for His "reflection."

We don't have to be great to do great things, do we? It takes so little really to let others see their "candlepower." Sometimes a little word of praise. Sometimes a smile of acceptance . . . a warm clasping of hands . . . or a wave to a new neighbor.

To Think and Pray About: What other ways can you think of which will let Christ shine through you? We are on His team, you know. So let's start the day with a glow. And share it, so that others will turn on and glorify our Lord. And if you are retiring this year, don't let that flame be extinguished. You have time now to be more creative in thinking up new ways to serve with a glow. God bless you as you flip on the switch for Him!

Love Without Measure

Genesis 2:18   June 29
Matthew 19:6-9

JUNE, traditionally, is the month for weddings. Mine was in October, so a friend asked teasingly how an autumn wedding had managed to survive. My answer was the usual response one makes—sharing, auditing the books together, and a little help from my grandmother. "I never thought of divorce as a solution," I ended.

"Oh, me either!" Mert said quickly, "*Murder* maybe . . ."

Seriously, marriages always lasted in our family. My grandmother took all the credit. The high incidence of marital success was due, she claimed, to her little "love note" practice.

These love notes were as traditional as "something borrowed." Grandma saw that every bride received one in her personal handwriting (the "Palmer Method" of roll-your-muscle penmanship). And here is what the notes said: "It takes two 'I-love-you's' to survive a marriage; four to maintain; six to grow; and an infinite number for love to reach maturity." The measurements were her daily dosage recommendation.

"What the world needs now is love, sweet love," say the lyrics of a once-popular song. Why, then, do we sometimes hesitate to express that emotion to each other? I, for one (and perhaps due to Grandma's teaching), like to be told. I know that I am loved by my mother, my husband, my son and his wife, and my friends. I like to hear the words "I love you." I want to do more than survive—more even than just maintain. I want to grow and mature—because of the love of others and my love for them.

To Think and Pray About: Oh, I left one out, you say? Right! The greatest love of all—in fact, the blessed One who created it. "The true measure of loving God is to love without measure," wrote St. Bernard. That would be Grandma's "infinite number." Tell someone "I love you" today. And yes, God would like to hear it, too.

The Crown of Wild Olives

JUST YESTERDAY, it seems, we were knee-deep in June, the month so honey-sweet with flowers and harmonious with the call-and-answer of mating birds in the meadows.

And now, we must bid it farewell. I watch the bees gathering the last nectar from the fading pinks. I listen for the short before-dawn serenades of the parent-birds (and perhaps their babies) and their sleepy good nights at dusk. But no more do they entertain the world at noon.

It is as if they have stored their song as the bees stored their honey and as we, hopefully, have stored remembered traditions. July, the "sensible month," is ready to enter.

Wherever you are, your senses are piqued by the season's abundance. Here in California, black olives are purpling the ground and I am recalling a legend, so sacred in tone, by John Ruskin speaking to the hearts of us all:

> No jeweled circlet flaming through Heaven above the height of unmerited throne, only some few leaves of wild olive, cool to the tired brow, through a few years of peace. It should have been gold, they thought; but Jupiter was poor; this was the best the god could give them. Not in war, not in wealth, not in tyranny, was there any happiness—only in kindly peace, fruitful and free. The wreath was of *wild olive*—the tree that grows carelessly, tufting the rocks with no vivid bloom, no verdure of branch; only with soft snow of blossom mixed with sharp embroidery . . . but earning great honor and sweet rest . . . serviceable for the life that now is . . . and promise of that which is to come.

To Think and Pray About: In the blessed gift of God's time, the wild olive has been tamed, its thistles removed, its fruit now nourishing. May it be so with our hearts! Else the crown—and the cross—were in vain. Honor the sacred memory.

My July "Wake-up" Prayer

WAKE ME UP, LORD. Shake me into an awareness of the inequalities around me. Call my name. Jar me if you must. But don't let me slumber until things are right in my country, the world, and me. Alert me to the small things—which are not small at all—that are overlooked. The just-within-the-law deals which rob new citizens of their inalienable rights. The conniving sales and contracts with those who do not know our laws. The arrogance which wears a courteous face to thinly veil the intolerance . . . the snickers . . . the leers . . . the acceptance of the ethnic slurs.

Wake me up, Lord, in this month so fat with good food and drink that I am groggy—this month so warm and right for dozing that I take no time for meditation or repentance when I let these wrongs go unrighted. Give me an early wake-up call, Lord, before I become conditioned to the meaningless flattery given and received.

Pry my eyes wide open, Lord. Make me see that every right I use in this Land of Freedom is a right of all others—too often denied. Draw my eyes back, when I would turn away, to the bruises on those who are stepped on. Make me care more about the families trapped in the ghettos . . . the hungry who are too proud to ask for help . . . the children who are misfits at school . . . and the elderly who are crammed into "rest homes" where there is no peace.

I am slow of speech, Lord, when I should be ministering to those locked away from society—men, women, and children who are sometimes forgotten by loved ones who are ashamed of the barred windows. Put the words in my mouth. Lay the burden on my heart. Ignore my excuses. Deny me my rest until I become involved in making all Your children free. Only then, Lord, will they be receptive to the message of Your love. Wake me up, Lord. Make me care!

The Voice and the Echo

July 2 John 15:14-16
1 John 4:10

IT TAKES a while for friendship to mature, they say. Not in some cases.

I loved Echo from the moment I met her—even her name. We were a part of each other. I was her voice, she said. And she was my echo.

We were little girls then, but the memory remains. My friend . . . what she meant to me . . . what I learned from her . . . and the feeling of having known each other forever.

"Did we ever meet—before now, I mean?" I asked once.

Echo shook her dark Dutch bob. "But I knew you anyway."

It was from Echo that I learned one of life's well-guarded secrets. Friendships are made when two people meet who have a mutual need for each other. Then, somehow, length of the association makes little difference. Each recognizes in the other a warmth not found heretofore . . . that special something which makes them one voice. And true friendships (rooted in love) grow sweeter as the years go by. It is almost as if they were preordained. Someone loves us and is out there searching until at last we meet.

Anyhow, that's how it was when I met another Friend! Had I met Him before? No, but He knew me anyway—and loved me before I learned to love Him. Then He became the voice; I, the echo. And now we are "one!"

Have you met Him? Jesus is His name. He's waiting to meet you and offer eternal friendship.

To Think and Pray About: Perhaps you have met that blessed One. Then introduce Him to your other friends. "Friends are like the hands of God reaching out to us here on earth," says Billy Graham. To this let's add that friends are the *echo of His voice.*

No Tomorrow?

"WHAT would you do if I told you this was your last day of life?" The professor asked in a doomsday voice.

Most of us were startled to silence. But one fellow student responded immediately: "It would depend on our ages."

True? Maybe to some degree. Younger people, feeling they had never really "lived," might crowd what they consider essential ingredients of happiness into each fleeting moment. Those with families would seek out their loved ones surely, and the hard-and-fast livers would go on living hard and fast in their eat-drink-and-be-merry ways. More practical folk would set their houses in order.

But should our activities on a designated "last day" vary that much? Any earthly day is a potential last one. Is age the factor?

The human species can learn much from nature. Consider the Marvel-of-Peru, the tropical plant sometimes known as the four-o'clock bush. The star-like flowers—white, pink, red, yellow, or variegated—open late in the afternoon of a summer's day. The little blossoms must learn patience in their infancy. The parent plant is thickly covered with bright green leaves which are overprotective of their young. Each bud must wait its turn for the sun to touch it before its eyes are opened for a short day of life. Could God have created the wee blooms, granted but one day, to communicate in flower language?

"I have this day—a few short hours—to feel the warm sun open my eyes to earth's beauty and teach the value of each moment. I can demonstrate serenity and strength in case of storm or I can tremble, shortening my time of joy and instilling fear in the hearts of others. The departing sun will close my eyes forever. I can fold gently or curl in despair when I face the dark. But I give praise for this hour!"

To Think and Pray About: Is "last day's praise" enough? We are to praise God always!

The "Indivisible" Dream

*I know three things must always be to keep our nation strong
    and free:*
*One is a hearthstone bright with cheer with busy, happy loved
    ones near;*
*One is a ready heart and hand to love and serve and keep the
    land;*
Another is a beaten way to where the people go to pray.
So long as these are kept alive nation, people will survive;
*God keep these always everywhere—the heart, the home, the
    place of prayer.*

                                              J.M.B.

GOD CREATED the world beautiful. He created Adam
    sinless and with a controlled freedom which allowed
him to roam the Garden unafraid. And then He added one
freedom more: *freedom of choice.*

You know the story. You know the agony of a wrong choice—
and all the suffering and bloodshed that followed. We are still
trying to put the world back together for Him. He has smiled
with favor on the New World we call America. Truly, He has
"shed His grace" on us: *spacious skies* that offer a roof to the
oppressed of other lands; *waves of grain* so bountiful that they
feed us and the hungering nations; *purple mountains* that boast
of water, minerals, and forests; *fruited plains*, once a wilderness
and now another Eden; and *liberty.*

Again, we are the guardians. Is there hope? There is always
hope if our strength is in the Lord! Not in the Garden of
Eden . . . halls of Congress . . . offices of military officers . . .
atomic energy plants or stockpiles of ammunitions . . . soci-
eties or organizations. No, the beginning must be in *you*! Just
as God is our hope, we are His!

So here's to a new *you*! A more prayerful, more understanding, more loving you.

To Think and Pray About: Can we do it? Of course, we can!
Aren't we and our Lord "indivisible"?

Happy Birthday, Chosen One!

YOUR BIRTHDAY always starts me laughing and crying, Bryce. Laughing at my fears and blunders.

It occurs to me that I have never shared with you the events of the night which is supposed to be so special: "Bringing Baby Home."

With most parents, it's different. They know when baby is due. We had no warning since the judge, not the doctor, delivered you into our hands. The labor was all paperwork, so your father did his pacing across the floor afterward—while I checked wildly through Dr. Spock's *Baby and Child Care.* You were never a crying baby, so we had to take turns as he paced and I thumbed while we were listening for your breathing. You were so precious to us that we were sure you would not survive the night. We two were the ones who almost didn't.

I found I needed everything from *absorbent cotton* to *zinc ointment:* thermometers . . . cod liver oil . . . and diaper pails (no Pampers then) in between. But now, a bed we must have. A beautiful bassinet, lined with silk, with pig's-hair mattress flashed across my mind.

And then I remembered Mary's plight. She and Joseph had none of these "essentials" and the Baby Jesus didn't care. A manger cradled the King . . . so a clothes basket should bed the world's second greatest male child.

That was the "In the beginning" night. And there followed so many other beginnings—and endings. Your first hiccup undid me; your first smile undid me again (in a different way). Later came peppermint kisses—followed too quickly by "I love you's" crayoned at school . . . loss of a first tooth . . . telephones and crew cuts . . . then a breaking away.

And a homecoming—as our most cherished friend. Thank you, my darling, for your patience . . . and for the pride in saying, "I was chosed!"

To Think and Pray About: The "essentials" are the same for all children: Love and more love!

My Slogan

GARBAGE IN—GARBAGE OUT!
The puzzling sign hung just outside a neighbor's back door. Finally, my child-curiosity won out.

"What does it mean, Mrs. Nelson?"

The wise lady smiled. "My way of training my eight," she said. "You'd be surprised what they bring in—mostly junk, mind you—and leave for me to clean up. I don't out and out forbid its coming inside, since they've got to be learning some responsibility. But there's a rule that goes with it." And she pointed to the sign as a reminder.

What would Mrs. Nelson think of the "garbage" we are bombarded with today? It appears in print. It appears on TV screens. We hear it. We see it. We smell it on our streets. How much do we internalize? Not a lot if we follow Mrs. Nelson's rule. Right? It takes courage, but . . . well, let me "demonstrate."

It had been three years since I was able to attend an outdoor theater performance. What a thrill when I sat holding hands with my husband beneath the stars above the bowl, our son and his wife on the other side. Had it always been so lovely . . . the lights . . . the music? Oh, how excited I was—until the show began!

How could things have changed so much in such a short time? The play was bawdy (downright filthy) and filled with oaths and obscenity. "This is too much," George whispered in my left ear; "Mother, I'm uncomfortable—shall we leave at intermission?" Bryce whispered in my right. Something inside me exploded.

Four vacant seats after intermission would go unnoticed. Why wait? I've no idea what "Miss Manners" would say; but we walked out in protest. And others followed. *Garbage in— garbage out!*

To Think and Pray About: Point to the rule when others violate it today. Be gentle but daring. Jesus was!

Star Gazing

M AKE today bright. The star of humor can help resolve problems. But you may have to stand on tiptoe
to see one—like children do.

Lee and his brother, Don, who live next door, are learning
the constellations. Recently the boys had trouble locating the
North Star.

"I see it!" Lee, the taller one, exclaimed suddenly. "Mr.
Dubbins says the earth's axis points right to it."

His brother was having trouble with the Scout Master's
assignment. "You have to show me."

"There—just above the avocado tree!" Lee pointed skyward.

But young Don made no effort. "I can't see—I'm short—"

"Stop complaining—stand on tiptoe if you want to see the
star!"

Maybe today isn't exactly "a platter of goodies" and every
word you say turns out as dry as casserole left in the oven too
long. The boss wants 1000 copies of Z-9 Revised; and the
computer balks. Or, you're reading an exciting book and baby
has torn out the last chapter. The plane you were to take is
grounded, compelling you to settle for one less dependable-
looking than the Wright Brothers came up with. Or maybe it's
less dramatic—just a bogged-down day when your head feels
struck by a woodsman's axe.

How can you look on the bright side when you can't see over
the problems? Well, you have a choice. You can indulge in a
"pity party" or stand on tiptoe and let the shine of a star
penetrate the gloom. There you will find that God has tucked
away a sense of humor to be plucked out for just such days.

To Think and Pray About: It is a silly myth that any day can
be without pressure. We learn by it, we grow by it, when we put
our lives in the proper perspective of God's light. Praise Him
for the gift of humor and find something glad about the day—
even if it is only thankfulness that a letter reaches you the year
in which it was mailed! There—see the star?

Have a Good Day!

M Y HUSBAND and I repeatedly assured each other: "This is the year we make the move." And, repeatedly, something prevented it. The year we decided that *nothing* could stop us, something did. That's when I lost my patience—even my hope. An unfamiliar sense of depression closed in each time I thought of another wet Oregon winter with California's sun so near—and yet so far.

Great Uncle Henry chose that time to visit, bringing news of his friend Barney. Barney lived on a family homestead near the Oregon-California state line in the Siskiyou Mountains. Naturally, George's uncle explained, his friend thought of himself as an Oregonian. Then came the highway surveyor crew, announcing that the property was actually over the California line.

"Now, that was mighty bad news to old Barn—what with the California sales tax and all, but (Uncle Henry paused to chuckle) you know what he said? 'I'm powerful glad to hear the news fer I'm mighty tired of this Oregon rain!' "

There's really little we can do about the weather. But the old gent spread a ray of sunshine on my mood. How silly of me to fret over something I was unable to control—either the rain or the intended move which, hopefully, would alleviate my chronic bronchitis. But I could do something to brighten my mood.

That "rainy winter" went away. And now, years later, I need to remember to turn my thinking around when my mood is rainy. After all, every day is lovely in its own way with God in it.

To Think and Pray About: How's your mood today? Make a list of the things you would like to change. By all means, change them if you can. If not, decide how you plan to cope. God will help on request. And remember: "It's not the way the wind blows, but the way you set your sails"—*Sunshine* magazine.

Legend of Love

Romans 8:35; 5:9; 7:25   July 9

WHEW! It's hot. Everything is weeping like the willow except for the holly bush in the neighbor's yard. The leaves are glossy and the little green berries are soaking in the sun in preparation for Christmas.

Preparing for Christmas in July? Christmas recognizes no calendar. The thought of it warms my heart and cools my brow. The berries will have blushed scarlet by then.

Did you know that, according to ancient legend, before the birth of Christ holly berries were white? At the time of His crucifixion, the legend says, His cross was made of holly wood and the crown placed upon His head was woven of holly branches. The sharp-pointed leaves pierced His flesh and the white berries were stained by the crimson flow of the Lord's blood.

The story of the holy birth—beautiful though it is—leads to the cross. And that would be tragic had the story ended there! But the spilling of Christ's blood is followed by His glorious resurrection—and our salvation. So Christmas is forever!

Now, I doubt that holly berries were ever white. I think God painted them red "in the beginning." But would Christmas seem complete without the red-berried evergreen? I can look at it and know that it is no legend that once my sins were as scarlet as the berries and now they are "as white as the snow" because of Jesus' sacrifice. Can anything be more wonderful than that—at any season?

Romans 7:24 begins with "O wretched man that I am!" But we can praise the Lord with Paul for changing that. Misery changes to glory when "I" disappears and Christ appears. Even the summer heat seems more bearable!

To Think and Pray About: Have you chosen your Christmas cards? There are some wonderful half-price sales. Choose a design that spells out the Christmas miracle. Some people may never have heard the message.

An "Older Glory"

TODAY as I watched a colorful parade on TV, with our flag waving proudly in the procession, the words of Thomas Gibbs came back to me:

> Every man has leaned upon the past. Every liberty we enjoy has been bought at incredible cost. There is not a privilege or an opportunity that is not a product of other men's labors. We drink every day from wells we have not dug; we live by liberties we have not won; we are protected by institutions we have not set up. No man lives by himself alone. All the past is invested in him.

How true the words are of the glorious red, white, and blue symbol of our country. Be there a heart so dead that it does not beat a little faster at the sight of "Old Glory"?

And yet there is a greater glory, a glory which reaches farther into the past—so far, in fact, that even the most astute scholars are not sure exactly when God created the land upon which that parade marched this morning. An *"Older Glory."*

Is it, then, the flag which makes America great? Or America which makes the flag great? No, its God's children that makes America great.

We are living up to our forefathers' heritage. We welcome those immigrants seeking refuge from evil rule. We use our engineering skills to train faltering hands to serve as husbandmen in the vineyards of foreign lands. We send highly skilled nurses and doctors to teach them to bind up their wounds, teachers to teach, and ambassadors to encourage democracy. How good, how right it all seems, unless we forget the words of Dr. Gibbs—taking them all the way back to the origin. We (and they) can do only so much. God of the Older Glory must do the rest.

To Think and Pray About: Give God the glory for our freedom.

The "Devil's Toehold"

Matthew 5:21-26   July 11

MY HUSBAND who offered to lay his life at my feet before our marriage was now afraid to sample my new casserole! It was high in protein, low in fat, and designed to "save a man's life"—which might end abruptly! Statistics fail to take into account men balking at eggplant.

It's tough to fight when there's no opponent, however. George happily made himself a peanut butter sandwich and encouraged *me* to have my *Egg Plant Au Gratin*—it was probably safe. I am not the type who breaks cups or lashes out with biblical words used in away-from-the-norm context. I simply left disappointment unexpressed and retreated to a world of fantasy where a wife is never, ever annoyed—especially over her husband's food tastes. (Or shall we say a sullen silence?)

The pent-up emotion blew like a munitions plant when "Champ" from next door buried his bone in my petunia bed. The dog had always been welcome and was remorseful when I said, "Bad dog!" *because* I was hurt at my husband's behavior *because* I had a toothache and the dentist was out.

Actually, of course, the *because* of things goes back farther. The formative theology of my childhood conditioned me to repress wrath . . . never deal with it . . . forgive without coming to terms with the inner dragon and slaying it once and for all. As a result, the walls of my defense had caved in and the poor dog was the victim of my hostility. But in lashing out, I had broken the "devil's toehold." I felt drained but cleaner. Having accepted that I *was* angry was the first honest move. Now I was ready to forgive and be forgiven. *Why, oh why, Lord, do I close the wound without removing the malignancy? Forgive me.*

George found my silly hiding place (just as God had done). But my job was unfinished. "I wanted you to try the casserole—" but I got no further. "I will—" There was no time to tell him I threw the tasteless thing away. The dog was at the window waiting for a hug.

To Think and Pray About: Do you express or repress? Talk it out. Break the "devil's toehold"!

No Right to Be Angry?

July 12   Ephesians 4:26
                         Proverbs 15:1; James 1:16-20

TWO OF MY FRIENDS are at odds. Each thinks the other has violated her territorial rights if she so much as crosses the path of her thinking! It is uncanny—almost comical, were I not caught in the middle. Not as a mediator, mind you—but as a sounding board.

"You have no right to be angry!" Erin is apt to say. "But I am!" Leah will fire back. The next encounter finds them using the same lines, changing speakers. If I could get a word in edgewise, I would suggest that they are on their way to a settlement.

No right to be angry? Who said? It would be hard to get through life without righteous indignation. Slow to anger, yes, but being angry is instinctive. We all entered the world with a howl of protest and it takes a lot of love to teach us to handle that rage in an orderly fashion. Look at Erin and Leah. Still protesting, each undoubtedly carrying a heavy sackful of guilt, and yet, how many sermons do we hear giving us permission to be angry, saying it might be a healthy thing if handled properly?

God was angry with the children of Israel. Jesus was angry with the Pharisees who used the temple as a "den of thieves." So we have a God of wrath if we inflict hurt upon others and ourselves. That kind of anger is a turning away from God. Poor Erin and Leah. Unknowingly, my friends have taken two important steps: 1) recognized anger; and 2) acknowledged it. Can we help them out by suggesting the next steps? Would you agree with: 3) settle one issue at a time; 4) bury the past; 5) ask for and offer forgiveness; 6) respect one another's differences; and 7) prepare to grow?

To Think and Pray About: Ignore anger and it will go away? (You will end up with a headache and a heartache.) Talk to God about the rejections you feel. He has felt them, too!

Management

"MANAGE" is too often maligned. It sounds auto-cratic and manipulative. But where would we be without *management*? Like the color red, though bold, wouldn't we be lost without it?

Management requires skill combined with art. It is the means of accomplishing an end. We manage our time, money, and emotions. We manage homes, classrooms, jobs—and we manage our automobiles going to and returning from these places. In summary, we are all managers.

I was wondering how to manage a certain person in my life (yes—we manage people, too) when I ran across an item in *Sunshine* reprinted from an old magazine. It is as valid today as it was so long ago. Modified here and there, consider the sound advice offered in relationships with mates, children, friends, neighbors, employers, and employees. Some excerpts might even work well if you manage to pleat another driver's fender at an intersection!

> WHEN you marry a man, love him, then study him.
> IF he is honest, humor him.
> IF he is generous, appreciate him.
> WHEN he is sad, cheer him.
> IF he is quarrelsome, ignore him.
> IF he is noble, praise him.
> IF he is secretive, trust him.
> IF he is confidential, encourage him.
> IF he favors society, accompany him.
> IF he does you a favor, thank him.
> LET him think how well you understand him,
> BUT *never let him know that you manage him!*

To Think and Pray About: "Managing" requires patience, diplomacy, caring, and sharing—necessary and fulfilling in our lives. Its definition is *love!*

The Daughter of a King

July 14   2 Timothy 1:12
                              Psalm 45:9-11; Luke 12:31-34

AS A CHILD, I enjoyed hearing my grandfather tell of his friend's courtship. It seems that the chap (shy by nature and "faint of heart," Grandfather said) was not winning Fair Lady.

My grandfather suggested that his friend must be bold as a lion. "She should know what you are!"

The young man took the words literally. On bended knee, he looked up into the face of his beloved and asked, "Martha Jane, what am I?"

Martha Jane fanned herself and made no reply.

In desperation, the suitor cried out, "Martha Jane, please tell me—*what am I?*"

The fan stopped. The young lady rose. "If you don't know, I hesitate to tell you!" And with a swish of her skirts she walked out of his life.

Those "Who Am I?" and "What Am I?" games seem immature and "I"-centered. Yet it is important that we know ourselves, our strengths, and our weaknesses. So, who am I? I am known as "George Bacher's wife," "Bryce Bacher's mother," "Gussie Masters' daughter," somebody's friend... the writer... a former English teacher... a neighbor.

But when I look into the mirror of my heart, what do I see? What do *you* look for? A Ms. America with hourglass measurements? The girls who *could* have won Mr. America—you know, the Golden Boy whose biceps, when contracted, split his shirt seams? A person of great wealth, great fame, great power (all of which you may possess)? Or do you see yourself stripped of all these, as we will be one day?

To Think and Pray About: Recently a group clustered around me at the Christian book convention for autographs. Another person stepped up and asked innocently, "Are you somebody important?" Amusing—but yes, I am! I am the daughter of a king!

He Lives!

Life is real! Life is earnest!
And the grave is not its goal;
Dust thou art, to dust returnest,
Was not spoken of the soul.

Longfellow

FIRST CHILD: "I wish *I'd* lived when Jesus was on earth."

Second Child: "I don't! I wish *He* lived while *I'm* here!"

The two little boys drifted away and I went on with my playground duties.

Basically, the two children's wishes were the same. Their desire was to have Jesus live while they live. And I have never outgrown the notion that it would be wonderful to sit down and talk to Jesus in the flesh, ask Him the questions I so want answered, and follow Him in His ministries. But maybe He has an even greater need for me here and now—beginning with such small incidents as that which the children illustrated.

For them, the episode ended. For the rest of us, the story begins where they left off—they and so many countless others who do not know that Jesus *does* live. For just as surely as He walked the shores of Galilee, He left footprints for us to follow. Footprints that lead to the grave, you say? *No!* To eternal life.

To Think and Pray About: Remember the beautiful hymns of the "summer revivals"? Maybe we are in need of a revival:

He lives, He lives, Christ Jesus lives today!
He walks with me and talks with me along life's
    narrow way.
He lives, He lives, salvation to impart!
You ask me how I know He lives?
He lives within my heart.

I Can't Do It Alone!

July 16   1 Corinthians 1:25
                                2 Corinthians 12:9,10

SOMETIME during the gray hours following spinal surgery I groped my way back to a state of consciousness. In pain, but proud of outwitting the pain-killing drugs, I tried to move, couldn't because of a suit of armor called a cast, and let out a moan. That did it! Strange about hospitals—they command you to wake up then jab you with a needle to dull your wits. Five minutes later, somebody shines a light in your face and asks, "Are you sleeping?" Say "no" and you get another shot. Say "yes" and you get it anyway. Doze and they need your blood pressure (they have an absolute fetish about that and just *try* and sleep through it!). A patient down the hall has a coughing spell... another drops a bedpan and your nerves jangle louder than the sound it makes rolling down the hall. And all the while, *the pain!*

"I can't do it alone, Lord," I mutter... and maybe it's the morphine that brings a memory back...

Fascinated, I am watching my husband inspect a piece of machinery he had located in a shed. Nobody used the building we stumbled upon during a walk in the woods. George cannot stand seeing anything broken without trying to repair it. So he put a connecting pin here, a wheel on a shaft there, then picked up an enormous gear wheel that had dropped from the massive shaft. It is as broad as my husband is tall—6'2".

"You're not going to try to *lift* that?" I gasp.

He gazes at the overhead rafters. "I'd need a chain hoist, a block and tackle—or six Marines. *No, I can't do it alone.*"

Now, nobody except my husband cared about restoring a piece of antiquated equipment. Not that I consider myself "antiquated equipment" exactly, but I identified with his situation. Well, I outsmarted those hospital folk. I fought off the drug, so I was fully awake when the Voice said, "You aren't alone!"

To Think and Pray About: Praise God for His glorious assurance. Through Him, be strong!

At Close of Day

James 4:13-15; 5:7,8   July 17

I've come to the end of a near-perfect day;
I sit down to rest—alone, in a way...
My heart is so tired... what words can it say?
I watch the sun setting—a dear friend departs—
Yet I know that somewhere a bright, new day starts...
The words I can't find, but God hears our hearts.
He knows the joy each lovely hour brought...
He hears the prayer my weary heart thought.

J.M.B.

MY THEN-YOUNG UNCLE and I watched the sun race toward the western horizon. I wasn't ready for sunset to end our play. "I wish it were tomorrow already," I said.

"Well," he said with all his six-month-older wisdom, "it is in China. When we say 'Good-bye' here, the kids over there are saying 'Good morning, sun! Welcome home.' "

I pictured the happiness of the waiting children, no longer saddened by my loss. It made parting with my playmate easier, too. When I said "Good-bye," and T.J. hurried up the hill to his home, my grandmother would be waiting with a "Welcome!" And she would be proud of her son for making good his promise to come home.

That was many sunsets ago. Each day brings its challenges, its commitments to fulfill. It is good for me to remind myself that even when the face of the sun is invisible to me, it is rising for someone else—maybe, just maybe, because I have done my work well.

To Think and Pray About: Harder for us all are the "sunsets" that close a chapter of our lives before we are ready to let go. Especially the departure of a loved one. But how comforting to know that even in the final agonized whisper of "Good-bye," we know that God is waiting with outstretched arms saying, "Welcome home!"

A Common Deed—Uncommon Sparkle

THE SUMMER we were nine, my cousin Marie and I found a cheap, variety-store ring. A buried treasure she claimed, having seen the sparkle first (her version). But I dug it from the dirt.

I kept the ring but felt a twinge of childish guilt which does not prompt a proper purging. Bothered by the feeling each time I showed the worthless trinket, I stored it with my other valuables—tin foil, a used-up lipstick, rocks, and a thunder egg.

In the fall, members of my father's family planned a camping trip. As I sorted books, crayons, and toys for the outing, I ran across the ring. "If she's nice, I'll let her wear it a while," I promised the ancestral lineup of family portraits who always looked on me with such stern displeasure. Then, turning away, I muttered, "If she's not, I'll wear it just for spite."

But Marie had something that captured my attention before I could test her. "A charm string," she told us cousins. "I'm supposed to turn my back and pass the string around. If you love me, add something to make it sparkle."

"And if we don't?" Maurice teased.

Marie shifted from one foot to the other miserably. "Then you take something away," she said.

When my turn came, I was sorely tempted. Why, that string was loaded with gems for my treasure box.

And then a growing-up sort of conscience nudged me. *Supposing all the cousins took something and the string was stripped bare of love?*

I slipped the ring onto the string. I don't know if that's what made the string sparkle. But my heart was aglow.

To Think and Pray About: "Give according to your means. God will make your means according to your giving," writes John Hall. Think of examples in your life. Common deeds can glow in the dark!

An Engine or a Motor?

2 Samuel 22:29-36   July 19

IT BEARS REPEATING: There is something about the relationship between men and motors that we women usually fail to understand. But I know their source of power because my husband told me.

Until last Sunday I used the words "engine" and "motor" interchangeably. George called my attention to the difference and . . .

Well, read the little account of our conversation and see if you can answer the question posed at the end in a way that would meet with God's approval.

A city bus passed us on our daily walk. Without turning to look, my husband commented, "Diesel-powered."

"Why do their motors sound different from cars with gasoline motors?" I asked of my husband (as Paul says I am supposed to do).

"Engines," George corrected.

I saw no difference until he explained in lay terms. Roughly translated, it went like this: "An engine operates by internal combustion. A motor needs a source of power."

Interesting. "Like what?"

"Well, take an electric fan, for instance. It has a motor and has to be plugged in." He lost me after that—and anyway, I had my information.

"You aren't listening," my husband kidded a minute or so later. "Want to tell me what you're thinking?"

"That we're like motors. You know, we have to be plugged into another Source of power."

"I do believe you understand," George smiled.

To Think and Pray About: So! Which are you? An engine or a motor? Consider Abraham Lincoln's words: "I have been driven to my knees many times by the overwhelming conviction that I had nowhere else to go." *Lord, You are our Source of power—our only Source.*

A Gift That Cost Nothing

WHAT happens when we smile? Well, there is a change of facial expression. A brightening of the eyes and an upward curving of the corners of the mouth. But there's more. A smile is a sort of giving—a giving of oneself.

Smiling is inherent with me. We were a laughing sort of family. But the item below reminded me that God's gift of a merry heart is not intended for the receiver alone. It must extend beyond the family circle to include others in the larger circle of God's family.

This smile piece was distributed at an educator's convention. It changed the tone of the meeting. It changed my thinking. It can change yours when shared with the "needy" (the world's population!).

> A smile costs nothing, but gives much. It enriches those who receive, without making poorer those who give. It takes but a moment, but the memory of it sometimes lasts forever. None is so rich or mighty that he can get along without it, and none is so poor that he cannot be made rich by it. A smile creates happiness in the home, fosters good will in business, and is the countersign of friendship. It brings rest to the weary, cheer to the discouraged, sunshine to the sad, and it is nature's best antidote for trouble. Yet it cannot be bought, begged, borrowed, or stolen, for it is something that is of no value to anyone until it is given away. Some people are too tired to give you a smile. Give them one of yours, as none needs a smile so much as he who has no more to give.
>
> —Reprinted from the First American
> Title Insurance Company

To Think and Pray About: Mark Twain said, "Wrinkles should merely indicate where smiles have been." And a smile, the whisper of a merry heart, leaves footprints on the heart of the beholder. Can smiles be taught? No, but they can be caught! Spread them everywhere.

Love Is Such a Busy Word

*LOVE is such a busy word; it's always on the go; If someone's
   sick across the way, Love's always first to know.*
Its eyes see neighbors moving in and helps them to unpack;
*Caught unawares, Love's latchstring's out and begs each
   guest come back.*
Love bends an ear to childish fear and elderly complaint;
When accusations come its way, Love answers with restraint.
*When Love must taste dregs of defeat, one never hears it
   grumble;*
And when it drinks from victory's cup, Love is ever humble.
Love will forfeit any race by taking time to pray;
And Love will aid the injured one as others race away . . .
*Love must be a "Friday's Child," both loving, yes, and
   giving—*
And a Child of Saturday, working for a living!
Love uses silent wings to serve—God and humanity—
With willing hands and heart that know the joy of charity.
J.M.B.

TONY MELENDEZ, the armless guitarist whose performance for Pope John Paul II drew a spontaneous embrace from the visiting pontiff, urged other handicapped persons to pursue their dreams.

"Don't quit, don't quit," the young man begged. "I say to everyone of you that you can do just as much, if not more, than I can."

The 25-year-old (a casualty of the thalidomide drug) was born without arms. He plays a guitar with his toes. At the end of each performance, Tony flashes his famous smile. He has done more than entertain. He has inspired.

To Think and Pray About: So many times we say "no" to life, believing that it involves more strength than we can muster. Doubt is a coward. It fears analysis. So face it, take it apart, and turn the small core remaining over to Jesus.

Prison Break!

CONVERSATION between my friend and myself slowed down and then stopped. We were nearing the California State Penitentiary.

Strange that there's little to talk about. Why wouldn't we discuss the well-manicured grounds, the spotless red-tiled roofs, the gardens that seem to grow more lush than those of home owners in the vicinity?

No, not strange really. Both Hazel and I are deeply aware that the men within the confines of those walls are prisoners. And there is something about the situation with which we both identify.

It was a long time ago that we began taking the shortcut to the supermart which led by the prison. I remember our conversation well.

"I wonder if I'd panic inside those walls or just succumb to hopelessness?" I said.

Hazel looked at me in surprise. "Why, I wouldn't do either! I'd be looking for a way out!"

Now, I doubt if my friend meant scaling the walls or bribing somebody to bake her a birthday cake with a saw inside. No, of course not. She meant something more uplifting— something we've put to work in our lives. We're all prisoners, you know— prisoners of greed, jealousy, worry . . . Need I go on? But there's a way out. Just as surely as we have let life put us in prison, God can open the door, break the chains, and set us free. He's waiting to help.

To Think and Pray About: Single out one facet in your life you want changed today. Don't neglect it, for habits are cheap to come by and hard to sell. Soon it will imprison you—make you its slave. But God doesn't want you convicted. He will spring you from prison. Ask!

18 Ways to More Joyful Days

HAPPINESS CLUB is the name of the group. They spend a lot of time pursuing instead of enjoying. Nevertheless, one of their pursuits captured my attention. Hooked, I jotted down some spiritual addenda which I think turn happiness to joy.

- Lose the blues by reading a good book (*the Bible*).
- List everything making you unhappy (*and give it to God*).
- Make a list of what you are happy about (*and praise Him*).
- Decide to watch only a little TV (*include some sacred music*).
- Take a walk (*and invite a friend along*).
- Declare a Be-good-to-yourself day: Take a bubble bath, buy a new hat or tool, etc. (*and wrap your family around you*).
- Buy yourself a bouquet (*and take it to a sick acquaintance*).
- Just this once, spend more than you can afford (*for someone else*).
- Eat energy-giving food from the seven basic food groups (*then gorge yourself on the "bread of life"—see a reference Bible*).
- Bake a cake (*with someone's special recipe and share it*).
- Call two special people in your life (*and express your love*).
- Plant some bulbs (*in a few pots for giving*).
- Do at least one good deed (*anonymously*).
- Complete one unpleasant task (*for somebody else*).
- Forgive yourself (*and others*).
- Invite a friend for coffee (*and say a prayer together*).
- Smile (*at a stranger*).
- Reorganize your closets (*and your priorities: God first*).

To Think and Pray About: This kind of thinking and doing comes with a warranty for a richer walk through life. It is an extension of the Golden Rule—with the Lord at your side. *Our pursuit is You, Lord, knowing that all else will be added.*

Reasons—or Excuses

Psalm 122:1

"HONESTLY! The flimsy reasons—no, *excuses*—people give for not coming to church," Leah commented as we folded church bulletins. "Some are so feeble they tickle my funny bone."

Funny, huh? Well, maybe we should treat them as such. We could circulate a notice of a promised cure for some ills:

- Sleeping bags for the late sleeper.
- Sports updates for those who had to leave a game on TV.
- Cotton balls for adult ears or gags for babies for those bothered by the joyful noise of children.
- Earplugs if the minister shouts.
- Amplifiers for those unable to hear the choir.
- Trading stamps for those who say they're not getting their money's worth.
- Paper bags for women who had no time to get their hair done.
- Taped bird calls for men who "find God in nature."
- Bullet-proof vests for those who feel that the minister aims at them.
- Wool socks for those who tend to get cold feet at the door.
- Live bunnies for all who attend only at Easter.
- Long-range smoke detectors for women who leave roasts in the oven.
- Screened areas for those who "prefer worshiping in private."
- Aspirin for the headaches some get in crowds.
- Hammocks for those who "can't stand sitting" (*Can anybody?*).

To Think and Pray About: *So what's my excuse, Lord?* Yes, you can (and *should*) worship God other than in a formal service; but without church you miss the fellowship of those who love Him—and love *you* through Him. Go to the church of your choice this Sunday!

Dr. Saint Says, "Think You Ain't!"

Proverbs 23:7   July 25
Psalm 107:19,20

HOW POWERFUL is a right attitude? We have scarcely tapped the natural resources of the curative powers God gave us.

I remember a country doctor whose approach was revolutionary for his time. He would say briskly to a patient, "Here, take this paper and jot down all the things that are right about you."

Caught offguard, the patient would mumble, "Now, Doc, I came here today to tell you what's *wrong*."

But Dr. Saint wanted to hear about the strengths. Why? Because it was with those weapons, he said, that his patients would combat the aches and pains of creaking joints and coated tongues.

How wise he was. Recently I read a report on research conducted in Manitoba, Canada, involving some 3,000 persons. Asked to rate the state of their health, those who wrote "Excellent" or "Good" had a higher survival rate than those who wrote "Poor." That figures? Wait! There's more. Even those with physician diagnosed poor health outlived the more healthy ones.

Doesn't this carry an implication in regard to our spiritual lives? If we trust in God's strength, we will become strong. So how is your spiritual health today? Feel weak? Dr. Saint would say, "Think you ain't." And God has said (through Paul) that in our weakness we are made strong. Yes, we need good doctors. But doctors need good patients, too!

To Think and Pray About: God knows our weaknesses. But He wants us to recognize the strengths He has given—and to recognize that He is the Almighty Source of those strengths. And He will never give up on us!

Words That Hurt or Heal

"**D**ID you know you spoke 4800 words yesterday?" The question from my son lifted my eyes from the typewriter to his face as I prepared to add to the total. I relaxed when I saw there was nothing personal in the question. He had lifted it from the Trivial Pursuits game (remember when it was popular?).

But did I? I wondered then. Did I actually give voice to nearly 5000 words? I turned back to my work. But my thoughts had wandered from the written words to the spoken ones. Had they been kind? Had they been loving? Had I comforted someone... reassured another... encouraged... or coaxed a smile? Or had I been too busy getting my thoughts on paper to share them aloud?

Somewhere in my piled-high library I have an old copy of *Doing It Now*. Sort of an interesting book if one is inclined to procrastinate. There is some validity in the clichés, "Use it or lose it," "Doing beats stewing," etc. But, confronted with the news on my word-count, I recall my mental question as I laid the book aside. *Aren't some things better postponed?* Angry letters... hasty words... notes of resignation... giving voice to worry...

If words were scarce, I guess we would not misuse them. We would do well to consider the words of F. W. Robertson:

> You may tame a wild beast; the conflagration of the forest will cease when all the timber and the dry wood are consumed; but you cannot arrest the progress of that cruel word which you uttered carelessly.

To Think and Pray About: God's Word has a lot to say about words: how we are to comfort one another with them—and that we are accountable for every idle word. Can our speech patterns be changed? Yes, by prayer. *Let my 4800 today count for something in Your kingdom, Lord.*

A People Diary

E VERYBODY thinks Mr. Mac is peculiar. Doesn't his behavior in the garden prove it? Why, the man spends more time squatted on his haunches writing than he spends on spading. But, they agree, the recluse gardener does seem to have a way with growing things. Now, how could this be?

Too bad they never bother getting to know him. There once was a hole in the hedge between his house and ours—just big enough for a stick figure like me to crawl through. Untroubled by his behavior, I wriggled through the tunnel to investigate.

"Hello, what are you writing?" I asked.

I was preparing to tell him I enjoyed writing, too; but he spoke before there was time. "My Flower Diary," Mr. Mac said as matter-of-factly as if flower diaries happened every day. "That way I can learn from last year's mistakes."

As our friendship matured, my friend shared some of his notes. The ones making the greatest impression included:

- Never get discouraged. Keep planting. Keep reading. Keep asking. Become acquainted with the subject's likes.
- Review often. Think back on what went wrong or right. Learn why. Learn when to do and when not to do.
- Don't be afraid to experiment. Keep up with new ideas.
- Don't set too many goals—but stick to them.
- Learn to identify. Flowers are your friends. You should be able to call their names when you visit.

Yes, it's too bad more folk never drop by and chat with Mr. Mac. He has only flowers for friends; and yet, he has a timely message for us Christians.

To Think and Pray About: The planting season is gone for this year. But Jesus tells us that the harvest season is always with us. How about starting a "People Diary"?

Oh! Those Bad News Henrys

I T IS a paint-peeling day. Only air-conditioner repairmen and deodorant manufacturers could appreciate this heat. I must visit a friend and cheer her right out of a body cast like the one in which I all but expired. I am remembering Bad News Henrys who cheered *me* . . .

The man who sculpted me into the wee-wee-waist thing (fiberglass so you can't breathe below the belt) led me to think I would be out of it before going home. My visit in the world's most expensive motel (called a hospital) was so long that I began to think he was right. And there was so much to learn. Like how to breathe when my 24-inch waist was reduced to an 18-inch one. Like accepting the sadistic orthopedist's holding me for questioning without my attorney. And like trying to outrun (in my mind) the soothing words of an endless line of expatients who trooped in when my sentence was extended.

I thought I had internalized all my learning—until the news that I must remain incarcerated over Easter. Talk about down-*cast*! The mercury soared . . . air-conditioning failed . . . and lilies filled the halls to use up the oxygen and mingle hothouse breaths with the septic smells. See people? No! I, who had always been so tidy, now felt unfeminine and undesirable. But they came—ignoring the NO VISITORS sign and bringing chocolate bunnies (which I was too nauseated to look in the eye) and news of those who had undergone similar surgeries and never recovered. Spinal surgery was much worse than those on legs and arms which can be amputated if gangrene sets in, they said. But a backbone? Well, you know . . .

I was doing a meltdown . . . sinking into a bottomless pit of despair. . . . Until a Pink Lady, whose name I will never know, peeked in to say: "Once I was in a cast, my dear. But Jesus resurrected me—made me whole again!"

To Think and Pray About: Take the Good News of what He did for you when you visit the sick.

Some Sick Summer Series

P RETEND YOU'RE A DOCTOR making rounds on the television program ward. (Names below changed to protect the guilty.)

Patient: "Folly." Anemic musical variety featuring country star afflicted with chronic cuteness. Often delirious. Prognosis: Poor.

Patient: "My Two Moms." Admitted with seemingly terminal premise. Responding to script treatment. Prognosis: Fair.

Patient: "Siam Spice." In final stages of recovery from massive stroke last year that left it paralyzed from shoulders up. With continued treatment, may be able to express whole thoughts soon. Prognosis: Encouraging.

Patient: "Monday Tomorrow." Weekend version of weekday show. Suffering from *déjà vu.* Prognosis: Who cares?

Well, doctor? What's your recommendation? Turn the knob when one of the above TV programs comes on? Have our electricity shut off? Move to the other side of the mountain beyond their reach? It's a problem and it isn't going away.

I find myself embarrassed and offended often by the Cyclops. But condemn programs too heavily and we separate ourselves (and our Christian influence) from our children, grandchildren, and friends. We can refrain from viewing. But would that avoid the impact TV has on others around us?

It seems that the answer lies in being well-informed. How can we recommend without knowing? And remembering (alas!) that they reflect our American culture? Preview tonight's programing. Nothing on except those warning of "adult language" (an insult!) and "nudity"? Then (privately) complain to the stations (they *have* to get the ratings) and (openly) suggest a "prognosis" game as a family. You may have so much fun you won't need TV. Then you have won!

To Think and Pray About: Discuss programs objectively with those you love. Then gently prescribe. Relax. Be able to laugh. And, above all, ask God for insight.

The Borrowed Cup

THERE is an old story about the woman who lent her neighbor a cup of sugar. She then complained bitterly to her friends because it was not returned. By and by the neighbor knocked at the door. "I brought back what I borrowed," she said.

Embarrassed, the lender said, "O! I can't accept it now. You see, that would prove me wrong."

Ridiculous? Yes, but it happens—in our thinking if not in our acting. We refuse to forgive others. We refuse to forgive ourselves. We want to change and find that changing our minds is harder than changing our ways. We lose our freedom.

Why? Because when we feel guilty, we feel unworthy in God's eyes and in the eyes of others and ourselves. Ironically, the borrower was probably so guilt-ridden that she found it hard to forgive herself for dilly-dallying or forgive her neighbor for not allowing her to set things right. Oh, how human we are!

There's a solution, of course. We see only the wrongs in ourselves and others unless we allow Christ to carry our burden. He bore our shame once and for all. Now, He needs unashamed workers. Don't you wish we could remember that?

To Think and Pray About: "Of him that hopes to be forgiven it is required that he forgive himself and others. On this great duty eternity is suspended; and to him that refuses to practice is the throne of mercy inaccessible, and the Saviour of the world has been born in vain," wrote Samuel Johnson. So let's forgive and treat the wrong like a canceled note. Tear it in half. Burn it. Then neither the offender nor the offended can see it again. Why suffer? If there is someone in your life with whom you have a problem, right it. Why let it spoil your day? And why risk God's disapproval?

Mid-Summer Meditation

I T IS TIME to bid farewell to July, Lord, and we scarcely have made its acquaintance. It is time for the ripe days of August—those days that tempt our minds and bodies to become languid and lackadaisical. We know You would have us rest, Lord, but lead us away from the temptation of a lazy, laid-back attitude that becomes a lifestyle. Remind us that Your work knows no season.

We pause now, Lord, as we prepare to turn our calendar, remembering the glory of the month just past. We praise You for the memories we stored along with the sun-ripened grain, the fruits we preserved, and the vacations the month afforded. We praise You for the lessons learned right in our own back-yards. For we know that a happy life need not depend on tours abroad, journeys on busy freeways, or even leisurely holidays, but in the little things You provide. The small clumps of violets along the roadside—so shy, so small, and (purposely, Lord?) almost hidden away, so that only those who have Your peace and love in their hearts will find them. They are Your whispers from the spiritual world. The daisies blowing in a golden mist in the meadow are Your warm gleams of sunshine upon our backs as we work. And the Big Dipper and Little Dipper, in the navy-blue of the nighttime sky, remind us that You are ever watchful over us as we sleep. Thank you for Your foreverness.

As we pause, Lord, let us reflect on the blessings we too often take for granted . . . the feet which transport us among the moving shadows of the full-blown trees . . . the eyes through which we view Your wondrous handiwork and read Your Word . . . the hands to do our daily tasks.

We praise You, O Lord, for our families, friends, and *free-doms*! Freedom to climb, to achieve, to choose, to grow. And, most of all, to worship—each in our own way. For all this awesome splendor, Lord, we praise You, as together we step through the August door. . . .

My Prayer for Understanding

LORD, I am imprisoned in this cast . . . smothering . . . gasping. And yes, Lord, all those professional mourners who "visit the sick" with their accounts of those whose dry bones never healed have done their work (*not Yours!*) well. I, like David—a man after Your own heart—find myself wondering why You have not delivered me. And it is so jarring, Lord, for me, the indispensable one to my family, friends, students, readers, publishers . . . the *whole world*, Lord! . . . to see that life is going on without me. Woe is me, Lord, for my bones are less crushed than my spirit. And only You can heal me. Let me be still. Let all the world keep silent, so I can hear Your voice . . . and come to understand.

That's *it*, Lord! I can feel myself smiling with a joy that overrides the pain. Your answer is but a single word, but it is loud and clear: CAST! I am to cast my burden upon You and You will sustain me.

It all seems more bearable now, Lord. I am to help and bless others, thereby glorifying Your name. So I surrender myself anew to You—*all* of me, including this cast! Take away the debilitating encumbrances heaped upon me by those Ambassadors of Bad Tidings. My days are numbered? Yes, Lord, and so are theirs—as are the hairs on our heads—but they forgot Your promise of the new bodies in that Land-of-No-Casts!

For we are all in casts either by the nature of the flesh or created by our own folly. I see that clearly now, Lord, and I praise You for the insight. Who says I must be "whole" to serve? And so it is for "the others" that I pray, those who—not understanding Your ways—wear the dark cast of despair. Reveal to them, I pray, that the good days outnumber the bad . . . and that ultimate delivery is theirs for the asking. Let them understand.

A Different View

AH! LAZY AUGUST... sort of dangerous really. Becoming too lackadaisical leads to boredom and we start complaining. As the old song goes: "Open the door and the flies come in; shut the door and you're sweatin' agin...."

All too quickly our view of life is distorted and dusty with familiarity. In a restaurant, one can ask for a different seat, shift to a table with a view. In real life, we have to do it for ourselves. And, ironically, that is difficult. The familiar, no matter how distasteful, is a reassuring rut. So our August world narrows. We languish, take on weight, and slow our steps. Need we?

Not if we realize how little it takes to enlarge the view. A fresh perspective emerges when we do something new. Read a different kind of book. Invite a new acquaintance for coffee. Volunteer to work at the hospital one day a week. Take up a hobby. Try a new dish (at home or at a restaurant). Walk instead of riding. Open your eyes to the world around you. See it in a new way. And slowly, ever so slowly, that excitement for life will return. You have given birth to a new attitude—God's! Now, use it.

Do remember, too, the powerful gift He gave us—memory. "Looking back"—yes, but more. *Memorizing.* Try to commit to memory one of today's biblical passages of praise. Let it paint your new view with prayer.

To Think and Pray About: Others' "points of view" help, too. Here are some favorite Chinese proverbs: "A bit of fragrance always clings to the hand that gives the rose." "Little acts of kindness are stowed in the heart to sweeten objects around them." "No matter where one travels, he has not seen the world if he fails to look into the hearts that inhabit it." And "The world is too small for anything but love." August can be a lovely month—with a God's-eye view!

To Fill Another's Shoes

Psalm 17:1-5   August 3
Luke 9:57-62

W E CALLED it "barefootin' " and children practiced
it all summer in the little rural community in which I
grew up. Shoes and stockings, except on Sundays, were shelved
between June and September.

Ohhh, the wiggly-warmth of the sand between my toes and
the welcome cool of meadow grass on a hot-breathed day. And
I was about to lose those things I realized when my mother
said, "Really, June, don't you think you're too big to go places
barefoot now?"

No, I didn't. Not until I looked around me and saw that
others my age were breaking our hard-and-fast rules. Well, let
them. I, for one, was not sacrificing my freedom. Need I be a
follower?

Then came the fateful birthday party. My hostess-friend
was done up in ruffles and every guest was wearing shoes.
Except me!

Now, maybe I would have gone on being the maverick
except for the kind of election we held. Our group of little girls
had a sort of president who presided over all get-togethers
(purpose of which was to decide where the next party would be
held if nobody had a birthday).

Elizabeth Ann, our new choice, said royally: "Now, it will
be hard to fill your last president's shoes—"

And I was mighty glad I wasn't elected. I had no shoes to fill!

Today I find new meaning in the words. It would be one
thing to leave no "shoes to fill" while I am *Here*. It would be
another if Someone asked me *There*: "Who filled your shoes?"

To Think and Pray About: We toss the phrase "filling another's shoes" about glibly. Consider what it means to assume
the responsibilities passed on to you by another person. How
can you perform so well that you set an inspiring pattern for
your successor? "Are ye able," asked the Master, "to be crucified with Me?" *Lord, we are able. Let us walk in Your shoes.*

Encore!

August 4
Romans 12:9-21
Hebrews 13:8

"SNOW WHITE" came back . . . encore . . . *encore!*
Some adults had bonafide reasons for seeing that 50-year-old movie again. They have children to share popcorn with and comfort when the tale gets scary or too sad. There are viewers, however, who have no children to hide behind. They pay a theater call to see "Doc" or "Sleepy" or more bluebirds than nature ever intended just because the world, according to Walt Disney's cartoon, was irresistibly near the ideal.

Sure, there were the dreariest of dungeons. But there were royal castles and the coziest of cottages as well. (And, face it, we women are captivated with the beaver that is a dab-tail at housework!) In the "Snow White" world, justice prevails, goodness ultimately triumphs, and true love will find a way. Just look at those seven dwarfs who whistle while they work. Look at Snow White's conviction that (never mind the statistics!) some day her prince will come. She's right—see the prince combing the countryside for the face he once saw? There is evil, of course . . . evil in the form of the Wicked Stepmother . . . evil destroyed by innocence, a posse of birds and bunnies and deer. There, go ahead and cheer with them!

"Snow White" is only make-believe, some will tell us. Just a fairy-tale. A mere *cartoon!* I disagree. It is an extraordinary series of drawings, melded with an extraordinary score which brings out the good in us all. A good that neither time nor cynicism can tarnish.

To Think and Pray About: Some values are timeless—as real today as when our Creator set the world in motion. This children's movie (for all ages) utilizes them instead of featuring bedroom scenes, alcohol, drugs, and violence. Draw some parallels with the plot and biblical stories of justice, goodness, mercy—and, yes, waiting for the "Prince!" Consider, too, the dignity of work—and approach your tasks with a "Heigh, heigh ho!"

Dog Days

1 Peter 1:1-10   August 5
Romans 5:3-5

S AN DIEGO COUNTY heated up to the 90's this week.
It looks as if fair-weather fans will have to sweat out
another week of near-100 temperatures before we can go back
to boasting about our coastal climatic wonderland. The Dog
Days of August are here!

Once upon a time this hottest season of the year was
attributed to the rising of the Dog Star (Sirius) just before the
sun. Something has happened to change that, having to do
with precession of the equinoxes. But we retain the name. It
remains the hottest time.

Some people like August, or so they say. But I react to it like
the farm animals. Pigs stop putting on weight. Chickens take
afternoons off and egg production drops. Tornadoes strike
where they have never touched down before. A mass of hot air
(the world's largest uninvited guest) sits on the face of North
America—frying us all. Dad's temper operates on a short fuse.
The children are too silent (always a danger sign!), only to let
out howls that well might herald the beginning of World War
III. They blame one another for everything—until confronted
by a parent. Then united they stand! Circuits are overloaded,
so there is a "brown out," which means that every hour our air
conditioner is off for 15 minutes. The gentle dog (either
because it's cooler out than in—or in respect to Dog Days)
turns vicious and snaps at bumblebees. Who says bumblebees
don't sting? In trying to rescue the dog *I* fall prey! One of the
huffy insects buzzes down the neck of my blouse. It has no
knowledge of rescue-by-tissue so stings me right through the
Kleenex. Now, I guess the environmentalists are on my trail.
What do I do with a day like today, Lord?

To Think and Pray About: This is a good day to bury the dead
(thoughts) take ice-cold lemonade to the new neighbor, pray,
and smile! It will be funny this winter.

The Many, The Proud—The Sloppy

TRIUMPHANTLY, my husband pointed to the article. Only those who once held down jobs outside the home and yet found time to scrub the grout from the kitchen counter, pull weeds (and pull strings to get our children's help), and still had energy to dab some of Liz's "Purple" behind our ears for our husbands—and then became a handicap (not as in golf)—can appreciate the title. *Dull Women Have Immaculate Houses*, it read!

The movement toward "sloppiness" started from the ground floor, a floor from which one would not choose to eat (*Whoopee! that includes mine! A.C.—After the Cast*), the item said. You see, there are so many of us in the work force that nobody is bothered by knowing that the granola dropped on the sofa bed will still be there when next we unfold it for an overnight guest. Back when women began their 40-50 hours away from the house, we tried to catch up which was about as futile as waiting for Tennyson's brook to run dry.

Now there were a lot of statistics about the number of hours women (the proud) spent housecleaning as compared to those "related home-care tasks" in which men engaged. Piles of useless statistics collected by researchers who do not know my George. He *always* ran the vacuum sweeper and turned the mattress. In fact, he wouldn't complain if he found something growing in the vegetable crisper. But *I* cared! Not that I was ever among the proud. But then, I was never among the sloppy either. We picked up chunks. And, unable to do that, I felt so guilty. This man of mine had proven himself biologically capable of creating order—alone!

"See?" He still wore the mask of triumph. "Who wants to be *dull*?"

To Think and Pray About: Whatever your job, relax. The mildew will wait . . . but *do* share the yoke, as Jesus invites. Life need *never* be dull!

The Innocent Bystander

Luke 10:29-37   August 7
Matthew 27:22-24

MAYBE the summer heat brings out the worst in us all. Or does it go deeper than the sweat glands? Love knows no calendar.

Today, as I neared an intersection, I saw a group (we call them "gawkers") gathered around the scene of an accident. Damage to the two cars was slight, so why was everybody so disturbed? And then I spotted the twisted remains of a bicycle between the two automobiles and the outline of a small body beneath a blanket. To my dismay nobody was administering first aid until paramedics arrived. The two drivers were more concerned with who had right-of-way and the others were debating heatedly as to which of them was right.

Police cars and an ambulance arrived simultaneously and, as the child was lifted onto the stretcher, the officers began to interrogate witnesses. But, alas! Now that there was a need for their help, those witnesses who had claimed to have "seen it all" were silent. Not one in the crowd came forward.

"Who was first to arrive on the scene?" an officer asked.

Still silence. But several fingers pointed to the same woman.

"I don't know a thing. I was just an innocent bystander!"

How could anybody do that?! I asked myself. *How could any witness refuse to cooperate—and still claim to be "innocent"?*

Then suddenly the accusations churning inside me pointed a judgmental finger my direction. *How many times, Lord, have I neglected to step forward and become involved as a witness for You and deceived myself with flimsy excuses? Forgive me!*

To Think and Pray About: Supposing Jesus had come to the world as an "innocent bystander"? Supposing He had witnessed our sins but refused to become involved? Find a way to speak out today!

Spiritual Fitness

" WHEN should we read God's Word?"
The leader of our Bible study's question hung unanswered. Morning, evening, at meals?

It was Miss Mollie who chirped, "*When?* I'll *show* you when!"

And she pulled a crumpled envelope from her knitting bag. Squinting, she began to read from the spidery jottings.

- WHEN in sorrow (John 14)
- WHEN others fail you (Psalm 27)
- WHEN you have sinned (Psalm 51)
- WHEN you worry (Matthew 6:19-34)
- WHEN you are in danger (Psalm 91)
- WHEN you are blue (Psalm 34)
- WHEN God seems far away (Psalm 139)
- WHEN you are discouraged (Isaiah 40)
- WHEN you are lonely or fearful (Psalm 23)
- WHEN you feel down and out (Romans 8:39)
- WHEN you need courage for a task (Joshua 1)
- WHEN the world seems bigger than God (Psalm 90)
- WHEN you need peace or rest (Matthew 11:25-30)
- WHEN you leave home for work or travel (Psalm 121; 107:21-31)
- WHEN you feel bitter or critical (1 Corinthians 13)
- WHEN you are considering investment and return (Mark 10:17-31)
- WHEN you are looking for a great opportunity (Isaiah 55)

To Think and Pray About: So when should you read? How about today? You'll feel richer for it. We read so much about physical fitness. It is important to get that heart rate up, those bodybuilders tell us. So let's exercise our hearts—by helping others! How? Pass along one of these readings to someone with an unresolved problem. Let the follow-up be a prayer for that person. Then take a "cooling down" period of meditation. Don't you feel just great?

Prayer Is:

DOES ANYTHING "just happen"? I am beginning to question that. Some of my most positive experiences have come during my most negative moments. Just little things—like my frustration at locating a reference I needed. In the midst of my exasperation, I ran across some definitions of prayer which put wings on my heart. Read and rejoice!

• Certain thoughts are prayers. There are moments when, whatever be the attitude of the body, the soul is on its knees.
—Victor Hugo

• Prayer is not overcoming God's reluctance; it is laying hold of His highest willingness—Trench.

• I have lived to thank God that all my prayers were not answered—Jean Ingelow.

• Our prayer and God's mercy are like two buckets in a well; while the one ascends, the other descends—Hopkins.

• I have been benefited by praying for others; for by making an errand to God for them, I have gotten something for myself.
—Rutherford

• In the morning, prayer is the key that opens to us the treasure of God's mercies and blessings; in the evening, it is the key that shuts us up under His protection—Beecher.

• Prayer is the wing wherewith the soul flies to heaven.
—Ambrose

• More things are wrought by prayer than the world dreams of.
—Tennyson

• Blessed be God, I not only begin praying when I kneel down, but I do not leave off praying when I rise up—T. Adam.

• A soul without prayer is a soul without a home—Herchel.

To Think and Pray About: What is prayer? It is all these things and more. It is the sacred moment when we give ourselves to God just as we are, allowing Him to love, to put us together again. Is there a seemingly hopeless situation in your life today? Pray! No relationship is so strained, no habit so fixed, no body or mind so weak that God cannot repair it!

Needed: Carpenter's Helpers

A NEW POLICEMAN was assigned to our block's Neighborhood Watch group. "Let's introduce ourselves," the hostess suggested as an icebreaker.

Officer Newton nodded approval. "And it would help if you give me an idea of any office held or responsibility you assume in the group."

Some of the reports sounded impressive. Inside I curled into a little fetal ball of embarrassment, dreading my turn. What did I do really but bake cookies, make a few telephone calls—a few small services on a few small occasions?

It was Alex, sitting next to me, who set my mind at ease. "I'm a diver!" He surprised us all by saying.

Silence. A few confused chuckles. "Did you say *diver?*" Officer Newton struggled to keep surprise from his voice.

"Diver," Alex repeated. "I just dive in and help wherever I'm needed."

Well, wasn't that what I did, after all? Come to think about it, God could use a lot of divers—people who don't see themselves as high-aptitude persons in a general sense. But they are willing to tackle menial tasks. I can't paint letter posters anybody could read, but I can type . . . bake cookies . . . telephone.

Paul spoke of the need for apostles, prophets, and teachers, then stressed that they, too, needed helpers. Come on—you can dive!

To Think and Pray About: If Jesus were among us, what would He be doing? He loved traveling as He ministered. He used His hands for healing and He used them for swinging a hammer to build. Just a carpenter's son, He constructed the stairs to heaven for you and me. And now, skilled or unskilled, young or old, we are needed as "Carpenter's helpers."

The Problem with Tulips

Galatians 5:13,14   August 11
Luke 11:13; Psalm 100:2

T HERE'S A PROBLEM WITH TULIPS. They bloom such a short while then have to be taken up each fall, bulbs separated, and replanted each spring. I used to watch my mother spade up the little brown nuggets, wondering where they hid the blooms.

"How do they grow so many baby bulbs?" I wondered aloud.

"My mother used to say it was because she shared. 'Things multiply when divided' was her way of putting it," Mama said.

She shared little-girl memories of helping Grandmother sort, sack, and label according to color then tagging along for sharing with the neighbors. And the tulips kept multiplying.

Years passed. I grew up and married. When my husband and I built our first modest house, I could hardly wait until I could plant tulip bulbs on each side of the front walk. The purple, pink, and yellow waxen cups (holding dew for the fairies, my mother used to say) were my very favorites. But, to my surprise, bulbs were expensive that year. A crop failure in Holland made them in short supply, as was money. So I ended up with only a half dozen in my three favorite colors. They bloomed in remembered glory; but I was unable to bring myself to separate them. Let alone share. If I let them lie dormant in the ground, wouldn't they be better off?

In a word, no! The plants looked sick from the time they speared the ground. The stems dwarfed because they were overcrowded and undernourished. Only a few bloomed. Worse, no new bulbs.

Yes, there's a problem with tulips . . . they demand to be shared!

To Think and Pray About: Can you think of some situations in your life in which your blessings multiplied from sharing? God had a hand in that. When we look away from ourselves we behold the needs of others. Meeting that need brings a new bulb of gladness which blooms on and on and on—as long as it is shared.

Learning, Laughter, Love, and Law

"TALK to your children," the child specialist told us. I drove home wondering if *he* had children. We do talk . . . and *talk* . . . and TALK. The man had skirted the issue of getting them to listen, of course.

I found my own solution shortly after the lecture. My son, whom my husband and I had "trained up in the way he should go," had departed from it. He had mastered the skill of leaping trash cans in a single bound (those set out for him to empty). His bedroom closet smelled like a gym locker. And obviously an unmade bed was a teenage status symbol.

It was bad enough that this once-tidy lad would not hear me if I used a megaphone. Then I came down with what surely was terminal laryngitis. *What now, Lord?*

I remembered a memo pad my school principal distributed to the faculty. DON'T SAY IT; WRITE IT.

But just try writing the details it takes to run a house, be well-groomed, and retrain a self-turned savage. I developed writer's cramp and heart palpitations. And then I recalled how small those memos were. I must be frugal.

Then and there I was converted from the omnipresent judge to the guardian angel with a sense of humor. Sorely tempted to hang a DANGER sign on Bryce's bedroom door and refuse him bathroom privileges until he gave up the junior-caveman life-style, I concentrated on notes that brought learning, laughter, love, and law.

In his jacket pocket he found this note: "No Kleenex in the wash. Has your nose given up running?" In the dust on his desk, this: "Nobody dies from inhaling such. But I'm pleased you open the windows at night." When he left a note in the bathroom, "Look Mother, no toothpaste on the walls," I knew it was working. "Love covereth all sins."

To Think and Pray About: Love notes are better than laws on deaf ears. Try them and you *will* find time for talking! About problems. About joys. About faith for the anxious heart.

Prophets with Wings

WATCHING my grandfather erect the martin box was like having a year-round spring. All winter he'd whittle doors and windows for the miniature home for the little birds. "You just never know," he was apt to say in the midst of a blizzard, "when the prophets of spring will come flying in."

Lovely thought. But prophets? Weren't they bearded men who could unlock dreams and tell us what to expect before the world ended?

"Not always," my grandfather explained. "The martins come to give us the word that it's spring. The prophets you're talking about are those who brought God's Word."

The *Bible*, I thought he meant then, and most likely he did. But since that long-ago time, I've thought a lot about his application and its application to life nowadays.

Those little birds that winged their way to our part of the world lacked the scientific evidence that our weather forecasters have. And yet they came with regularity. And, sure enough, they were accurate. Nature gave them the gift of prediction as God gave the prophets of old the gift of prophecy with fresh revelations. And those prophets brought the Word down to us.

Doesn't it follow that we each have an obligation to spread that Word? To become "prophets" to those around us? God ordains some to preach and teach, of course. But I am thinking of the little ordinary ways in which to scatter news of God's goodness and mercy.

To Think and Pray About: Do you want to be a prophet? Read to a blind person. Tell the story of Jesus to a child. Help a stranger with directions (who knows but that your kindness will change the direction of the lost one's life?). Isn't it wonderful what you can do? And say, wouldn't a bird house be fun to build as a family project—or in a group as a gift for a shut-in who loves bird-watching?

Habits to Shed

"WHY, MOTHER?" from my then-young son used to irritate my every nerve ending. An intellectual why-of-things was one thing. Having each request or decision questioned was another.

However, something positive came from it all. I will always remember the little scene which went something like this:

"Bryce, bring me the hammer."

"Why, Mother?"

Angrily, balancing myself on a chair as I tried to hang a picture, I said, "Because I said to!"

"There's gotta be a reason."

We talked. And yes, he brought the hammer. But he did have a point. Everything I do should have a reason behind it— a good one.

Recently I was thinking about how programmed I am— moving forward like a wound-up toy and seldom examining purposes. So, I have started a list of habits I would like to shed. Beside each entry, I pencil a question.

- Taking tomorrow's work to bed with me. (*Do I really think I can accomplish the job in the dark with my pj's on?*)
- Comparing cost of living with last year's. (*Can torturing myself bring prices down? And won't the Lord provide?*)
- Weighing "old ways" and "new ways." (*Were mine really better?*)
- Hurrying. (*Would the Lord want me to be first in the grocery line—allowing no time for the friendly exchange with other shoppers on the way to the front?*)

To Think and Pray About: Snakes have it made, don't they? They can shed their old skins and underneath is a nice new one. We have to work on ours. But the Lord will help. Let us pray (as we extend that list) that every word and deed has a purpose—*His!*

Following

H ENRY FORD said: "Too many people say 'Look what I have done!' instead of 'Look where I have been led!'."

I wonder if the remarkable man who made it possible for virtually every American to own an automobile spoke with evangelical fervor. If so, did he ask God where He was going before following? Would he have said: "Well now, Lord, You tell me about the trip, then I'll decide if I want to tag along"? or (*Oh, my!*) would he have placed a collection of travel folders in the outstretched hand, asked God to think about the options, then to check His favorite?

Does following God mean any of those things? Or doesn't it mean offering our companionship before we know where He will lead us? *That would be surrender.* There are those who, not knowing what a wonderful tour guide God is, sometimes balk on the word *surrender.* The pronoun *He* is just too much. "No man's going to order *me* around!"

How do I tell them, Lord, that You are not a MAN (with whom they may have had some shattering experience)? Reassure them that You are not going to ORDER them, but bid them follow if they trust You?

What will God's answer be? Why, that He wants to talk with them, of course! And just a simple little prayer will do. And then the listening—God speaks to each of us *individually!* In a whirlwind . . . from a burning bush . . . on the road to Damascus (see today's reading). Some of us need a tumultuous thundering, I guess; others, a whisper of the pines. And (surprise!) sometimes He wants us to stay put. Who, pray tell, started the rumor that God's will is always contrary to our own—that He wants us to be miserable? Somebody who failed to listen—that's who! Somebody who professed to trust, then searched instead of listening.

To Think and Pray About: God has a personal message. Listen and be led—happily!

Lessons of Love

August 16   Psalm 25:1-10

I think God teaches love to us on mountains high and cool;
In lakes, and fields, and shaded glens, I think God holds His
* school...*
The spikey green of new-born grass; small children out at play;
The homeward pull of wayward feet at closing of the day...
The call of coyotes in the dark in search of missing mate;
The quiet joy that fills the heart when night has closed its
* gate...*
All these are teaching tools of God: the songbirds sense it, too—
They gather in their well-matched robes and sing from every
* pew;*
To enslaved hearts of low estate who seek a new degree:
"Come learn of love with us;" they say, "His truth can set
* you free!"*   J.M.B.

- God shows us the direction to heaven by pointing the fingers of the tallest mountainpeaks upward where dark vagabond clouds linger to teach of a silver lining.
- God reveals His caring for the creatures He created by watering the fields in softly singing rains.
- God demonstrates how He can cast away our cares by planting fields of wildflowers, so bright of spirit, so gloriously robed, and taking no thought of tomorrow's changes.
- God illustrates His own desire to pull our wandering feet home to His kingdom by magnetizing the hearts of His lesser beings so that they are drawn to the nest, the burrow, and the glen.
- God whispers of foreverness in the drop of the sun—its golden hush reflected in the wings of birds in homeward flight—the brief twilight, and then the resurrection of a new day.
- God shows His infinite caring when He allows our lids to droop. "Come to me, you who are weary," He says, "and I will give you rest."

To Think and Pray About: Do your feelings lie too deep for words? Then God has set you free!

Self-Examination

Observe thyself as thy greatest enemy would do, so shalt thou be thy greatest friend—Jeremy Taylor.

"PEOPLE PERCEIVE IN THEMSELVES what they see in me," a well-known actress answered when questioned how she had soared to stardom. I snapped off the radio. What would others see in *me*? I was standing one-legged, like a stork (shifting one's weight is a must for us lamebackers). I went on peeling potatoes for the pot roast—and thought about her provoking (but provocative) words.

Unbidden, the memory of a hospital chaplain's visit to my "cell" came back. The well-meaning man took one look at my mummy-like wrappings and selected a passage from Job. "My bones cleaveth to my skin," he said as if administering a last rite. He left me uptight—more because of the effect I'd had on him than about my own demise (which he so obviously expected). Poor fellow... I must check on him and see if all his bones are still intact. You know the old saying about being so scared "I jumped out of my skin." Oh dear...

The vision faded as the words of Matthew came to shoo it away. We are to "let our light so shine" that it brightens the path of others. But how to "so shine"? By words? Deeds? Both, I am sure. But isn't there a certain glow that goes with them?

Smile at someone and that person perceives himself or herself as acceptable—perhaps admired. "Hello" to the stranger at the bus stop and that person sees himself or herself as a bit more worthy.

Then and there I put down the uplifted foot and stood full height. No longer a Job's daughter, I belted out a few stanzas of "Stand Up, Stand Up for Jesus!" And I did it with a smile. Others should see a bit of God in me and perceive it in themselves... a smile... a glow.

To Think and Pray About: We women are instructed to examine our anatomies for lumps. We should examine our spirits, too. How will you glorify Him today? Oh *yes*, you can!

Casting Out Demons

August 18   James 3:11-18

THE ZENIA BED is possessed by weeds, I see. Hard work—weeding—but those demons have to be cast out.

It was Mrs. Foley who taught me about demons that lurked in a garden. Her place next door looked to my child-mind like my vision of heaven. No demons could lurk there. "One did," the fairy-godmother-like lady told me, "until the Lord cast him out!"

Mrs. Foley had me hooked and she knew it. "Now, this one," she said, taking hold of a pigweed, "is 'evil thoughts' and it's an enemy of growth. This one's 'unkind words' that kill buds."

"How do you recognize demons?" I asked.

She admitted that it was sometimes hard. "That's why we have to be careful. Demons come in all shapes and sizes—and they're sneaky. Have to learn to identify the enemies, then work hard at eliminating them. And the pesky things keep trying to reenter."

My friend pointed out "negativism," "nit-picking," "moral confusion," "doubt," "indifference," and lots of other demons. We had the garden weeded in short order. But the demons reappeared just as she said they would—I knew by her bent-over back. No matter. I'd learned to deal with them—even taking pride in helping my mother weed.

Putting on a wide-brimmed hat to protect myself from the heat of the noonday sun, I pluck a demonic weed up by the roots. "There's no room for you, 'evil thought'," I say with a smile. If my heart is to be a lovely garden—even a little glimpse of heaven—I must be cautious what I sow, yes. But I must make unworthy thoughts and unkind words unwelcome, too. Then only love and joy can abide.

To Think and Pray About: Identify a demon in your life. Ask God to help you cast it out. And remember: God made your heart for His own garden, so He could walk with you each day; make each thought and word so gentle, demonic shadows slink away—J.M.B.

A Matter of Attitude

2 Corinthians 1:4   August 19
John 20:21

THE DAY BEFORE I had told my doctor I was unwilling to share my "case history" with outsiders. I stepped up my pace as if to escape guilt's clutch. I would give the pain to anybody who asked. But *share* it I wouldn't.

Whether by chance or God's design my walk led me to a huddle of "snowbird" oldsters who were soaking up the sun on a park bench. "Don't know if I could handle the sun shinin' every day," one of the men twinkled. "What do these folks talk about? Weather reports would lose meanin' if you'd never seen traffic stuck three hours in a blizzard." (*Now, wait a minute, Lord . . .*)

Then they all began chattering like a flock of blackbirds. " 'Think it's gonna get worse?' you say to the guy you don't know well. 'Always does,' he says, 'then it gets better.' And it's all so friendly-like, sharing. We understand each other—no strangers."

There was laughter followed by a chorus of voices. " 'Cold enough?' we ask, then if it's a newcomer, 'think this is bad, just wait'll tomorrow,' before pitchin' in to help" . . . "Help? You bet! One family hitched his collie to a sled to get his neighbor's pregnant wife to the hospital" . . . "Polar bears in the zoo won't stick their heads out in winter; but I figure I've earned the right to be one of the 'Old Guys' who tells how pretty spring'll be . . ."

Their voices drifted off because I had turned around. It was time to tell the doctor that although life is not all sunshine, maybe we learn from the contrasts.

To Think and Pray About: How can we go about sharing another's burden without unloading our own on fragile shoulders? Can you lend a hand by listening compassionately as another talks, cries, is silent or angry even while your own spirit limps? God needs you.

Bagging One Bird

Psalm 90:16,17
                                                 Galatians 5:9

M Y DAD was a bird hunter—much to the despair of my
mother and me. Mama objected to the time and money
hunting demanded. I objected to the slaughter. But, if pheasant
season coincided with corn shocking, corn went unshucked.
And "A-hunting He Would Go," a Nimrod, the Mighty
Hunter, in his eyes only.

Poor Daddy. He never had a very good audience when he
tried to tell of the excitement of seeing a family of pheasants
rise right in front of him, or of his aiming, firing, and bringing
down his target! But I do remember a lesson his hunting taught
me—one which had to do with picking out a single target and
following through.

"Now, I know I'm a good marksman," he would say. "I know
I can bring down a single bird—providing I give no thought at
all to others that are getting past. Bagging one bird at a time is
enough. I'll get my quota later on."

So many times I've thought of what my father had learned
through experience. When tasks pile up and I'd like to take a
scatter-gun approach, I tell myself: "I know I can bring down a
single task—providing I give no thought to all the others that
are getting past."

So, today I try to bag one bird. I take aim at the job I know
is important. I concentrate on that one target and follow
through. That finished, I get on to the next until my day's
quota is reached.

Of course, I must be selective. I doubt if Daddy would have
aimed at less than the most promising-looking bird. So, knowing that time is of essence, I shall choose the task with most
promise . . . something love-oriented . . . a trophy worth bringing home!

To Think and Pray About: Bagging one bird at a time is
enough. "Aim" to please God.

A Dose of Friendship

I need someone whose eyes are closed to human frailty;
I need someone who looks within and sees the good in me.
I need someone who beauty sees in flowers, trees and birds,
Who understands the tender thoughts for which I find no
*   words.*
I need someone to share with me when I must shed a tear;
Who may not speak but strengthens me by simply standing
*   near.*
I need someone who shares my joy when I have won a game—
Who's disappointed when I fail but loves me just the same.
I need someone who holds me close when time tears us
*   apart...*
I'm sure God fashioned friends for this, my fragile, human
*   heart.*

                                                    J.M.B.

IN NEED OF A FRIEND? Of course, you are. We all are. God created us with a need for each other, born (I believe) from His need to love and be loved. Loving friendships draw us near to the heart of God.

Friendship is so much of the quality of the mind and the soul that there is no artificial or superficial value through which one may purchase friendship. Loyalties may be required and demanded through force or power; but only out of the heart can the sentiments of friends be born, grow, and flower. They are God's gift to us.

You can make do with what you have—with a friend. You can endure the unendurable—with a friend. You can get through this life in all circumstances—with a friend. A friend is a buoy to keep you afloat; an anchor when you are adrift.

Isn't it great that we are *commanded* to love one another? First, God; then others. And all other commandments then fall into place. I read somewhere that the Ten Commandments first came in tablet form and by following directions we could avoid swallowing others.

To Think and Pray About: Seek God. Seek others. Take your medicine—and get well!

Can't Change How You Feel?

I F YOU BELIEVE that, skip our visit for today. Stand in the corner and flip your own suspenders to add to your misery. It's here to stay!

But look—God believes in you. And He gave you the power to change. In fact, He does it for you! What woman doesn't want a "make-over"?

Let's examine some common problems. Then identify your own.

1. *Do you fret over past mistakes?* (I know a woman who can't remember where she parked the car five minutes ago but recalls the scolding she gave her daughter who fed the goldfish to the cat 40 years ago. Can she change how she feels?)

2. *Do you dwell on your shortcomings and/or weaknesses?* (I grew up in the "small feet" era and struggled like Cinderella to wear what felt like glass slippers. Can I change how I feel?)

3. *Do you set unrealistic goals?* (A woman in our church invariably says of her absences, "I was there in spirit." That . spawns images of grieving ghosts in search of their bodies! She obviously wants to be two places at once. Can she change how she feels?)

4. *Do you compare yourself unfavorably with others?* (My neighbor has pounds of hair that would qualify for an "I'm worth it" commercial and twists it into a tortuous knot because it refuses to stay in place like "other women's." Can she change how she feels?).

5. *Do you develop anxiety over others' opinions?* We all wrestle with inferiorities heightened by guilt because we "aren't supposed to feel this way." Can we change how we feel?

YES! Are any of us preordained to be losers? How can we be when God created us in His image? But the "human hand" inside keeps pushing little negative buttons to lower us in our own esteem. But not in God's! He sees us as all we would like to be—and more! Yes, you *can* change the way you feel!

To Think and Pray About: Put God in control. No, we are not perfect—yet. But He is perfecting us.

Today Is the Day!

M Y PARENTS brought me up in a beautiful world of anticipation. Be it ever so small, I looked forward, counting days, hours, and minutes. Then, awaking before dawn on the Big Day, I would whisper over and over: "Today is the day!"

So, today *is* the day for the dictates of your heart. It is God's gift, the chrysalis of eternity. There is no statement more shocking than: "I do not know what to do with my time." Such words would have been ill-fated if spoken by Methuselah in his 969th year! So take this day which cannot last and consider:

TODAY is the day for giving, forgiving, creating, recreating, singing, and praising.

TODAY is the day for smiling, laughing, learning, adventuring, touching, and meditating.

TODAY is the day for thinking, planning, listening, sharing, healing, and encouraging.

TODAY is the day for sowing, growing, searching, dreaming, discerning, persisting, and thanking.

TODAY is the day for choosing, trusting, sympathizing, empathizing, loving, caring, and giving.

TODAY is the day for playing, preparing, attempting, producing, daring, and doing.

> Hours have wings and fly up to the Author of time and carry news of our usage. All our prayers cannot entreat one of them either to return or to slacken its pace. The misspents of every minute are a new record against us in heaven. Surely if we all thought thus, we would dismiss them with better reports and not suffer them to fly upward empty-handed . . .
> —Milton

To Think and Pray About: Solomon tells us that there is a time to be born and a time to die. Today is an interval-stone in the bridge between the two and that bridge is of infinite importance. Yes, today is your day. How will you use it?

Mollie Pitchers Don't Pitch

August 24   Matthew 10:42; 25:35-40

THOSE WERE THE DAYS when women were "discriminated against"—only I didn't know the phrase. How, then, did I, a girl, make it on the boys' baseball team?

I had two young uncles who insisted. They had taught me to "pinch hit" anywhere, they said (and besides, they owned the only baseball so their opinion hit a homer). Of course, I was only on probation, a big, red-haired boy told me in an "Ah, shucks!" manner. "Now you gotta learn to take orders."

What a workout they gave me! I was a willing learner. The first match-game was coming up and I hoped to make the first string.

Then the day before the game, the big redhead sauntered over and pointed a stubby finger at me. "She don't play." My uncles challenged "Buster" (just the right name) and a free-for-all followed. Then came a caucus from which I was barred (illegally probably).

But the announcement was a triumph. "You can play if you want to be Mollie Pitcher."

Mollie *Pitcher*. What a beautiful title! Me, a girl, pitching in the major league. Only it didn't turn out that way. One of the boys handed me a jug and told me I was to be water girl. Holding back tears, I stumbled to the sidelines where my grandmother, who never missed a game, stood shielding her face from the sun with a newspaper.

"Mollie Pitcher was the valiant woman who quenched the thirst of dying men on the battlefield. What an honor!" she said. I did what she knew I would—marched back to my call of duty.

At the end of the game, Buster came over. "Hey, Kid, you saved my life today." I was the heroine—the one who had won the game.

To Think and Pray About: What's your batting average? High, if you are willing to do some task beneath your dignity and capability today for another's sake.

A Family Visit with God

PEACE. That's what we women crave. There are days when we want to scream, "QUI-ET!" hoping it will bring that moment to ourselves—that moment with God. A time to prepare for the next obstacle course, juggling babies, meals, church committees, P.T.A., with jobs, in order to bring the *family* together after a day that has been blown apart like a dandelion in the summer wind. Not that we homemakers hold the monopoly. Singles have their built-in set of problems in arranging a time for devotionals and maybe in attracting a few friends. Let's begin on common ground. We want it to be a happy time—a time to take off our shoes and relax and enjoy ourselves, our loved ones, and God. So out with the "dismal duty" attitude and in with the imagination.

Do you want to be that one family in 25 which worships together? Yes? Then, we'll need to set up a time, place, and plan. Sound rigid? Rigidity is what we want to avoid. So, consider a carelessly lettered announcement taped onto the refrigerator door—a sign-up sheet, really, as it will ask for suggestions and volunteers to lead. Ideally, the man does this? Men differ as much as women. Father no longer wears a high collar and carries a big stick (just as Mom and Gram no longer wear hooped skirts nor are children "seen and not heard").

Now, what you do is less important than how you do it. Each recite a Bible verse, make music, share a Bible story, say a one-line prayer. *Use your imagination!*

To Think and Pray About: I like games! Remember the ancient story poem, called "One, Two, Three"? An elderly lady and crippled lad sat beneath an old maple tree. Grandmother closed her eyes as the child "hid" in some imagined place. Grandmother got three guesses as to where.

Where has God hidden a new blessing? Oh, children will love this (alter games for adults). Make it a learning time—but joyful. For you are visiting with God.

Finding Nourishment

"I NEED a pair of good workers," my grandfather called to my young uncle and me—oh, ever so long ago. But T.J. and I were busy building a fort in case the Martians invaded. Leaving our newly-split kindling and taking up the spade to work in the garden offered no appeal.

"We were building a fort," I said.

"Couldn't this wait?" T.J. asked, following my lead.

My grandfather explained that the ground was just right for setting out onions. But T.J., trying another approach (bolder this time), pointed out that he saw no need in spading beforehand.

I trembled, but Grandpa Owens showed neither irritation nor amusement. Instead, he laid down the garden tool and motioned us to him. "See this?" He leaned down and picked up a handful of just-spaded soil. "It's surface dirt. There's no life left in it. The spade goes deep and finds soil that will nourish seeds and make them grow."

When my ideas won't take root or the bloom fades from a relationship, I remember the incident in the garden. It is then that I ask of myself: *Have you been working with surface dirt?*

It is much easier to shake our fist at a withering plant than to dig down and find the problem. So much easier, too, to sow carelessly without preparing the soil. Jesus had something to say about that, cautioning us to sow seed on fertile ground and to keep it watered if we expect to reap. That requires sharp tools. It requires work. It requires patience and the willingness to try again.

To Think and Pray About: How can you apply this to your association with others in the home, on the job, in the church, and in social situations? Do you dig below the surface of your own negative reaction to a new acquaintance, preparing yourself to be more receptive so a friendship can germinate? How do you nourish it and help it grow? Reread the parable, digging deeper, finding more nourishment.

The Wonder Worker

GRATITUDE is a wonder-worker. Whatever you're doing, *stop!* It only takes a minute for you to make two people happy—and you are one of them. Just push the buttons that dial a person who has enriched your life and say, "I'm grateful you are my friend." Now, as you were—and have a happy day.

The beauty of that small act is that it becomes a globe-trotter—traveling from that friend to another gathering smiles with the miles. Look, it all began with you and it is heaven-bound.

Now, *you* are the wonder-worker! Have you ever seen a truly joyful person who was not brimming over with gratitude? And have you ever seen a miserable, complaining person who was truly grateful? Charles Dickens had wise words for both of them: "Reflect upon your present blessings, of which every man has many; not your past misfortunes, of which all men have some."

What are your present blessings? If you have another minute to spare, count these—then add them to the ever-growing, ever-glowing list:

You are still here, aren't you?—alive and capable of breathing, laughing, and loving in this beautiful, magical world.

You have friends (try counting, beginning with the one you called).

You possess all or some of your senses: eyes to view the majesty of the sunrise; ears to hear the brave call of a meadowlark in the rain, a whippoorwill at twilight, a baby's coo at dawn; a set of nostrils to smell the first wood hyacinth, noon sun on the meadow, freshly turned earth, and clove-spiked ham; a mouth with which to sing, praise, and take in palate-pleasing food for sustenance; and the sense of touch with which to communicate affection, allowing you the sweet joy of feeling with both the hand and the heart.

To Think and Pray About: Something like a miracle has happened—right? Together you and I have discovered Who the *real* Wonder-Worker is. *Good morning, Lord!*

I'm an Heiress, I Am!

August 28

Luke 12:16-21
Matthew 19:21

THE GROCERY LINE was a traffic jam. Everybody seemed to be stocking for the "Big One," the quake that's going to take California out to sea. Most customers paid with credit cards, the plastic-money kind of economy that demands more self-discipline than most people have. The others used checks, listening for their total then asking: "I want to make this out for ten dollars more, so I can buy lottery tickets. Okay?"

The heroines-of-tomorrow talked among themselves, a huddled mass of rags-to-riches dreamers. They passionately believed they would join the ranks of the wealthy.

Had they never heard that the world-median shelter is a mud hut? I can identify with that to a lesser degree. I grew up thinking that anyone owning an automobile was "well-to-do."

Lights changed and the shopping carts pulled ahead. Two men moved out of the parking zone and stopped behind me as the line stalled again. They talked stocks and bonds in seven-digit figures. The "haves" undoubtedly, but no more possessed than the coveting "have-nots."

Can anybody explain the fatal fascination with money? Why are people so irrationally bewitched by the stuff? And why is no amount enough? Is there a rehab center for money-holics—a support group which helps victims rid themselves of its eerie, demonic grasp?

Stocks and Bonds resumed their conversation. "What's old Ben worth now?"

Worth? Money determines *worth*? God entrusts money to meet my needs. But it *belongs* to Him. A far greater gift was His Son, with whom I am a joint heir. Millionaires can't buy that!

To Think and Pray About: Where will the baubles that money can purchase be when the "Big One" comes? But nothing can separate us from God's love: neither death, life—nor coffers of gold!

Those "Sincere Pumpkins"

Philippians 1:8-11   August 29

HAVE you looked at your garden lately? Flecks of gold are showing on some of the fat-cheeked pumpkins as they squat beneath the wilting leaves of summer. Soon now those freckles will merge and the uncarved jack-o'-lanterns will light up the fields with their blush. Halloween capers and pumpkin-pie visions will come alive.

Pumpkins are interesting fruits (and must lead an exciting personal life according to their rate of reproduction!). Being rovers, they trailed their way through history from Europe in the 1700's and have been trailing ever since—dumping their offspring all over the globe. Because they are so plentiful, we take them for granted—forgetting how useful they are. They're a youngster's delight on Allhallows' Eve, of course, and a culinary delight in pies. But did you know that once they were essential to the royal household? Cleaned of their insides, pumpkins were inverted and placed over the king's head as a haircutting guide (and I think we've seen some examples here!). They are used in some medicines...to feed stock ...for canning...and to inspire writers in countless numbers.

"Peter, Peter, pumpkin-eater..." (remember the nursery rhyme?). "When the Frost is on the Punkin'..." (remember Riley's poem?). And how practical the golden fruit was as Brom Bones' head to scare poor Ichabod Crane out of his wits. Then, there's Cinderella's coach...

But, looking at an especially large pumpkin so perfectly grooved by nature's hand, its stem prominently enlarged and flattened like a button at the top, I am thinking of more contemporary literature—Linus's search for the "sincere pumpkin." It goes on like Diogenes' search for an honest man. Sincerity and truth go hand-in-hand. The world searches on and on, little knowing that God is both! Somebody please tell Linus!

To Think and Pray About: Make us sincere in our relationships, Lord—as sincere as we know You to be. Let it shine golden in both pulpit and pumpkin patch.

Though the Waters Be Troubled

SUMMERS along the banks of the Umpqua River in Douglas County, Oregon were a teenager's delight. We picnicked beneath the giant firs, sunned on the white, sandy beaches along the water's edge, and gathered armloads of ferns and larkspur that grew beside the mossy logs. We swam until the giant river became a slender stream—so slender that we could pick our way across to the other side by walking on a path of natural stepping-stones. One by one we would file to the opposite bank—only to file back, laughing, singing, and safe.

Winter rains tore down our playhouse. The stream became an angry, roaring river which flooded the lowlands and covered our stepping-stones completely. It was a bad time for farmers, too. The waters removed their topsoil and deposited logs and debris in yards, gardens, and fields. "I wish spring would come," everyone said.

"It will," said Gammie Winston, the regal, little lady who was a grandmother to us all.

"Sometimes it's hard to believe," I told her. Of course, she had seen a lot more springs than I, and her faith was more firmly established.

Gammie pointed to the murky current. "Right there's where your little crossing is," she reminded me. "For nearly 80 years I have kept that in mind. I know that somewhere down deep the stepping-stones remain intact. The rains will stop. The water will recede. And you will cross safely to the other side."

To Think and Pray About: When the floods come into our lives, threatening to take away the rich loam of faith we've built up and replacing it with debris of doubt, fear, and dread, we can rest assured that God has kept the stepping-stones intact. We are to pray. We are to believe. We are to *know*, for God has told us. The storms will pass. The waters will recede. And we will pass safely to a brighter day! Remember this today—"though the waters be troubled."

The Golden Rule of Change

Psalm 15   August 31
Matthew 7:12

AUGUST is nearing its end... closing the door of summer... opening the door to autumn. Leaves are freckling with gold—nature's way of announcing that autumn's golden rule of change is near. So today I reread Psalm 15, because it is golden-toned with change—change in the attitudes of people.

David writes of the qualities of the citizens of Zion, making no mention of race or skin pigmentation. Rather, he concentrates on the spiritual requirements: righteousness, truth, honor, and the sharing of possessions. Enemies, as he views them, are backbiters, faultfinders, and those who are reproachful of others. His words are a pre-Christian Golden Rule, a good preparation of the reader's heart for a different approach to the Scripture from a children's version I overheard recently.

The Sunday school teacher had assigned Matthew 7:12 as a memory verse. All the children recited the Golden Rule. Asked to explain it, one child said: "It means I can hit everybody else and they can't hit me back." Another protested. "No!" he said. "It means we gotta treat other guys like they treat us."

A sad reflection of adult attitudes...

To Think and Pray About: We know that children reflect our attitudes. And yet today—enlightened, desegregated, and acceptant as we like to think of ourselves as being—there is a lack of tolerance and understanding. It exists in regard to race, creed, code—and yes, social mores including dress. How can we go about reteaching the Golden Rule? The change must begin inside ourselves. Talk it over with the Lord. Tell Him your desires. Then put your trust in Him and persevere *now*—while we have the "golden opportunity!"

An Autumn Dilemma Prayer

A FIRST PINK blush of the sweet gum shows Your autumn signature, Lord, while other trees around it refuse to to respond to the coming tide of color. Do they, like us, turn deaf ears to Your Voice and cling to summer? *Rest,* You whisper to us as the year turns autumnward. But the pace of our civilization is against it. We have no time, we say, no time for thinking, a gift we give ourselves, and no time for praying, a gift You gave us, Lord. Why then, do we try to hold back the season? I ask, Lord, and yet I too am holding back . . . fearing.

You know my dilemma, Lord. September opens the schoolhouse door and I—like the trees—hesitate. More and more I must call on You to help me deal with teaching. For something has happened to our families, Lord—something has ripped the lives of so many of these little ones apart. I know that in many cases it cannot be helped, Lord, but that knowledge does not ease my caring and coping. Where have the beautiful commitments at the altar gone? And how can I mend the broken spirits of these innocent victims?

They are so afraid, Lord—afraid of losing other family members through another broken relationship or the explosion of a bomb. I am afraid, too. Yet, I must appear serene even as my eyes (conditioned by responsibility) search the skies for a mushroom-shaped cloud.

The blessed hope is You, Lord. So let me draw new strength and divine inspiration from You, the Master Teacher. You had no classroom and no tools—and yet You captured attention quickly and kept it. Teach me Your simple language, Lord, that somehow I may bring Your peace to these small hearts. Show me new ways, Lord, to ease their troubled spirits with Your love, the greatest teaching tool of all, as together we bring to them the golden glow of hope.

Take Up the Sickle!

Luke 12:34
Proverbs 6:6-8

JUST outside my window is a small brown squirrel bustling about busily, his tiny pouches filled with delicacies for the coming winter. He darts forth through the crisping leaves, pausing frequently to dig frantically, then burying one of his chosen morsels. These will be his sustenance in the cold, sometimes bitter, days to come.

These beautiful autumn days would be wonderful times for the wee creature to frolic and romp with his many squirrel companions. But the Master has provided him with wisdom and instinct to make provision for the bad times ahead when choice acorns and other nuts are less readily available. No matter how severe the weather, this furry creature will find food and nourishment stored away.

Is this not the Almighty Plan? Shouldn't we, too, prepare ourselves in the times of fatness for the lean times ahead—not only in terms of physical needs but for spiritual ones as well?

Just watching the perky little fellow inspired me. Some gray day I would share the incident with a shut-in. And there! That last golden leaf which left the parent oak would be beautiful pressed away in a book—together with an appropriate passage of Scripture or a brief prayer. Such a cheerful bookmark could brighten someone else's day. It takes so little sometimes!

To Think and Pray About: Let us thank God for providing food for even the least of these—thank Him, too, for the daily opportunities of storing up beauty for ourselves and for others. And now, we are ready to harvest packets of sunshine— memories to share in His name! Winter can be a time of plenty.

Labor of Love—and Love of Labor

Proverbs 13:11   September 3
Psalm 139:23

LABOR Day! Never mind the date. Just know that it will come this month. The second Monday will be a legal holiday. There will be weekend trips, picnics, and parades to herald summer's end. But probably few will consider its real meaning, how far labor has progressed, and the dignity of work. Maybe in some dark shelf of the mind there will be an awareness reflected in "I don't have to work today."

Yet, there is no denying the value of work. It fattens our purses. It flexes our muscles and sharpens our wits. Also, doctors now recognize work as "good medicine."

But is this enough? Perhaps this is a time to search the heart.

I am remembering a little story my mother used to recite in narrative verse. Three little sisters in the story each claimed to love their mother. Then one skipped away to play with friends. Another, annoyed by some petty incident, went out to her swing and pouted all day. But another saw love as more than words.

> "I love you, Mother," said little Nan,
> "And I will help you all I can."

I am remembering, too, the old hymn, "Let Us Labor for the Master." Shouldn't every day be Labor Day for Him—by our doing at least a small task?

To Think and Pray About: "Faith without works is dead," says James 2:20. And "faith worketh by love," says Paul (Galatians 5:6). But, he warns me, no matter what I accomplish, "without love, I am nothing" (1 Corinthians 13:2). Is it the quantity of work that counts for the Lord? Is it the quality? Both perhaps, but something more—something much more important. Motivation! So, motivated by love, what are you and I going to do today? A jotted-down reminder might help. But remember, pray first! My prayer is: *Search me, O God, that every single work of my hands be one of the heart.*

Vacation's End

It seems we left a year ago; you say it's just ten days?
Why, this old house has changed so much in, oh, so many ways!
Somebody left the sprinklers on the pink petunia bed;
They're blooming like it's spring again; we thought they'd all be
*   dead.*
This is the key—and I know it is—so why then won't it fit?
Oh, here's a note from Great Aunt Sue—I've got to answer it.
You children bring the baggage in—I felt the door key budge—
And throw the windows open please; the house still smells of fudge.
Just toss the laundry in the chute; and, yes, the mending, too;
This table needs a coat of wax... a million things to do...
Here are my last year's comfy shoes; I think I'll put them on;
Pick up the mail... empty the pail... there goes the telephone!
The lawn has grown a foot, I think; look, autumn pears to can...
Here comes the neighbor from next door—I'm glad we're home
*   again!*

J.M.B.

WASN'T IT JUST yesterday that school let out? It's time to switch from hot dogs at the beach, backyard barbecues, and family jaunts in the station wagon to shopping for the latest fads in clothes that you and I wouldn't have weeded the garlic bed in! Daughter is ready to wave pom-poms. Son is coming out for track. And the little ones? Where on earth is the health record showing immunization for whooping cough, tetanus, mumps, and measles?

With all the scamper of the months to come, think to yourself: *I think I can.* That line from the children's story, "The Little Engine That Could," is prophetic.

To Think and Pray About: You thought you couldn't survive the summer. But you did. Discuss the changes ahead. And face them together—remembering always: "I can do all things through Christ which strengthened me" (Philippians 4:13). *Welcome home!*

Into Your Hands

Matthew 22:16
Mark 12:14

September 5

DEAR TEACHER: My son will be a little late. And it is I who is unable to let go on this, his first day at school. You see, it is into your hands that I place a new star in your universe. I guess it is no secret to you that, in the galaxy of human relationships, a baby has always been the center around whom all other planets revolve in the home. And never has that little light shone brighter than during the last six years. You see, this is a "designer baby"... exclusive... shown by appointment... only one to a family...

Only he isn't a baby anymore. And that, dear teacher, is what hurts. His infancy is gone. Before me stands the beginning of a man—a chubby-cheeked child fighting for his independence. I postpone the moment of his departure, knowing that when he returns today a part of him will be beyond my grasp. That part will belong to you—you who will open the door to his new world as I close the door on the memories he left behind. I long to postpone the moment of transition... and, yet, I know that it is in progress...

We, his father and I, have tried to prepare this little one for school, with its inevitable briar patches of love-hate conflicts.

We have created for him a nest lined with patience, humor, and love. He brings with him an Alfie lunch box containing the essentials from all the food groups—and some other essentials as well. I hope you'll overlook his holding sandwiches in his left hand. We concentrated less on that at the table than listening to his rambling prayers. Lately those prayers have been about you... and today I will be praying for you, too. He may stumble over the ABC's, but he knows the Golden Rule. Use it in whatever language the law allows. He is no "latchkey kid," so I will be waiting to hear, "Teacher said"—and to support you, as time pipes him away.

To Think and Pray About: We did not "create." Neither will the teacher. God did! But we must nurture. Be ready to comfort, rejoice—or just listen—and pray for child and teacher.

The Letter Not Written—or Received

D EAR PARENTS: Won't you help me—*please*? I look out on this roomful of shy creatures with their look-alike Buster Brown bobs, their fly-away hair, and shining eyes so filled with anticipation—each so unique and so precious—and am humbled. I listen to their unguarded words, beautifully natural, and face the challenge of refining them into sentences without destroying their beauty. It is I who must widen their world, soothe their anxieties, bind up their wounds, and prepare them for the generation of the bomb. And yet I cannot take your place. A teacher is not a person to lean on but a person who must find a way of making it unnecessary to lean. These little ones try to be so brave, but no amount of bravado can mask the internal bruises. I look at the records spread before me and wonder how I can help without interfering—their fears and hurts go deep, to the feeling of abandonment. For some, the nightmare is a reality—they have lost one parent or both. Fear spreads quickly in a crowded room. It has happened to others; it can happen to them. How can I ease this fear, knowing that once parents had many children but now there are children with many parents? So I take my moment of silence . . . even though my lips are sealed by law as theirs are sealed by fierce pride. These children are worth any sacrifice. Can you sacrifice time to pray?

To Think and Pray About: This is the dilemma of Christian teachers. They have an assignment from the State concerning the child who is an assignment from God. When the Founding Fathers separated Church and State, no one could have foretold a future in which 50 percent of marriages collapsed and children would be born out of wedlock with a shrug of society's shoulders. Neither could early scientists have foreseen the bomb. What a burden for a child! Heavy but not hopeless. Assure each child of your love and protection. Encourage the sharing of fears. Visit school. Your child's teacher needs your support. Make your home a haven. *Our hope is in Thee, Lord.*

Make the Choice—and Rejoice!

Habakkuk 3:18   September 7
Deuteronomy 12:7; 26:11
1 Thessalonians 5:16

YOU HAVE WORN the new shoes, so they are "used" (never mind the blister on your heel). Some well-meaning (?) person has told you that the guest towels you gave a friend turned up at a rummage sale (and you embroidered her initials on them!). The telephone shrills while you are stir-frying the vegetables...

We have those days! How to handle them? My grandmother would have recited all the books in the Old Testament to simmer down. Her mate would have driven nails in the gatepost. Me—well, I like to recall a rainy autumn afternoon when I finished reading *Pollyanna* to my fourth-grade class.

"Well?" I smiled, inviting comments on the characters.

The group sat silent. Then one little boy I'd noticed looking sort of teary-eyed 'round the lashes, raised a timid hand.

"I was thinking about Mrs. Snow. She made me sad."

"Why, Eric?" I asked about the minor character.

"Well, she was never satisfied with anything Pollyanna took her—the jelly, soup, and stuff—and I was thinking it would be nice if we all liked everything we got—even if we don't!"

Teachers learn to unscramble meanings. Yes, it would be nice if we considered the gesture more than the gift.

Too bad about the shoes. But salesmen have an obligation to fit feet properly. Try for that. If there's a policy against such exchanges, aren't you glad that the store welcomes your business, so will find you something more comfortable or reorder for you? As for the towels, your friend is the "Mrs. Snow." Forget it! And let's suppose the person who called was concerned about the headache you had yesterday. Are you going to tell her about today's or thank her for caring? In short, we must choose between Pollyanna and Mrs. Snow.

To Think and Pray About: Rejoice. Rejoice. Rejoice! We are told in both the Old and New Testaments. A beautiful commandment worth rejoicing over.

Listen—It May Be God

September 8

Hebrews 3:15
Psalm 116:1-15

"IT HAD been a hard day and a light drizzle had slickened the roads. If I hurried to make the next light and stayed with the flow of traffic, I might stay ahead of the homeward-bound San Diego traffic." *Home* to my pastor meant the greeting of a loving wife, a warm fire, inviting smells from the parsonage kitchen, and the contented sound of children-home-from-school. So *hurry,* hurry!

He accelerated slightly and made the light. Then, suddenly, an uneasy feeling centered in his chest. Should he pull over and stop? Even as he asked himself, his foot eased up on the gas.

On the emergency shoulder, he waited. The feeling went away; but he felt powerless to move. Then he heard a name called—only it was not his own. "Mary Milam!"

"I was relieved that there was nothing wrong with me," he said later. "But what did it mean? I'd met the lady—even considered visiting her that day. But I was late and hardly a friend—"

But the minister was to get to know her better—much better. In fact, he was about to save her life. Suddenly feeling a sense of urgency, he made a U-turn and headed back. He found the lady standing at her front window frantically motioning him inside. "Oh, I'm glad you came. I begged God to send you—to make you hear His voice. I—I couldn't have faced life another minute." She was near suicide . . .

My mother and I are targets of a lot of good-natured teasing in our family. We constantly hear "voices" and get "feelings." We just smile knowingly, for we know their Source. It can happen to you!

To Think and Pray About: God speaks to us through the Holy Spirit. It is not always when or where we think it should be. If someone says, "I *knew* you'd call!" ask yourself, "How?" Form the habit of listening without embarrassment—and smile knowingly!

What We Do This Day!

1 Chronicles 28:9   September 9
Hebrews 6:10-12

EACH Labor Day I am reminded of my grandmother. "What we do this day we will do the rest of the year!" she declared, her words carrying a word of warning.

Consequently, there was a flurry of activity. Rugs beaten, windows washed, lawns mowed, hedges trimmed—you get the general idea. Labor Day was literally translated.

I was thinking of the grand lady's philosophy this Labor Day as I (yes, from childhood training) cleaned a neglected closet. When I picked up a book to dust beneath it, this item fell to the floor (undoubtedly from her scrapbook):

> Are you willing to consider the needs and the desires of children; to remember the weakness and loneliness of people who are growing old; to stop asking how much your friends love you, but rather to ask yourself whether you love them enough; to bear in mind the things that other people bear in their hearts; to trim your lamp so it will give more light and less smoke; to make a grave for your ugly thoughts, and a garden for your kindly feelings, with the gate wide open—*these, even for one day?*
>
> Henry Van Dyke

So, remembering my grandmother, the immortal words of the American author, and challenged by the Author of my faith, I shall work on *me* today. How do I seek transformation and renewal? I ask God's help.

To Think and Pray About: A change in attitude brings about a change in behavior. We must honestly evaluate the diet of the mind and eliminate any "junk food" that displaces our allegiance to God and our service to His children. Now, with a "willing mind," think of ways in which our labor will be for God's cause today . . . tomorrow . . . and forever.

Grandparent Proverbs

ONLY A GRANDPARENT could think like this:
Lizards are really quite all right when you get to know them.

I need someone underfoot whenever I'm hammering.

Snack-time is enhanced by dill pickles, green apples, and peanut-buttered crackers if washed down by 7-Up.

The dark is less frightening than a tidied-up house.

I am a lot greater than I used to think I was—and no longer have to throw my back out of whack to prove it.

Loud singing is less bothersome than it used to be—even when my hearing aid is turned up.

Sugar-coated cereals are a good bargain if there's a prize in the box.

Scary shows on TV do not cause insomnia.

Dessert *does* taste better before a meal—and why not wash up afterward instead of before?

Clothes hangers bent out of shape hold clothes intact just as well as the satin-covered ones that nobody is allowed to touch.

Another spot on the rug makes no difference.

Soiled clothes are okay—that way you won't get them dirty.

Bible stories are fun when acted out, so every "David" needs a sling.

"No" is a poor answer in most cases—why not negotiate?

Reading the newspaper aloud makes sense when there's a squirming body in your lap, feeding you melting sugared doughnuts.

Stick horses enjoy their hay best in the living room.

Being a cowboy is better than being President.

Rain *could* be angels' tears—because my day went sour. And the rainbow very well *may* be God's smile when a grandchild turns it sweet again.

To Think and Pray About: Today is Grandparents' Day by proclamation of President Carter (1978). Just hold an older person close today. God will bless you for it!

Believe the Beautiful

1 Corinthians 6:20   September 11
Mark 9:23

Last night I heard the wild geese fly; they sounded far away,
And yet I see the countryside is turning gold today.
The sunrise wears a misty veil of Indian Summer smoke;
And on brown hills the cattle graze beneath the speckled oak.
I never knew when summer left; her exit was so calm,
She must have told the wild geese, though: last night I
     heard their psalm.

                                                    J.M.B.

WHY IS EVERY AUTUMN a glorious surprise? Did we
not know that the beard of the wheat would burn
golden? That the cider-ready apples would intoxicate the
nostrils? That the goldenrod beside the pasture fence would
tattle to the pumpkin and the squash? Why is it that when
colors become so vivid they blend their scarlets, russets, and
yellows to wash the landscape and confuse the eyes that we
stand in awe?

We see, but we do not believe.

Autumn traverses the breadth of the nation, speaking a
different language to each locale. *Change.* We see transformation in the rain-drenched Smoky Mountains... the grain-
rich Plains states... the snow-covered Appalachians... the
sun-kissed Pacific shores... the mapled majesty of New
England... and the blue-fingered marvel of the five Great
Lakes. We are moved by its song.

We hear, but we do not believe.

Autumn is a celebration of nature, its rarified air tugging at
our senses, begging for praise to the Creator. Why do we
butterfly back to summer or incant lamentations for the ice-
bound winter to come? Because the eyes of the human heart
are blinded to beauty unpaid for?

To Think and Pray About: We are conditioned to suspect
anything which cannot be weighed, measured, and repaid.
God gave His all—freely! Believe and rejoice!

Women at the Wheel

"ENJOY YOUR TRIP—you may not be coming back." What a way to start a day! But I read the article about women drivers out of morbid curiosity. Chances are, it was written by a man; but there's something we can do about our mortality rate.

- Check heel heights like you check the oil gauge. Toothpick heels thrust the foot forward. As the toe goes, so does the heel—catching on the accelerator, slipping off the brake, or triggering a cramp in the arch—any of which can lead to disaster.
- What about clothing on that quick trip for diet margarine? "Running down in my housecoat" could mean you won't be running back. Catch a heel in the hem—and you know the rest.
- "I'll wear my sunglasses. Nobody will recognize me." Maybe not—afterward! Unorthodox shades may be fun, but foolish. Dark shades distort color. One glance over your shoulder...blind spot...WHAM!
- Flowing scarves are unsafe. You may not hang yourself, but you can hang up traffic with your neck in a noose suspended from the steering wheel. You may survive while gawkers perish.
- "What am I going to do with this hair?" is a valid question when you're driving. If it's long, wear a cap or secure it with a rubber band. If this turns you off, consider the alternative of catching your crowning glory in the gear shift or signal lever.

We-e-ll...God has no need of unexpected dropouts. He created this temple and I am to maintain it (avoiding as many repairs as possible). We are a nation of vitamin-gulpers, exercise addicts, and health-food-fad-followers. But "death on the highway" stalks us.

To Think and Pray About: How responsible a driver are you? How would you apply the Golden Rule here?

We Hereby Resolve...

SKIP this page if you have kept all your New Year's resolutions! Otherwise, ponder with me a question in a friend's letter.

"Why should we all feel a need to clean up our act on January 1st, just because one year's gone and another's beginning?"

Yes, why? That question has remained unanswered (as has the letter!) for eight months. Now with Labor Day at hand I have come up with what I hope is a "workable" idea.

I believe the reason I have been unable to keep most of my well-meant resolutions was that I tried to "picture" the whole year. In other words, I used a wide-angle lens when I needed a microscope! Laying out a whole year's work is just too broad.

"I'm going to stop desserts," I say. Or, "I'll read the entire New Testament through... answer letters..."

By January 31st, I'm having dessert—*twice* a day. By Ground Hog's Day, I have read two chapters in Matthew. And you know about the letters! But everybody knows that on all counts it was somebody else's fault (Right?). So all the willpower in the world did not do the job.

Well, so what if it's Labor Day? Don't I need to work harder? First, I resolve to slow down. To work harder, yes, but on a daily basis. But there is more! I must not be too hard on myself—just recognize with John that without God I can do nothing and that He walks with me every baby-step forward. Eventually, change will come where it counts—in the heart.

To Think and Pray About: Are there things in your life that need changing? How many resolutions were you unable to make work (Be honest!)? Together, let's start anew. It is hard to change, you say? It is impossible! But the Jesus inside you can perform that miracle.

Confidential Survey

YESTERDAY'S MAIL brought a questionnaire from a doctoral candidate.

Instructions were to rate oneself on a scale of 7 to 1 on items listed. "No need to ponder . . . first impressions generally are best . . ." Good! One could do the thing before the stew boiled over. Dropping an onion into the pot was a mistake (I cried all the way through the dull paper), so I let my mind wander. How, I wondered, would most of us rate on a Bible-reading survey? Here's a sample question:

1. *I read carefully, pondering each word, praying for interpretation by the Holy Spirit.*
   7 = definitely most characteristic of you
   6 = very characteristic of you
   5 = somewhat characteristic of you
   4 = neither characteristic nor uncharacteristic of you
   3 = somewhat uncharacteristic of you
   2 = very uncharacteristic of you
   1 = definitely most uncharacteristic of you

How about taking just one verse and working through today's reading? It is imperative that we fit ourselves into God's Word as He spoke through the mouths of His prophets and scribes. Otherwise, we find ourselves trying to fit the words into a mold of our creation. In this case, we shy away from being 1 and strive for the 7.

To Think and Pray About: Sometimes Bible reading is so frustrating that tears come without the onion? Think of this as a recipe: 1. Set aside a definite time—and stick to it; 2. Try different translations (but hang onto your KJV and be aware of paraphrased versions); 3. Remember the tried-and-true rule of quality versus quantity (chew and digest); and 4. Talk with the Lord all the way through ("I hear You, Lord, You are telling me . . ."). Now, abide by His Word. He will make you a 7 one day!

Hope Lies Over the Hill

SEPTEMBER's gold fingers reached through the window to warm the waiting room. But Nita did not feel them. Her heart was a lump of ice as she waited to hear a third doctor confirm what the two before him had said. "Cancer."

With trembling fingers, Nita plucked an old magazine from the cluttered table. It opened as if by plan to a one-page account of a man's battle for survival.

The writer was riding horseback across an unpopulated stretch of Midwestern cow country when caught in a blinding snowstorm. He had only enough food for one day in his knapsack and, although he was warmly clad, no amount of clothing could button out the cold. No lodges. No houses. Just howling wilderness. Darkness came early in the blizzard. Could he stretch the rations to sustain him through the unexpected delay? Reaching for the knapsack, he found it was gone. And with it went hope. *No food!*

The rider grew weary. His horse stumbled. And the strange white world became a ghostly screen through which he could no longer see. He begged the Lord for help. None came. His eyelids drooped... and then his mind began to drift. In that exhausted state it was easy to imagine music...

He floated out. The music floated in—louder to awaken him to a lantern-lit hole in the swirling snow. God *had* heard. Help was just over the hill.

Minutes later, inside a snug wagon, he was the guest of a bearded Basque shepherd who knew how to fry beans, perk coffee—and dish out love. All the while, the shepherd strummed a stringed instrument, singing in a strange tongue. But to the lost rider, it was as if the Lord translated: *Never give up hope... I am near.*

My friend's heart grew lighter. She, too, had heard "music in the storm."

To Think and Pray About: Are you struggling with a problem today? Most of us are! So why should we sit parked in neutral when hope lies just over the hill? *God is near.*

Following a King

WADING THROUGH the "begats" of the Old Testament is a challenge. But we need our history lesson. We study the prophecies for what they foretell. (I am struggling with Kings!)

Verse 16 stood out in today's reading: "And he did evil in the sight of the Lord, and walked in the way of the father, and in his sin wherewith he made Israel to sin." I was remembering Jason.

My pint-sized student turned enormous, ripe-olive eyes toward mine. They swam with remorse. "I didn't *want* to take the bike, Teacher!"

I believed him. "Then why did you, Jason?"

"I—I saw my big brother take one just like it— only it was to get even with that bully, Manny, you know?" *Yes, I knew.*

I handed Jason a Kleenex and he went on. "He'd beat my brother up and I—I took *this* one to replace *that* one—"

I'd been through this before. *When will they ever learn?* I asked myself. Yes, when would Older Brother learn that Little Brother was watching—and following in his path? When would Little Brother learn that one wrong does not right another? And would he ever come to realize that somebody else is watching *him*, too? And imitating?

Startling as it sounds, we are all "kings" (or "queens" if you will) in somebody's eyes. To somebody within the family or outside the family circle. To some stranger on the street. Are you ready for *this*? Maybe we have a whole "queendom" watching, admiring, and making our ways their ways! So how can we prepare for such anointment? First, we must seek our own King to follow lest we be caught up like Nadab in today's reading or like Jason. We must strive to be like Jesus.

To Think and Pray About: *Father, we would walk with You, in each single thing we do; Lord, we know the victory's won when our model is Your Son!*

J.M.B.

Prophecies and Promises

1 Kings 15:33; 16:7   September 17
Psalm 48:1

THE NIGHT SKY is beaded with stars. A full harvest moon reflects the end of summer's growth and hints of bare-branched months ahead. In its pure white-gold light I am remembering another glory-filled sky which helped me with today's reading.

Newspapers had promised a spectacular show in the heavens for earthlings who postponed bedtime. "The moon will turn from silver to gold to red, then disappear."

Writers referred to the lunar eclipse which began officially at 9:22 P.M., July (my son's birthday), 1982, and lasted until 3:40 A.M. the following day. Astronomers predicted 106 minutes "totality" (time the moon was inside the earth's shadow).

Those witnessing the phenomena agreed that it was worth waiting for (aren't all good things?). Our family celebrated Bryce's birthday watching, awestruck. Words would have been a sacrilege. I wished to write a hymn similar to Boberg's "How Great Thou Art."

There have been other eclipses. There will be more. What's amazing, however, is the ability of learned people who can predict with total accuracy the exact moment of each phase of God's handiwork. Newspapers said the sky-watchers worked with "scientific facts." I like to think they were inspired as were olden-day prophets.

Today's reading speaks of an inspired man who predicted in detail the destruction of King Baasha's evil reign. Jesus' prophecy came to pass. God's prophecies never fail. Neither do His promises! And that is the greatest truth of all.

To Think and Pray About: Can you look around you and see fulfillment of the Scriptures? In what ways do the revelations affect your daily life? I find them comforting!

Oh Lord, my God, what power is mine when I consider how divine Your plan for this my human heart; O Lord my God, how great Thou art!

You Deserve a Break Today

September 18   Matthew 22:37-40

"GIVE ME A BREAK, will you?" used to be the plea for a chance. "It's time for my break," means that the saleslady, cashier, or other who earned a rest can't help you. And, of course, a nation of TV viewers recognizes that "You deserve a break today!" translates into a Big Mac just as "break a leg" says (oddly enough) "Good luck in the game." *Put them all together, and you have a wise suggestion.*

How long has it been since you sank into a tub of comfortably-warm water with bubble-bath frothing up to your chin? Bought a new album of your favorite music, leaned back with your eyes closed, and enjoyed it? Read a good book without glancing at the clock? Danced all alone, humming your own tune, until you were deliciously tired (never once giving thought to tonight's menu)? Went for a long, long walk in the woods thinking of nothing but the canopy of color above?

Give yourself a break today. Indulge yourself. Pamper yourself. Enjoy yourself. *Love* yourself! If you tensed up at the last thought, you need the break very much because chances are very good that you need to rid yourself of guilt, fear, worry—those destructive attitudes that hamper us all in their attempt to rob us blind. Blind to the joy God wants for us. Blind to the beauty of the world about us. Blind to the ever-loving Creator who longs to cradle us in His arms. And blind to the needs of others.

Yes, sadly, that's the way it works. When we predetermine molds for ourselves and become slaves to schedules and ideas, we begin expecting others to behave somewhat like ourselves. Deadly! Respect our own individuality and we will respect theirs. Let yourself go. Be unique (because you *are*!). Be creative. Surprise yourself. Surprise others. A smile here, a compliment there. Love yourself and you will love others!

To Think and Pray About: Friendships and family relationships are infinitely richer in a warm, relaxed atmosphere. We women possess the key. God put it there. What a break.

In His Own Way

Psalm 90:13-17   September 19

THE ONCE-POPULAR SONG, "Everything is Beautiful in Its Own Way," caught on. No matter what our handicap or station in life, somebody thought we were beautiful. Now, who doesn't want to be beautiful? Cosmetologists have busy schedules. Physical fitness classes are packed. And plastic surgeons have six of everything.

I imagine Eve was beautiful. Back in Garden-of-Eden days, all life was in perfect balance. Since then we have sampled or gobbled down fruits from the Tree of Knowledge, separating ourselves from our Creator. Seeing our nakedness, we were ashamed and sought to cover the imperfections with the temporal things. Deep inside there is a desire to get back to the beautiful. But the process is slow and painful—like removing unwanted pounds or putting luster back into sun-damaged hair. We moan, groan, join 12 health clubs, and still pick a quarrel with our reflections because we are working on the external. So beauty is only skin-deep, huh? We'd settle for that! Or would we? Not if we recognized what a miracle our beings are!

You see, I am persuaded that my being here is no accident... and the same is true of you, no matter what the circumstances of your birth. Scientists tell me that 400 million spermatozoa raced for the ovum and the winner's prize was *me*! Computers can't do that. I am no mere machine even though God gave me all my moving parts and assigned to each a job (sometimes two). My ears can hear as well as keep my hat from falling over my eyes. And my mouth—Wow! What it can do. Unlike my ears, I don't have two. And that's beautiful. Ask my husband.

God had a plan for us billions of years ago—before the sperm chased the ovum! We don't have to prove a thing to Him. He knows that we are capable of developing the spiritual muscle to take us home!

To Think and Pray About: Help others realize that they are acceptable. Change a life today with: "You're beautiful in God's own way"... "He loves you" and "So do I!"

Celebration of Life

September 20   Acts 26:16-18

MY SON came home laughing about a sign his friend has taped to the door of his bedroom:
Do not open this door. All the dark will leak out!

Clever, we agreed. But, once alone, I did some thinking about that sign. Maybe it would be a good idea if I lettered a couple of those warnings for myself. Then, on one of those days that steals my smile and leaves me with a frown, I could alert the world around me to let me be! Let me fume, pout, and enjoy my self-created darkness. I think Satan would have a heydey!

But what about God? Wouldn't that silly sign hurt Him deeply? He wants me to be happy, wearing a smile, and ready to make every day joy-filled for myself and others. He tells me so over and over in His word. How much more reassurance do I need than that given in John 1:5? "God is light and in him there is no darkness at all."

No, I'll not be wearing a sign like the one belonging to Bryce's friend. And my prayer is that you won't either!

To Think and Pray About: But what about the crepe-hangers around you? Those who respond to your "Happy birthday!" with "What's happy about it?" Pity them, comfort them if you can, but *don't* let the darkness seep out to dim your light. I know a lady who celebrates her birthday every week. That she has survived another week is cause for celebration. Share this with your killing-frost acquaintances if they are receptive. If not, hold it fast in your heart to rejoice about with those who know that life is a gift. In Jesus' time, His 30 years would have been middle-age. An added five years would have made Him "old." And look at us now. No meter can measure the light He spread! Now God grants us 70 . . . 80 . . . 90 . . . 100 years to carry on, *praise Him!*

Some Things Are Timeless

1 Corinthians 15:33,34   September 21
2 Peter 2:17,18

THE POOR COLUMNIST is aging. She has reached the big Three-Zero! In jest, the writer prepared a list of things every women her age is sure to have done.

Have a marriage proposal turned down... lose all your credit cards... fall out of escrow, out of love—and back in ... get a fuzzy perm by Mr. Joe who outdresses you and expects a tip... spend more than you can afford on a suit too good to wear... quit a job in a fit of righteous rage... rear-end somebody while testing your highly-leveraged car... alternate between panic and relief at being single... consider cosmetic surgery...

So much of life (and aging is a part of it—consider the alternatives!) is a matter of attitude. How about some timeless suggestions on how to enjoy every minute the biological clock is ticking away?

1. Step on the brakes of your tongue. Say less than you think.
2. Be frugal with promises (keep them); lavish with praise (give it away).
3. Show interest in the ideas and pursuits of others.
4. Never let an opportunity to praise and encourage slip by.
5. Preserve an open mind. If you must disagree, be gentle.
6. Keep the corners of your mouth turned up in a youthful smile (the best face-lift and also hides your pain).
7. Whatever your virtues, let them speak for themselves, and let the shortcomings of others do the same.
8. Protect the feelings of others. Laugh often with them—not at them or about them. The mark of a thoroughbred is to discuss strengths, not weaknesses.
9. Ignore spiteful criticism.
10. Give without counting the cost. God will reward you.

To Think and Pray About: These promise youth-everlasting—in the heart!

Oh, Those Quarreling Blackbirds!

THERE they are—quarreling again! Can they never agree on anything? This time the flock of blackbirds is debating loudly the propriety of the birdbath. There is a harsh *check* as a black creature, flashing purplish in the autumn sunlight, nosedives into the shallow basin. Rudely shoving relatives aside (malice in the white eyes), the bird shakes excess water from ruffled feathers and joins other freshly bathed birds in the avocado tree, only to meet with opposition again. *Que-ee! Que-ee!* The notes are harsh and wheezy, somewhat like a rusty hinge. And I am wondering how we ladies would have sounded to an observer this morning. There wasn't even a birdbath to quibble over—just the date of a meeting.

Disagreements lead to broken hearts, homes, lives, and kingdoms—yes, even the kingdom of God. Long ago Amos questioned, "Can two walk together unless they be agreed?" And Jesus tells us: "If a house be divided against itself, that kingdom cannot stand." But, back to the blackbirds.

Remember the fable about the farmer sowing grain only to see the pesky birds holding a feast behind him? The good man devised a strong net which he cast over the birds—already quarreling over the kernels.

Now, the blackbirds could have flown away with the net, landed at a safe distance, and walked from beneath it. But they lacked something vital. Agreement! The ladies began pecking at the net and the gents began quarreling. "East... West... North... South... straight up!"

Each flew a different direction and the net full of birds fell to the ground. So the helpless creatures may have been the four-and-twenty baked in a pie.

To Think and Pray About: It may take some ultimate daring to pull it off, but sometimes we win by losing! Find a compromise—lest you be caught in the deadly net of division.

All Over the Earth

John 10:9-11   September 23
Matthew 5:14-16

NATURE plays no favorites. No season is king or queen. Instead, each is of a certain royalty in its own right. There are those who would rebel against the heat and humidity of summer; others who would cross out the cruelty of winter's shutter-rattling gusts. But the summer rebels would rob individuals who find peace in strolling the quiet country lanes, lolling in the hammock, listening to the squeals of nut-brown children freed from school—as they, themselves, are freed from vexations. And those who would rob winter of its ermine robes would take away nature's rights to pristine beauty and sportsminded skiers' claim to the freedom they find in decorating the snow-iced mountains with loops and swirls in their race to the valleys below.

But nobody finds fault with the seasons dividing the two. God, in His infinite wisdom, surely knew that we mortals (complainers by nature) needed a time to rest our discontented tongues. So He gave us spring. He gave us autumn. And He announced their arrival by equinox. Once again with this autumnal equinox He has divided the light from the darkness and set His world ablaze with color.

The horizon appears pushed back as the sun ascends 12 hours, pauses briefly above the equator, and then begins the 12-hour journey to brighten the land "down under." In that blink-of-an-eye pause over the equator, the sun creates a significant moment: an equinoctial sameness *all over the earth.* It is as if God were saying: "I play no favorites. I am the light of the *world.*"

I have always assigned a certain intelligence to sunflowers. Their great, golden-bonneted heads follow their master from horizon to horizon. Would that we did the same for Him. Even when there is a fanning out of the light, He leaves reflected glory in the moon . . . and in our hearts.

To Think and Pray About: God has reflected His Light in our lives. Roll back the darkness for others *all over the earth!*

Fuel for the Heart

September 24

John 6:35,48
Mark 7:15

THE WORD *cholesterol* added a new wing to the structure of my vocabulary. I grew up on fried chicken, butter beans, and buttered biscuits. "Clean your plates," grown-ups told us. We tried to raise our children the same way. But along came a subculture with long hair, blank faces, and a passion for "natural foods." That excluded meat, sweets, and other "establishment foods." My husband, who never got away from the U.S. Air Force crew cut, saw to it that our son kept his hair out of his eyes so I could check them for focus. And, although we stuck with tossed greens and steamed prunes, neither of us considered dinner complete without a chop or a steak medium-well.

As it turns out, maybe that generation grazing the meadows had a point. "Lots of salt-free veggies," doctors tell us, "but no flesh-foods that don't swim or fly." The only cow that came close to flying was the one that jumped over the moon. And I've never heard of a hog with wings. I doubt if swine can swim either, according to the herd which housed a demon and perished (Matthew 8:31,32).

So, it's skinless chicken (why the chicken but not its fruit, the oh-so-delicious egg?), a flat fish, unseasoned vegetables, and skim milk. Sounds sort of like the old Mosaic law, doesn't it? My family goes along with it, balking only at seaweed. What convinced my two men were the doctor's words: "Hearts are machines. Want to keep them running, then use the right fuel!"

Fuel for the heart. Ignoring Bryce's questions about Methuselah's diet, I've been thinking about that phrase. What kind of "soul food" do we dish up for others—particularly those who do not know the Great Physician, Jesus?

To Think and Pray About: Make out a menu of ministries for today. Make each item simple, a little unsung service, but so nourishing for the heart. The *New* Testament Law of Love!

One Step Forward

THE WELL-MEANING "Angel" (a name assigned to volunteers in the children's ward) offered a pad and some charcoal to Ronald. An automobile-accident victim, the little boy had both legs in casts for what must have seemed longer than he had been alive (don't I know!). Now, today, the casts were to come off. And the child was scared.

"I don't wanna draw!" Ronald said irritably.

Of course, he didn't. I was thinking back on the friend who knows I'm all thumbs, yet brought me all that yarn to knit-and-purl while I lay mummifying in my body cast. "Cast off!" Ina said gaily. The only thing I wanted to cast off was that 100-pound corset. And, as far as I was concerned, knitting was for backbones and purling—well, wasn't that winding strings of oyster-made gems around one's neck? Oh, yes, I knew how Ronald felt. So I sat in the shadows and said a prayer for him instead of offering to read.

The casts were stripped away. So was the boy's confidence. "I'm afraid it'll hurt," Ronald said without moving.

"It may," the therapist said, "but it's going to help. Any step forward's a risk."

How true, I thought as the child, his courage bolstered by the therapist's honest approach, mastered a painful first step. Then another. And another. Triumphantly!

It is hard to step forward after we have been bound up by painful circumstances. We become discouraged, frightened, and tired of trying. We fear ridicule. We fear rejection. We even lose sight of the fact that God's loving arms are there to support us when we stumble, to reassure us, to make us whole again.

To Think and Pray About: Are you afraid of that first step? The risk is worth it! Jesus is standing by.

Preparation

IT HAS BEEN a long time since I ate watermelon-rind preserves. Watching my grandmother, then my mother, convert what most would discard into spicy, emerald-green, translucent slices of goodness, I decided the process simply took too much time. Slice. Soak. Drain. Cook. Cool. Repeat. But, of late, my taste buds will not behave. Neither will my memory. So here I am in the final step of simmering when a ring of the doorbell interrupts. Hoping the preserves will not stick, I rush to the door only to find a sheet of yellow paper poked through the latch. A little irritated, I am about to throw it away when the caption catches my eye: *A person may go to heaven . . .*

It is time to add the sugar to my boiling preserves, but I want to finish that sentence. So I read on.

Without wealth . . . beauty . . . learning . . . fame . . . culture . . . friends . . .

But no one can enter heaven without Christ!

Now, we know that, don't we? But the "withouts" remind me of something most of us tend to forget. God does not always choose the kind of people we would select to do His work. Look at John the Baptist. Just as my grandmother and my mother were the "forerunners" of my pickle-making, that strange man, clothed in camel's hair and a skin girding his loins, wandered in the wilderness eating locusts and wild honey as the forerunner of Christ! Imagine that—humble birth, little education, and dressed like a desert hermit!

To Think and Pray About: *Prepare ye the way of the Lord, make His paths straight* very well may apply today!

What Am I Laughing At?

John 16:33; 8:32   September 27

"WE'RE LOST! Can you direct us there?"

Our wonderful friends whom we had not seen for 20 years were here at last! In my excitement, I handed George the phone. My husband is better with directions. Anyway, I get all tongue-tied when I am excited. He greeted our friends warmly then asked practically, "Where are you now?"

Just a small incident. But something in the question sparked a memory as I popped an apple pie into the oven. Then, turning the control on bake, I remembered. *We have to know where people are before we can direct them*—a Christian quotation I had read somewhere.

It was a perfect evening. The pie was a tender-crusted, spicy success. Not that it mattered much. If the fruit had been tough and the pastry baked black, we'd have called it a "burnt offering" and whooped with laughter. You see, we know each other that well. We walked the stardusted trail of honeymoon years together. We laughed at our hard knocks together. We mourned the loss of their precious baby boy together. And we learned to laugh again, because we prayed together . . . loving more dearly . . . seeing more clearly. God was our starting point. We never asked where we were. We *knew!* And, in that climate, laughter just seems to bubble over. Shall I say "laughter born of the Spirit"?

But what about the others? Don't we have to know their starting point before we can redirect their course? I find myself guilty of urging non-Christians to do this or that without knowing if they understand. So what shall we do?

To Think and Pray About: Suppose you know a non-Christian gripped by anxiety. For starters, offer this:

> Fate used me meanly; but I looked at her and laughed,
> That none might know how bitter was the cup I quaffed.
> Along came Joy, and paused beside me where I sat,
> Saying, "I came in to see what you were laughing at."
> —Wilcox

The Sandman Calleth

Matthew 11:28-30
Matthew 6:33,34

THE WORST THING about insomnia is how stupid the sufferer feels the morning after. Toss...turn...recognize how wrung-out you're destined to be tomorrow... and try to recall the remedy for those carry-on bags beneath your eyes to be reckoned with. But there are so many life-and-death matters to resolve. What ran the gas bill so high? Why did you purchase that trendy dress just because it was marked down after Labor Day? Are there enough Cheerios for breakfast? *And why, oh, why can't you sleep? Maybe you're ill...*

There are those who are convinced (and will try to convince you) that you are heading for a breakdown when the Sandman refuses to answer your ring. But don't they say that about taking X-rays, under- or over-exercising, lack of fiber in the diet...salt...sugar?

Well, it's daylight and you feel a little silly. One of those dumb sheep must have got stuck as it leaped into the fold, because you slept in spite of the broken crockery in your pillow, the sirens that screamed out of sync, and the cramp that grabbed the right great toe. You'd deny that you dozed except for the alarm clock's invasion of your private dream.

The good news is that our need for sleep varies. Some, experts tell us, require ten hours (incredible) while others (like me) are bright-eyed and bushy-tailed on four. The worry the insomniac indulges in is worse than the problem. The bad news is that we very well may be making too much of our physical bodies. Now, we need to care for our health; but must we make it a gospel? God is our absolute, our hope, our promise of the "new body."

To Think and Pray About: The cure? Obey the first commandment. We are to love God with all our heart, soul, mind, and strength (who added "and sleep eight hours?"). We are to rest in *Him,* so count blessings (oblivious to time)...love ...life...and *sl-e-e-e-ep...*

Within Hearing Distance

"STAY within hearing distance," my father cautioned the day I went with him to haul firewood. But the dogwood was in full bloom, each tree a bit more beautiful—and a little farther away. I wandered on and on, forgetting Daddy's warning. Soon I was lost.

"Daddy!" I called. No answer.

Being lost in the woods is a frightening thing for a small child. I imagined great bears that craved little girls for breakfast and alligators that lived on land. Under the spell of such visions, I panicked and began to scream—hearing only a mocking echo that seemed to come from the four directions.

At last my voice and legs gave way to exhaustion. I sat down on the mossy bank of a little stream and prepared to die. But it was in that quiet moment that I heard a dearly familiar voice. Daddy was calling my name!

What had happened? I was able to hear only when I stopped my screaming. Then, as I listened, calmly and reassuringly, my father guided me to him.

How good to know that our heavenly Father is always within "hearing distance" even when we forget and wander away. No matter how far we wander, how lost we are, how frightened . . . panicky . . . even so in despair that we are "planning to die," God can and *will* lead us home if we will but listen for His voice.

To Think and Pray About: Your situation is not that desperate? It's only a frustrating day? God wants to hear. And He *can* help. When Jesus said, "Take up your bed and walk," I am convinced that He meant the words spiritually, too. We can be victorious over small and large things with Him as our companion. And He loved to walk as He talked. Remember? So stay within hearing distance—all the way home!

Found and Lost

September 30   Luke 13:34
                                               Matthew 18:12-14

MOTHER HEN was a source of amusement to all who watched her. The lady had hatched a duckling and refused to accept that any child of hers could swim. Baby duck's wandering away to the cattle pool was a constant source of frustration to the watchful hen. She'd run from bank to bank, scolding her peculiar, water-loving child, in an effort to warn him of what she counted danger, ever hoping he would learn.

The protective instinct is very strong. One sees it in the animal kingdom. And the person with a bit of sensitivity to nature, sees it in the plant kingdom. Today September bows out wearing a red-gold scarf. It is easy to imagine that beneath, held close to the bosom, is the golden grain for next year's crop. Soon the embroidered leaves change to russet and then to somber brown as October harvests the apples to store against the white shawl of approaching winter. But as one month gives way to another, none forgets nature's motherhood. Tucked snugly beneath that ever-changing scarf are the tight-fisted buds of another spring and, inside its secret pockets, slumber the fur-people of the forest. For nature, like other mothers, holds in her heart that beautifully sacred flaw of hope.

We human beings practice that protective instinct in our homes, holding fast to hope when the little ones change or stray. And how much more Christ looks out for us. Unlike the mother hen, He knows what is right for us—and it is we who are foolish. Remember the saying: "We have met the enemy and the enemy is ourselves?" Our Shepherd searches the darkness of our sin and pride while we try to make it alone.

To Think and Pray About: Study the parable in today's suggested Scripture reading. How can you apply it in a new and meaningful way? God wants us for His kingdom of eternity. He lights the way with bright October to lead us from self-willed dark.

An Anniversary Prayer

DEAR LORD, can it be October already? It is time to climb the golden stairs again. The way is lighted by orange flames of burning leaves heaped high in the gutter, the smoke rising to join Your white throne of clouds. We marvel at what we feel but cannot yet see, knowing that there—above the smog of earthly cares—You hold the key to eternal spring. We praise You, Lord of all seasons, for Your promise that we will join You there when we ascend the stairs one last time.

But for now, we know that October is another milestone reached . . . another harvest of blessings . . . another challenge to set new goals . . . a time to dream and set sail for the unknown shore, now a rim of far-flung sky—to be revealed to us as we venture forth. Deafen our ears to the jeers of doubters, sailing on as Columbus sailed when surrounded by a doubting crew.

He sailed in time of disbelief, Lord—not unlike our own time. Without the qualities You gave him—initiative, perseverance, determination, and faith—would the explorer have reached the shores of this land of plenty? Columbus, like Adam, looked upon an unspoiled land. As sin had not touched the garden, smog, squalid slums, prejudice, and evil in the high places of government had not touched America. These are the price we pay for moving from primitive pygmies to industrial giants.

But we have traveled far in other ways, Lord. With Your blessing, we have erected churches, synagogues, and cathedrals. We have built schools and universities. So preserve the good in us, Lord. Lead upward another step.

And, Lord, if I may have a word for myself? Today marks another anniversary for me. It was October 1st that you joined my husband and me in marriage, giving us all the tools You gave Columbus and adding one more, a love that deepens with each step—up the golden stairs. For this, dear Lord, I praise You!

Golden Moments

I've gathered as I traveled a part of every day
And precious are the keepsakes I've found along the way:
A field of purple clover... the cool of speckled shade...
A picnic by the streamlet where strands of moss were made;
Soft-spoken words remembered, a flash of loving eyes...
I think that I've forgotten then to my sweet surprise
The glint of golden moments come back to me once more
To shine in retrospection more golden than before. J.M.B.

THERE ARE GOLDEN MOMENTS in every day. Surely God planned October so we could recognize these moments more clearly. For when is the world more golden than in October? The forest paths, once shaded with green umbrellas, are beckoning with the bright fingers of autumn's sun—more visible now through the thinning leaves.

The air is spiced with apples—Delicious, Pound, Winesaps, Rome, Jonathan, Ben Davis (depending upon your region)—all begging that their sweetness be stored away. Do people still make apple butter—smooth as velvet with a sheen on top—for bringing back memories some wintry day? All of us can store the remembered smells, recalling them at will.

To Think and Pray About: Oh, the glory of the countryside. But city life need not be a barren path either. Even the noise of the traffic seems subdued as if to capture the golden moment of watching one last leaf drift down. Find a way today to clear your mind, to open your heart, to tune in on the senses for refreshing the soul with God's handiwork. Do you sense His presence? Walk with your family, your friends, or just meditate all alone. Invited, God will join you—and that will be the most golden moment of this day. Gone is the clamor. In its stead is the true peace of autumn.

The Be-Attitudes

1 John 5:4   October 3
Psalm 86:10; Matthew 5:3-11

L AWRENCE WELK, one of our local residents, is back in the "wunning!" That's right. The music maker once described by a critic as a man "loved only by his public" has taken up his baton again at 85 for that very reason, his tenacious grip on his fans. That and his never-faltering faith. "I always knew what I wanted to *be*," he said. "And I knew God would get me there!"

Welk's 27-year TV reign as a musical variety host came to an end in 1985. But his loyal legions remained. Deluged by letters, public TV stations aired a tribute as a membership campaign. Larry is a humble man; but, with his kind of faith, all things were possible. The result was more than $1.6 million in pledges. Public TV execs looked the gift horse in the mouth and decided to feed it reruns. Beginning in the fall of 1987, a series of 52 episodes began. Fans were delighted. Executives were overwhelmed.

But Lawrence Welk was not surprised. Hadn't he known all along that the curtain was not drawn on his BE-ing? God was his agent.

How long will his return to the tube last? Who knows? God will take care of his tomorrows. Of his todays, he says (what else?) "Wonerful, wonerful!"

To Think and Pray About: Yes, today *is* wonderful. Now, what do you want to do with the day God has handed you? You can make it more wonderful so let's:

- BE content with what we have. BE willing to share it.
- BE loyal to our friends. BE tolerant of our enemies.
- BE strong enough to face adversity. BE weak enough to seek God's help.
- BE charitable to those in need. BE frugal with our own demands.
- BE wise enough to know that only God is wise. BE foolish enough to believe all things are possible.

Trial by Fire

I T HAS BEEN five days of elemental fear. First a major earthquake and devasting aftershocks in Los Angeles revived in Californians the fear that their lives rest on an unstable foundation.

And then, after a gentle summer, a heat wave erupted into a series of fires, blackening more than 10,000 acres of timber, citrus, and avocado groves. Residents huddle together, awaiting the next weather bulletin or an order to evacuate and to pray for rain to drown the flames. "Inevitability" is of little consolation.

Santa Ana winds are a personal nemesis to those of us who live here. They howl like banshees through the passes, whine through the eucalyptus windbreaks, and work on the nerves. October is the month of fear. Hills blaze. Breathing is difficult. But—

Something special in human relations is taking place as the infernal winds heat the brittle chaparral to the point of explosion. God must be very proud of the heroic fortitude of public servants who fight those demonic flames every inch of the way—and win! The story begins with the coordination of thousands of fire fighters with their sophisticated machinery and its awesome achievement. It ends with everyday people banning together to tally losses, count blessings, and comfort one another. *Gone:* homes. *Saved:* lives!

"It takes a lot of faith, you know," says one resident. "But help came—and it will stay as we pick up the pieces."

Yes, it takes a lot of faith. Faith, courage, and strength to get on with their lives. And God must be even prouder of these "little ones," equipped only with faith, who show such coolness during this harrowing trial by fire.

To Think and Pray About: How do you meet adversity in everyday life? The key word today is *teamwork*. Teamwork with your families, friends, neighbors, and the wayfaring stranger. And teamwork with God!

Forsaking All Else

Matthew 19:6   October 5
John 15:12

"COME WITH ME," my husband invited, as he prepared to take the car to an adjacent town for repairs.

I was tempted. The 20-mile road to Ramona winds in and out between avocado groves as it crawls up a mountainside. The air was October-soft. The pumpkin patches and sun were trying to outshine one another.

But going was out of the question. "I have too much to do," I said with regret.

"Is it really that important?"

Something in George's tone caused me to stop and think. Could anything I had on my calendar be more important than spending this autumn day with my husband? I looked at my list, so trivial in comparison. Odd, because a minute before I was tilting the scale in exactly the opposite direction. A year from now, would the entries on my calendar matter as much as another memory, another chance to unravel the sleeve of care and reweave the golden threads into an even brighter design? My heart gave a reckless flip-flop.

"No," I said.

"No, you're not going?"

"No, what I have to do is not that important."

I meant it even before George gave a whoop of pleasure. It is so good for a woman to know that her company means that much. But another realization had swept over me. It is God who gives us the wonderful people in our lives to love and spend time with. Maybe when Matthew and Mark recorded the words of Jesus, "... let no man put asunder," they included those of us within a relationship as well as outsiders. And couldn't the same be applied to time?

To Think and Pray About: In what ways do you sometimes find it is *you* who's dividing yourself? Try today to forsake all but love—sharing time with others and with God.

World Judge

S URELY you've encountered a Miss Smothers—by whatever name. On my first job she had ascended the first rung of the rickety ladder to success and, as such, supervised the other girls.

The lady's qualifications were poor. Any completed government form came back marked for correction. When a light pencil-check would have served, Miss Smothers used a red pen so that the entire page must be retyped. Criticism was her way of life.

And, of course, like a stone cast into water, the supervisor cast ripples of meanness throughout her department. Soon we were all but snarling at one another in frustration. The climax came when Analee, the spirited redhead, went into Miss Smothers' office and overheard her dismembering all of us in a nonstop monologue. Analee had had enough.

"Who do you think you are anyway? World judge?"

I winced when Analee reported the incident but realized she had a point. One of the girls suggested that we should talk the situation over before it became a stone nobody could lift. We did.

We were a comfortable-together group so we decided that the resolution we formulated could be put to work among ourselves as well as presented to Miss Smothers: *Let's stop judging others and talking to ourselves and start judging ourselves and talking to others.* It worked!

To Think and Pray About: If you are the supervisor (in your home or on the job), how do you organize? How can you be decisive, yet lead without driving? If you work with a difficult person, do you communicate your grievances gently *to that person?* We all need to remember that God is "World Judge" and His judgments are righteous.

Understanding

With our chosen friends . . . and still more between lovers (for mutual understanding is love's essence), the truth is easily indicated by the one and aptly comprehended by the other. A hint taken, a look understood, conveys the gist of long and delicate explanations; and where the life is known even yea and nay become luminous. In the closest of all relations—that of love well founded and equally shared, speech is half discarded . . . and with few looks and fewer words contrive to share their good and bad and uphold each other's hearts in joy . . . Understanding has in some sort outrun knowledge, for the affection perhaps began with the acquaintance. Each knows much more than can be uttered; each lives by faith . . . and between man and wife the language of the body is largely developed and grown strangely eloquent. The thought that prompted and was conveyed in a caress would only lose to be set down in words—ay, although Shakespeare himself should be the scribe. Robert Louis Stevenson

M R. AND MRS. George Wilson Bacher request the honor of the presence of our Lord's Spirit and your prayers at a small supper party celebrating the wedding anniversary of our son, Bryce, and his wife, Sun, this day. Dress is informal as we will sit by the outside waterfall—which will serve as our orchestra. Fare will be simple—perhaps spaghetti and pineapple upside-down cake (their favorites). Please bring no gifts. God arranged for: a million blazing stars overhead . . . a slice of moon . . . a few delicate flowers . . . *and four hearts made one.* You will meet *Laughter* and *Love;* but *Prejudice* and *Criticism* are among the uninvited. The central figure will be God. He will bring *Understanding.*

To Think and Pray About: Renew your vows to loved ones. And rejoice with us!

The Lonely Crowd

October 8   Psalm 46:10

LOLA said she'd meet me at the Food Park of the new mall.

The *where?* "Take any one of the escalators, turn west, and follow everybody—or follow your nose and ears!"

My friend's right. Shoppers march like armies, breathing in French-fried grease and melted-cheese smog. Loud music struggles to drown the drone of a thousand conversations ricocheting against the cavernous dining hall. So shoppers do not live by sales alone . . .

"Everybody ends up at the Food Park sooner or later," Lola says, joining me with bags in hand. I can see why—I guess. It's the fast foodist's nirvana of neon and nachos, skylights and sodas, ferns and alfalfa. A glimmering string of take-out establishments corralling a slick communal seating area. "So pick your poison!"

I am too overwhelmed to move. And so they sweep right past me, shopping refugees all: your poor, your tired, your huddled masses, fleeing the kitchen, seeking corn dogs, Cokes—and companionship.

The people are as varied as the foods. High schoolers, weary couples pushing strollers, retirees, and far-from-home Marines. But it's a lonely crowd. Privacy, quiet, peace, and happiness are missing. I guess the closely packed tables don't allow them to squeak in.

I feel a surge of sadness. Not that I'm anti-mall or against the Colonel's coupons. It just seems to me that as the body cries out for a balanced diet, the heart hungers and thirsts for a quiet time we let slip away when we closed the door on the dining room. We lost our "Upper Room," our "Shangri-La," our refuge from the world. A place to draw closer to each other and to God is not available at Food Park.

To Think and Pray About: Find a way to draw the family together at least once a day for a time of caring, sharing, and "prayering." Hold hands. Sing together. Love will grow.

Detour!

YOU know the game. "Take this word," someone says, "and see how many words you can make from it." The word was anger.

My students knew the rules. However, the new boy did not; and I failed to explain.

"I have a good one!" The apple-cheeked youngster blurted, unaware that the rules forbade use of additional letters. "Put a *d* in front and you have *danger!*" Burton exclaimed.

Just one letter separates anger from danger. The thought was so overwhelming that, spelling forgotten, we spent some time with the idea.

How can you apply the lesson today? Think of that rise of adrenaline called *anger* as a warning, a flashing red light, saying: *Danger Ahead.* Then detour with a prayer. And don't be surprised when the Lord opens an avenue of escape. Have you ever thought of laughter as an antidote? Frustrations are not fun? No, but (remember the Lord is helping!) they can be funny.

Pick a number. I have a favorite recollection that doubles me up. I was seeing red lights, believe me—brought on by pain as I lay dying (I was sure) and trying to fight off the brain-dulling injections nurses give to make going easier! Suddenly, there they were, *three* of them this time: in white, black, and gray pin-striped suits. The Three Wise Men—on *Easter?* The Three Blind Mice maybe, since they obviously couldn't read the *No Visitors* sign. And then the awful possibility struck me. Good guys wear white (and yes, he was checking a roster). Bad guys wear black (so that black book spelled my doom). The one in gray must be the mediator as the other two decided whether I was to head up or down. "Go away!" I shrieked. "You know I can't travel in this cast!"

There was a burst of masculine laughter. Not angels or demons. *Doctors!*

To Think and Pray About: Angry? I have never been so happy! See? We *can* win the game!

In His Name

WHENEVER you receive a letter with the complimentary closing, "In His Name," what significance do you attach to it? Most of us think (and rightly so) that the phrase is like the closing of our prayers, "In Jesus' Name."

There is a history of the words, however—one worth reviewing. It all began in 1871 in Chautauqua, New York, when a group of young persons (influenced by Edward Everett Hale's story, *Ten Times One Is Ten*) established a religious Lend-A-Hand Club. The philanthropical club idea spawned any number of similar organizations—basically religious. Though some were social, all used the Hale motto:

Look up and not down, look forward and not back;
Look out and not in; lend a hand!

The badge of the club is a Maltese cross bearing the inscription, "In His Name." There would be no way of measuring the good deeds done by the Lend-A-Hand Clubs. Quietly, as if wearing soft-soled shoes, they move in while others are still attempting to map out a strategy and—often anonymously— "lend a hand" to the down-and-out, the "street people," the losers, the needy.

The author's name is undoubtedly familiar. Edward Everett Hale, a contemporary of James Russell Lowell, was a minister in addition to being a scholarly writer. The reverend gentleman possessed a rare insight into human nature (as exemplified by his best-known work, *The Man Without A Country*). But one wonders if he possibly could have envisioned the impact of his immortal lend-a-hand lines.

We *never* know, do we? God gives to each of us a gift and it is up to us. Imagine, if you can, His meeting you with outstretched arms and saying, "I gave my Son for you. Blessed are you for all you have done—*In His Name.*"

To Think and Pray About: Lend a hand today, looking up, forward, and out. Only God can measure its reach!

October Attitude

Galatians 6:1-9,17,18   October 11

D O YOU FEEL baffled by letters which recount every detail of Great Uncle Hector's prostate surgery, Cousin Elva's addiction to alcohol, and the man (you don't know) who salvaged his eight-foot sofa from his burning house—but had to let his wife perish?

We are to bear one another's burdens? Yes, of course, we are. But we are to bear our own also. (You *did* read today's passages?) Yesterday I received one of those doomsday letters and in the same mail came these excerpts of a letter from a friend in Florida:

> About this time each year I think of the red and gold leaves I haven't seen in 40 years; but I am content to spend my Indian summer [in Florida] . . . here is my peaceable kingdom with a series of blessings: 1. I was in the hospital this time last year; 2. It was a relief when Hurricane Emily fizzled to a "watch and beware"; 3. Yellow Bus No. 562 unloads its precious cargo of children in full view of my kitchen window (triggering little journeys of the heart, but I never hanker to get back into the dawn-to-dusk teaching career); and 4. Books! I'm pleased to travel vicariously. I have reached a comfortable acceptance of low achievement and as my wise nurse-friend advises "don't sweat the small stuff." The sun follows its course and time moves on whether I'm busy or dormant. I am comforted by my doctor's kind, quiet, unhurried manner, who hopes for remission. May your October be as bright as mine "With the yellow and the purple and the crimson beating time."

To Think and Pray About: Our friends want to share our tears as well as our laughter. But have we any right to make them into "beasts of burden"? Maybe it is all right to be a slightly reluctant patient (holding back unsavory details). It's a good reminder of where ultimate hope lies.

In a New Light

October 12

1 Timothy 4:15
2 Timothy 2:15; Proverbs 15:13

I T HAPPENED on Columbus Day.

"Now, boys and girls," I said to the children in my classroom, "who can show us where North America is?" Shawn, a rather advanced second-grader, was first to raise his hand. "Here!" he said, eagerly tapping the wall map.

"Right!" I said, pleased. "Now who can tell us who discovered our continent?"

Amelia spoke up quickly. "Shawn did!"

I bit my lip to discourage a laugh, shushed a few jeers, and went on with the lesson. But my mind kept going back to the little boy's "discovery." At the end of the class, I shared my thoughts.

"You know, Amelia was right. We credit Christopher Columbus; but let's say Shawn *rediscovered* our land by finding it on the map."

You see, I'd been thinking of the biblical significance of discovering and rediscovering spiritual truths. As growing Christians, we struggle with problems daily. What better "how-to" than God's Word in seeking solutions? And each reading brings new insight to heretofore hidden meanings. I feel closer to solutions and to helping others with facing similar problems once I have seen old truths in a new light. My spirit is unshackled. I feel a laugh of triumph coming on!

To Think and Pray About: Reread today's passages. Can you find a meaning you missed before? Discovery is fun! Do you think Columbus frowned or let out a whoop of joy when he saw the light of land? I did not laugh at Amelia for fear of embarrassing her. But now I take time out for an honest-to-goodness belly-laugh. Isn't it *fun* to be a Christian!

"Malice" in Wonderland

Titus 2:1-5   October 13

"WHY DOESN'T Erma Bombeck do a survey on grandmothers instead of tallying women in her neighborhood in regard to extramarital affairs?" Lucy (the newest to reach the grandmother status) said.

Others in the group folding church newsletters giggled. Lucy did not. "I'm serious! All these silly articles picture us with granny knots, creaking bones—and, well, too old to be included in the Bombeck survey!"

"Good point," Eva said, checking a well-manicured nail and glancing at her watch. "I guess writers see us as so obese we require a block and tackle to pull us from the upholstery. Never do I see a word about grandmothers who still work for a living!"

The folding went on. So did the conversation. Olga disliked her children's calling her "Grams" instead of "Mother" now. Chris said, worse, her *husband* called her "Grandma." Mollie said that any time she met up with an old friend the only question was "Any grandchildren?"

I glanced around the group at the table, understanding their desire for an identity. It occurs to me that grandmothers are younger, prettier, and more involved each year. The image is changed. Gray is golden! It's the media that lags.

"Who started the malicious rumor that we are neuter gender when we enter Grandmothers' Wonderland?" (Aha! Lucy again. The *alpha* of the rebellion was about to become the *omega*. "Wonderland" indeed!) "I guess if Erma took her survey she'd find us not so different, after all—90 percent might say 'Baby Talk's' a crashing bore; but our own would be utterly fascinating."

To Think and Pray About: "Grandmotherhood" may rattle our foundations. Are we expected to look different, act different? We grew up in an age of hardship and idealism, a time when good and evil could be identified. And now—? Why, we'll impart that wisdom to the world's finest baby just as God intends—and praise Him for the privilege.

Signs of the Season

MY NEIGHBOR is planting a border of violets along her walk. Although the breadth of the earth is gold with autumn, I am thinking of how lovely the harbingers of spring will look. And I am remembering another spring...

Incredible that one little violet could smell so sweet. Incredible, too, what a powerful message the solitary flower delivered.

Spring had made an unscheduled stopover somewhere else, surely, I told myself. March had roared in like the proverbial lion and, contrary to the proverb, roared out the same way. April brought floods instead of showers and my nerves were as raw as the weather. "If I could see just one sign of spring!" I fumed as my husband and I removed a few clothes we'd dared hang out to air between showers.

Then, suddenly, even though the shower developed into the promised downpour, I caught the unmistakable odor of violets. George must have thought I'd taken leave of my senses when I all but threw the clothes basket at him and rushed to our one clump of violets, sheltered against the fence. Once there, I was unable to find a bloom even though the scent was stronger than before. Disappointment washed over me. I'd so wanted to bury my face in the blue-bonneted flowers and take their sweet promise indoors.

So intent was I in the desperate search that I failed to hear my husband's footsteps. He leaned down and pressed the one purple blossom into my hands. "Your sign," he smiled.

"Sign?" I was skeptical. "It's only one bloom—"

George laughed. "How many would it take?"

Right! How many signs *do* I need? Browning was right: "God's in His heaven, all's right with the world."

To Think and Pray About: Check your reference Bible for instances when people (even Jesus' followers) demanded signs. Everything everywhere is a sign of His love and an eternal spring.

About-Face!

SUN, my son's wife did a totally acceptable job with my dry shampoo. She even coaxed my hair into a fairly becoming shape (considering I was lying flat—still in that cast, mind you). But I could have worn one of Dolly's wigs and felt unglamorous. I was sinking into another how-long-how-long-oh-Lord? mood which nothing but sudden healing could remedy. Only something else did!

Sun handed me the newspaper and what should greet my lack-luster eyes but "I had this big cast and all I could do was chip and putt..."

Cast! Somebody in this world understood. And God must have known just when to have Sally Little, the pretty South American golfer's, story appear.

"Sometimes a person must suffer a setback before moving ahead," I read on. "I was 15 when I broke my leg and couldn't get around; but I think it was that broken leg and dumb cast that really helped give me the golfing bug." What catching the bug did for Sally was to help make her one of the top women's professionals in the game.

Now, what if she had lacked the grit and gumption to shed self-pity? She would never have turned her life around. The world has need of those about-face people—lots of them. Not necessarily golfers. Just *people*-people who refuse to be "cast" into a valley of woe... like me!

What would Jesus say to me? Very gently He would remind me that our heavenly Father had numbered every hair on my head (even the ones that fell out when Sun used the curling iron). He would tell me how God looked after the sparrow... and, anyway, how many cubits would worrying add to my stature? Didn't I have more worthwhile things to do?

To Think and Pray About: Ezekiel tells us to do an about-face... crawl out of ourselves... become what the Lord wants us to be. Whatever your own setback today, He will take care of it. Didn't He promise?

God's Remnants

"I WILL GATHER you from the people, and assemble you from out of the countries where you have been scattered . . . and I will give you the land of Israel." Yesterday's reading of Ezekiel interested me. Today his words triggered a memory.

My grandmother always snipped a scrap from the bolt before cutting fabric into skirts and dresses. Those scraps were essential, she told me.

"Why, Gram'ma?"

"Because," she would say, adding each tiny remnant to the other bright-colored scraps in the sewing machine drawer, "they mend tears; help me match colors; brighten applique; then blend together for a patchwork quilt."

I could understand part of her answers. The tears baffled me as she pronounced tears and tares alike. Later I came to know that she had a point either way. One could mend rips (her *tares*). And one could dry away the sad-sweet memories that were handed down together with the quilts.

It seems that God used a similar plan. Always, as He explained to the old prophet, He preserved a remnant of His people then provided a sanctuary for His chosen few. Eventually, God's plan was to "piece" them together to right the wrongs, mend the hurts, and finally blend them into a coverlet made of His goodness and mercy.

My grandmother's quilts came down through the generations to her family. And God's Word has come down to us. So today we—His remnants—should mend a quarrel, brighten a life, and link hearts together in keeping with His purpose.

To Think and Pray About: The art of quilting is back. If you enjoy quilting, why not start a tradition in your family. You need not quilt in order to make the practice work in your life. You are surrounded by people in need of having their lives "stitched together." Use the golden thread of love.

Someone Heard a Voice

MARGARET grew up under the watchful eye of George Washington. The First President stared unwaveringly from the wall of Margaret's paternal grandparents' parlor. And neither flood, fire, nor Grandmother's new ideas on decorating could remove the painting, my good friend told me.

The words beneath, not Mr. Washington's cold stare, must have accounted for its honored place:

> For every right you cherish,
> You have a duty that you must fulfill,
> For every hope that you entertain,
> You have a task that you must
>   perform.
> And for every good that you wish to
>   preserve,
> You will have to sacrifice comfort
>   and ease.

" 'For every good thing, someone has heard a voice and heeded the call', Grandpa says," Margaret whispered, "and he points to that picture."

I have no idea who painted the Washington picture. But it is interesting that Ezekiel was an artist, too. He painted strange pictures—sometimes mystifying and frightening; but glowing with life and action. He talked about sin and punishment; but he talked about repentance and blessing, too. He painted with P's: parables, poems, proverbs, and prophecies. Now—what can *we* do? All of the above in our own way. The "glory of God" he painted many ways. So can we. In words. In deeds. Even in the radiance of our faces.

To Think and Pray About: I urge you to read through Ezekiel. It is for the Jew today. It is for the Christian today. But our hearts are intertwined. You will not find him in the Gospels or the Epistles. But he and John link arms in Revelation. They heard the call!

A Dream for Tomorrow

Psalm 34:14
John 14:27

RECENTLY there was controversy over the naming of a street in San Diego. Some wanted it to carry the name of Dr. Martin Luther King. Others did not. The issue was of no great significance; but the emotional reactions on both sides were. They were in direct conflict with what the great civil rights leader stood for: PEACE.

Dr. King, a dedicated man of God, wanted peace such as Jesus offered, for all peoples. But he was struck down by an assassin's bullet as our Savior was nailed to the cross.

Do you recall the once-popular song, "Let There Be Peace on Earth and Let It Begin With Me"? That's where it must begin, isn't it—right inside the hearts of you and me? If we can change our selves (meaning allow God to change us), we can have faith in tomorrow:

- And its sufficiency, through God, of erasing today's mistakes.
- For I shall recall today's brief laughter and know that it can be extended into eternity.
- Pulsing to God's promise that He can transform today's tragedy, restoring a multi-splendored effect to twisted causes.
- When I see candles of enthusiasm and uninhibited joy light up the eyes of children. They believe in the new.
- Knowing that the waning sun will rise warm conceiving new life from winter's barren womb and restore to birds their unfinished song.
- And its handkerchief of joy to wipe away all tears, its balm for the lonely heart, because God is love!

To Think and Pray About: Why has complete fulfillment of the Lord's sacrifice and Martin Luther King's dream been delayed? Think back on time squandered and love perverted. Now remember the small things we can do to accomplish the great. A moment becomes forever in the solicitude of a smile and the warmth of a loving hand.

Killing the Body with Kindness

1 Corinthians 12:14   October 19
James 2:26

"LAY down that electric toothbrush. Have the push-button garage door removed by the wise guy who was out to get you. They'll *kill* you—"

Quickly, I closed the magazine. My dentist recommended the brush. Would he want to lose a patient? The man who installed the door opener looked sane. I picked up the magazine.

1. Are you sitting? (I got up.)
2. Do you drive or walk? (Drive sometimes—40 miles for research.)
3. Do you avoid stairs? (Worse, we have none.)
4. Do you own an electric mixer, vacuum sweeper, typewriter, washer-dryer, hair blower, knife sharpener, blender...? (Yes, *yes*, YES!)

Then you're dying from lack of exercise...

Letting my adrenaline take over, I flew around unplugging everything. I munched a sandwich standing up then brushed my teeth—rejoicing that I had learned to brush manually in my youth.

Karen had a lo-cal carrot cake recipe. I could walk (no, run)—over for it. I beat the cake by hand then did a telephone survey among my friends while it baked. How revealing—and what fun! Annie dances while dusting. Mit "tippy-toes"... Ruthie went back to arm signaling (drawing circles)... Ev crawls on hands and knees...Liz gallops down the hall, bolting now and then.

"Did you know I'm killing you with kindness?" I asked George when he sniffed cake.

"Whatta way to go!" He said, kissing my hair with his mouth full of cake.

To Think and Pray About: How good to be alive, to laugh, and (yes) to learn. Christian fellowship takes many forms. Consider a "fitness survey." Include some laughter—and a prayer together.

"Club Dead"?

"WE'RE OUT OF IT and proud of it!" the slogan for the new so-called club read. Purpose of the club? To stay *un*involved.

Name of the organization is "Club Dead." Fitting, isn't it?

Probably most of us have made the out-of-it-all statement with a sigh of relief a good many times. I am beginning to understand that I need not feel obligated to say "Yes" to every cause and stick with it until I have fallen arches. After all, the body of Christ has many parts and each of us is only one of those parts.

But I *am* one! So there can be no room in my life for the Club Dead and its silly slogan. The members (and I am told that they are "dead serious") need to have a staffing (George says "clubbing"!) and face up to life's purposes. Come to think of it, the decomposed group did something unintentionally. It served to remind me that as one of Christ's "parts" (I prefer "sisters," under the fatherhood of God), I don't toss in the towel on tough situations and take a dangerous and self-centered pride in uninvolvement.

I think God would rather you and I organized a "Club Alive!" *Alive in Christ.* What a wonderful thought—and to think that it translates into *forever* . . .

Oh, yes, we will need a slogan—one which will be pleasing to the Lord in His work. How about: "I'm *into* it, Lord—involve me!"

To Think and Pray About: How do we stay involved? It is faulty thinking to suppose that we have no abilities—wanting to serve but slinking into the shadows. That is denying that we are, indeed, a part of Christ. Consider this: You are serving as an active member when you say "thank you" when a waitress gives good service, when a customer buys your product, when someone offers a hand. Now, what's on the agenda of "Club Alive" today—after you thank Jesus?

A Penny's Worth

Zechariah 4:10   October 21
Luke 15:8-10

FIVE PEOPLE passed the penny by, although its newly minted shine rivaled a precious stone. It seemed to light the street.

I had mixed feelings about those people. On the one hand, I was glad that they left it for me (I am a coin collector on our walks). On the other hand, I felt concern for a world grown insensitive to the little but vitally important things that go to make great ones.

"Pennies make dollars," our grandparents told us. True then. True now. All it took to pick up that penny was a slight stoop. One hundred stoops add up to a dollar.

I may have identified the problem with that thinking. Maybe most of us refuse to stoop anymore! At any rate, the idea stuck with me, enlarging as pennies enlarge into coins of greater denomination. I stooped for the penny. But what about the lowly tasks I'm called upon to do? Am I as willing as I should be to stoop to those? If the ocean refused enough tiny raindrops, one day the sea would be dry.

Awesome thought. But it is well for us to remember that we can "dry up" a life, too, just by refusing to do the little things we should be doing.

Look around you today for those in need. They will reveal themselves like bright, new copper coins just waiting for a lifting hand once we open our spiritual eyes and start "collecting" for the Lord.

To Think and Pray About:
> For April rain,
> For August grain,
> Warm winds that slant them gently;
> For shady trees,
> But more than these,
> Needy friends You've sent me:
>   *I'm thankful, Lord!* —J.M.B.

When You Can't "Gettuit"

October 22   1 Corinthians 7:29-31

A FACETIOUS little note in Sunday's church bulletin hit home. The "Gettuits" were ready for distribution, the announcement said. All we had to do was pick up a fistful after church in case we "had planned to come to choir practice and just couldn't 'gettuit'." All the things we'd needed to do, wanted to do, promised to do. But, alas, we just couldn't "gettuit."

Just this morning my husband wanted to wear his pale yellow shirt, but the button was missing. It had been missing two weeks, but not lost. I found it in the washing machine, planned to tack it back on, but—well, I couldn't "gettuit." I owe some letters and the Easter lilies need separating and storing, but, well—you know. Those things, like some services I was going to perform for the church this year are hard to "get to." Granted, but if nobody found time to serve, what kind of church would I belong to? Certainly, not one I could be proud of—and not one which would be carrying out the ministry of Christ.

Come to think of it, what if—just what if—God's schedule had never allowed Him to finish the Creation (He's busy, you know)? What if Jesus couldn't have found time to visit this earth? And what if the inspired writers of our Holy Bible had wanted to record God's Word; but they never found the time to "gettuit"?

So, I think (when nobody is looking), I'll pick up a few of those reminders the church provided. Like Paul said, ". . . time is short."

To Think and Pray About: Are there people in your life who need a narrow margin of your time? Are there little tasks that you postpone and secretly feel guilty about? Colton's quote had a timely message for us all. Let's rearrange our schedules with God's help: *Whatever needs doing for You today, Lord, let us GET TO IT!*

Without a Backward Glance

Matthew 6:25-34   October 23

THE LITTLE SPARROW-SIZED BIRDS cluster together, conversing in distinctive voices which defy verbal description. One wonders what secrets the swallows share as they hover there beneath the eaves of Mission San Juan Capistrano, California. Do they talk about the trials and joys of raising families in this busy, sometimes careless world—away from the security of their little winter island? Or about the perils of flying so many nautical miles over the often storm-tossed Pacific? Their language is so secretive, even to ornithologists, that one fancies the wee, feathered creatures whisper of the legends woven about Capistrano. The dark-robed Franciscan ghost. The bells that toll in spite of motionless bell ropes. And an Indian girl novice dying with the reverberations...

But it is easier to imagine a sort of sadness in the eyes of the tuxedo-clad flock. The children are grown up now and will be making the return trip with them. And, for just a little while, as tourists' cameras click, they hesitate like a last autumn leaf that is reluctant to leave the parent tree. They twitter, notes seeming to catch in their throats. They turn sooty heads from right to left as if photographing a memory. And then they lift off in slim-winged, graceful flight—homeward bound without the aid of a control tower. But, once airborne, there is never a backward glance.

Strange that the little birds should leave on St. John's Death Day. Do they sense a dying of the year? Or, is this terminology we human beings ascribe to autumn? I tend to think that once their *good-byes* ("God be with yous") are said, they are free spirits, looking ahead already to another St. Joseph's Day... another spring... another opportunity to perpetuate their kind and give them a "Christian education" in the beautiful Mission San Juan Capistrano.

To Think and Pray About: What inspiration can we glean from the trusting little swallows?

Consider the Ant!

October 24

Psalm 121:3
Proverbs 6:4-11; Mark 14:37

AN ANT stores up food against a time of need. The tiny insect surpasses most others (and some human beings!) in instinct and industry.

And yet . . . "Turn back the clocks. An extra hour of sleep!"

Over and over we heard the words by newscasters last year on the (then) next to last Saturday in October. "We've gained an hour" is the boast heard everywhere. And those who are of that mind can think of no more rewarding way of using those 60 golden minutes than "getting some extra Z-z-z's.

Time is relative. But let us say we *have* gained an hour. Supposing the Lord has said, "Here is an extra hour—yours to do with what you please."

Would you choose to sleep? Wait! Supposing He cautions, "It will be your last." Would your response be the same?

Sobering. And yet one hour is less important when we realize that *every* hour is His gift. The words of my grandmother come back each year when it is time to turn the clocks from Daylight-Saving to Pacific Standard Time. "Live each hour as if it were your last."

To Think and Pray About: Would you want to spend it sleeping (physically or spiritually) when there is so much that needs doing? Simple things to consider are: 1. Going to church if you've been "too pushed for time" until today; 2. Getting to church on time if you have "had too much to do beforehand" until you gained this hour. An hour "gained" is an hour in which we store up blessings. An hour "lost" is an hour in which our leaden feet refuse to respond to God's will; our heavy lids droop to close out His beauty. Let us keep watch with and for the Lord—awaiting His wake-up call!

Lesson of the Halloween Cat

John 14:6,7   October 25
2 Corinthians 6:6-15

I T SEEMED altogether fitting that the little black kitten should show up at our door on Halloween. Memory of "Captain Midnight," that irresponsible ball of fluff, reminds me of God's love and His concern over my own waywardness.

I truly think Cap meant well. He seemed to appreciate the bowls of warm, fresh milk, fish tidbits, and special pillow I provided. He wasn't much of a "mouser," my mother pointed out. But he was only half-grown, so we hoped he would learn. We went on pampering him. And he went on purring lazily with little white claws extended. There all obligation ended.

Time passed. Cap showed no interest in chasing mice from my father's corncrib. He snoozed, sang, lapped cream, and drove the other cats crazy swatting at their tails. Then he took to wandering away. First, he was chasing butterflies, then birds. And, finally, he would disappear for several days for no reason.

Each time he reappeared after one of the unexplained absences, Captain Midnight would be doubly sweet, rubbing against our legs as if begging forgiveness. And each time I would hold the warm little body close until he stopped trembling.

When the little black cat failed to return—ever—I thought my heart would burst. All family cats since those long years ago, although more deserving, just never took his place.

And I know that's how God is with me. I just "lap up" the good things He provides but neglect my responsibilities all too often. Now, singing praises is fine, but I forget that, too. And yet I belong to Him and it must pain Him when I wander away.

To Think and Pray About: God is the giver of all good things, the greatest being unconditional love. What do you think He requires of us? Prayer for one thing: *Forgive my waywardness, Father.*

Kellie's Rainbow

ON OCTOBER 26, 1987, God plucked from the earth our brightest and most precious jewel, Kellie Elaine Patterson. The brilliance of her life will shine on forever in the minds and hearts of everyone who were so fortunate as to have had their lives touched by her love. Kellie was a proud senior at San Pasqual High School. She was an active member of the International Order of the Rainbow for Girls in which she held the position of Charity. Charity is defined as "the good affection, love, or tenderness which men should feel toward each other; benevolent, giving." That was our Kellie.

Her never-ending smiles, laughter, and boundless hugs will be deeply missed by everyone.

We, her loving mother and father, beseech all parents to love their children as we so dearly cherish our one and only Kellie...

In loving memory,
Ken and Rosemary Patterson

THE ITEM appearing in a local newspaper went on to announce the memorial service. Beside the announcement was the hauntingly beautiful face of Kellie, caught in one of those senseless accidents in which the innocent driver is so often victim.

I never knew Kellie, but the parents' tribute touched my heart. Would I be invading their privacy to call? The urge was powerful. God's ways are so wondrously mysterious. He made it seem quite natural that two strangers should be weeping together by telephone a few minutes later. In their darkest hour of sorrow, God had given them strength to reach out to other parents, encouraging them to enjoy the richness of their children's presence. Some would have cursed fate... said God was cruel... reviled drunken drivers. But Ken Patterson said softly, "Our Kellie is with God now—but she left with us her glow."

To Think and Pray About: "Be thou the rainbow to the storms of life: the evening beam that smiles the clouds away and tints tomorrow with rays of hope"—Byron.

Dwelling Together

If we speak as a friend, we will be a friend—
And love for others will show; if we walk as a friend,
We will be a friend—wherever we choose to go.
If we act as a friend, we will be a friend
Who brightens another's day; if we walk as a friend,
We will be a friend—journeys seem shorter that way.
If we build as a friend, we will be a friend
Who helps the world understand that in loving a
*   friend,*
We're leading a friend to reach out and touch God's
*   hand.*

                                             J.M.B.

E SCONDIDO (Where my husband and I "dwell together" in peace) has rarefied the streets with perfectly magical trees. Standing in proud lines, the trees defy the seasons. It is as if they whisper together: "Let us ignore the fads and fashions and bring out-of-season beauty to passersby."

In autumn, when the rest of the world is crimson-decked, these trees (leaves still green) bloom out to rival a spring-orchard's glory. Then, as others don catkin wigs, our ornamental fruit trees garb themselves in scarlet and gold, as if to say: "See what it is like to be an out-of-season friend?"

Christmas cards are exciting. But they are in season. Birthday cards add excitement to our special day. But we have come to expect them. Convalescent cards only come when we are ill. How about the days in between? Isn't it wonderful to receive an unexpected card?

To Think and Pray About: Surprise someone in your life today with an out-of-season note, gift, or deed. And remember that "There Is a Friend that Sticketh Closer than a Brother..." Aside from your daily devotional time today, send Jesus a series of out-of-season words of love.

A Bridle on My Tongue

TODAY I am preparing treats and remembering last Halloween. I do not associate the celebration with the occult. But if I did, I would have been sure that all the demons were released from wherever demons dwell.

"Please do *not* come back for any more treats tonight!" I said sharply to the three little girls who lived next door. They had rung the doorbell repeatedly since the first trace of twilight... to show their ghost, goblin, and witch costumes... to get their bags of cookies I'd baked... to show what somebody else had given them... to borrow a safety pin to hold a cape together... and, finally, to report that someone was threatening to soap our windows. Each time they expected a reward. Now I was out of cookies and patience.

DING-dong! I opened the door a crack. And there they stood! "I *told* you—" I began, then stopped, feeling near tears.

They were holding out their sacks to *me*. "We brung *you* some treats this time," the littlest goblin said.

A long time ago I earned a double-dip ice-cream cone during a summer revival meeting for arranging names of the Old and New Testament Books in alphabetical order. I committed them to memory in hopes of an extra scoop. I can still do fairly well down to the J's. At that point, I begin to stumble. My grandmother used to recite the Books of the Old Testament to control her temper. Remembering, I began a review of my alphabetizing: "Acts, Amos, Chronicles (1)..." I may never get to James through Judges. I will be ready for Halloween!

To Think and Pray About: How do you handle your little irritations? Seneca wrote: "The greatest remedy for anger is delay." How can you control your anger (and your tongue) according to Paul's definition? Maybe *that* is what we should commit to memory and put into practice. Then we could throw the bridle away!

Fall Back!

John 9:4   October 29
Mark 5:24-32

*Walk softly through the goldenrods; for all that glows, you
   know, is God's...*
*Walk softly lest you step upon His memories of a summer-
   gone.*   J.M.B.

I T USUALLY HAPPENS on the last Sunday in October. "Fall back," the media tells us. "You have gained
that hour lost last April!" Flight attendants announce the loss
or gaining of a full day when we cross the International
Dateline by plane. And we adjust our watches (hinging on that
airy transit over Greenwich) here in our own land: Eastern,
Central, Mountain, and Pacific Standard Times. The measurement of time is based on the motions of celestial bodies
(according to physicists and astronomists). But it was God
who hung the brilliant instruments of measurement in the
firmament and set them in cyclic motion. And it was He who
breathed into our "earthly bodies" the gift of life—its measurement being known only unto Himself. We have gained no
bonus heartbeats. We have lost none. We can set our clocks
forward or back; but we have neither lost nor gained *time*.
   Time is a favorite subject for poets and philosophers.

- There is a time to be born, and a time to die, says
  Solomon, but there is an interval between the two
  times of infinite importance—Richmond.
- We sleep, but the loom of life never stops—Beecher.
- Time well employed is Satan's deadliest foe—Wilcox.
- "TIME IS," said Henry van Dyke, "Too Slow for those
  who Wait; Too Swift for those who Fear; Too Long for
  those who Grieve; Too Short for those who Rejoice;
  But for those who Love, Time is Eternity."

To Think and Pray About: Bear in mind that today is the
chrysalis of forever. "This is the day the Lord has made; rejoice
and be glad in it!"

A Final Reward

THE GENTLEMAN FARMER with a smiling face, kind eyes, and a straw hat has seen a lot of Halloweens. But he never grows tired of "treating" local school children to the biggest pumpkin they can find in his patch. Commercial harvest is finished by workers instructed not to glean. Mr. Bates then notifies parents and teachers to bring children to help him clean the field because he "can't stand seein' punkins lay out there after Halloween. Saddest thing I ever saw."

Bates Nut Farm is straight from the Dick and Jane storybooks—a quiet place of red barns, white fences, and green meadows dotted with chickens, goats, and cows that probably give chocolate milk. The philosophical host smiles indulgently as hoards of Dicks and Janes, as if guided by radar, choose pumpkins too large to carry.

These innocents know nothing of ancient druids' bloody rites. Nothing either (as pagan practices turned to gaiety) of buggies arranged to block country roads. (What mindless creature would attempt to blockade a freeway?) And it is unlikely that Gramps would admit to mounting a "comfort station" atop somebody's barn—pointless, since today's are portable and rented out for construction projects. Even the more recent trick-or-treating is forgotten in the search for the orange globe whose future begins with an impish, gapped-tooth face and ends in a pie!

"Some of these little tykes never seen a farm," Mr. Bates says a little sadly. He surveys the near-barren field. "Me—I've had my last reward."

Maybe—in a worldly sense. But somehow it strikes me that God will look with favor on the country-shouldered man with calloused hands and a giving heart. "I am pleased! Your sacrifice was a sweet savor."

To Think and Pray About: Jesus used children and the harvest in many of His parables. The beauty of His illustrations was in their simplicity. What kind of parables can you formulate from the farmer's giving?

Happy Birthday to a Halloween "Mommy"

Isaiah 49:15; 66:8-14   October 31

O N HALLOWEEN, when we indulge in fun-fantasies with the children, cemeteries seem a proper setting for the ghosts, ghouls, and goblins (in costumes designed by their mothers' loving hands). And where better than in New Orleans, land of the Mardi Gras?

It is there that one finds a monument which has captured the hearts and imaginations of tourists from all over the world. The gray stone represents a ship fighting and losing the battle with a storm-tossed sea. A mother and her child cling together on the sinking vessel. And on the base there is an inscription telling the sad story of their drowning on July 4, 1900. The two of them had been the sole survivors of the large estate and the inevitable question was: "Under whose name shall the estate be administered, the name of the mother or the name of the daughter?" The court ruled that it should be in the name of the child, reasoning that she went down last because, they said, the mother would hold her in a place of safety until the end.

How sad, but how beautiful. A fitting tribute to a mother's love! And so it is that I share the story as a tribute to my own mother, whose birthday comes on Halloween.

I was an only child, but my mother never overindulged me. Neither did she indulge *herself* in being a sacrificial martyr. She sacrificed for what I needed, instead of what I wanted. She was firm but fair. And (although I used to think she was too strict) I came to realize how important that was and how parallel with true love. Hardworking, my mother (I now know) "went down" on many a ship for me—wearing a smile because I called her a Halloween "Mommy."

To Think and Pray About: While you fashion yourself or your children a costume for a make-believe hour of fun, consider the hands that fashioned your childhood. Express your gratitude to mother if you are fortunate enough to have her yet. Express your gratitude to God either way.

Beauty of the Harvest

Oh, spring, with all your emeralds about which poets rhyme,
Do you think you're a match for rich gold of autumn time?
Oh, youth, with all your promise, your laughter and your
tears,
How can you know the peace of the fruit of autumn years?
The beauty of the harvest is joy in work well done;
And jewels of life's seasons lie in a victory won.

                                                    J.M.B.

A LMIGHTY GOD, we thank You for differences in our lives which You created so majestically. In my part of the world orange trees, still laden with last year's sweet fruit, refuse to wait for spring to pen their perfumed waxen blossoms. Overhead, triumphant honks of wild geese announce their safe arrival from colder climes. I praise You for their safety along the flyways, Lord, and for the instinct You gave them of remembered frost. Somewhere else You are whispering to other migratory birds. And, as people watch, they ascend from a field of golden grain, their trusting wings silhouetted against a patch of their native sky. In another corner of our land, colored leaves are dusted with first snow to caution hibernating animals to scurry underground. Oh, the beauty of the season, Lord, its glory reflected in each state—different, as are we, Your children.

We praise You for our bounty and for the brave pilgrims who, in face of hardship and death, found heart to feast and fellowship with their own—and those who were "different." Surely this was another of Your messages that You ask not *uniformity*, but *unity*.

We thank You, too, Lord for our nation's First President's proclamation that a day be set aside, acknowledging You as author of peace and liberty. Bless every human heart lifted in praise, Lord of the Harvest, in different ways!

All Saints' Day

I T WAS an interesting—and sobering—discussion centering around All Saints' Day. Zella, the skeptic of our
little group which shares coffee on the rare occasions anybody
finds time to bake cinnamon rolls, shrugged off the celebration's significance. "Now, I know it dates back to the seventh
century to honor the departed saints. Me, I'd prefer honoring
the living ones—if there were any walking around."

Winnie stirred Sugar Twin into her coffee thoughtfully. "I
guess there are lots, according to my minister."

Zella's mouth flew open. "Yeah? Show me a few!"

Winnie pointed a finger at Zella wordlessly.

We were all glad that Zella didn't wear dentures. She would
have swallowed them for sure. "Saint Zella!" she sputtered.

The rest of us laughed—but a little uncertainly. Just what
was a saint anyway? Did any of us really qualify?

Suddenly, everybody was talking at once. "I thought you
had to die to be a saint"... "And then be canonized"...
"Canonized? Only God could decide that"... "Well, they're
all dead, aren't they—and weren't they men?" *Men* set Zella
off. When the saints went marching in, women would lead the
march!

Fortunately, someone thought of a dictionary and we studied the definition. A living saint is one of God's chosen (*Well,
weren't we?*) ... one belonging to the entire company of bap-
tized Christians (*ditto*) ... a holy or godly person (That took
some thinking, but yes—not because of *our* goodness but
because of His!). Charity is our bond of perfection.

To Think and Pray About: In many American churches a
custom has grown up making the Sunday nearest November 1
the occasion of a service in memory of those who have died
during the year. Whether we attend a formal service, we can
thank Him also for those saints who have added substance to
our lives. We need not be martyrs. We need not die and be
canonized. We are saints by mandate of our Lord and Savior.
Piety? God forbid! Just walk in His grace.

Be Thankful—Whether You Are or Not!

John 16:33   November 3
1 John 3:18

"MERCY!"
The gasp came when one of our neighbors told my husband over the fence that "By gum!" he was going to be grateful whether he was up to it or not, come Thanksgiving. Now, I've learned from a good many years of eavesdropping that men often come up with a great deal of wisdom. So, hoping that Jim didn't hear my word of shock, I slunk back behind the hibiscus. One couldn't force gratitude... could one?

It took only a minute to find out—and you know what? Jim's pretty smart. Not as smart as George. But smart.

"You know, when I was in seminary, an instructor used to say, 'No matter *what* the job is, you get into the mood when you start it.' I figure on using mood control."

Mood control? Jim and Sue had had a tough year. About all that kept them going was anticipation of the gathering of the clan. Now, for various reasons, that fell through.

Somehow I got the impression that our neighbor-friend felt happier already just from having expressed a willingness to be thankful. Oh, the formula? Serving others. Not the way they'd planned but in other ways

"You know lots of people see us Christians as negative and dull. We need to change that image. So do I dare act less than grateful?"

So Jim and Sue were going to take some football fans to Murphy Stadium to see a game—taking along soft drinks and noisemakers!

George said very little since Jim needed to talk. But that night we talked up a storm as we listed some things we could do: clean Jim's walk while he was gone... have coffee and cake waiting... and so much more!

To Think and Pray About: Who says Christians don't have fun? To be grateful is to be happy. That "Mood control" works.

How Many Thanksgivings?

COLORED leaves. Wood smoke mixed with ovenly scents. The warm glow of togetherness. And the linking of prayerful hands. That's Thanksgiving.

"Wouldn't it be nice," we say among ourselves, "if every day could be like this?"

There was a time, however, when there were those who declared that we had "one Thanksgiving too many!"

In 1939, during the Great Depression, President Franklin Delano Roosevelt made an unpopular decision. Wouldn't it be practical, he reasoned to inch the holiday up from the last Thursday in November to the next-to-the-last? This, he hoped, would bolster Christmas sales in a faltering economy. Perhaps. But Americans, steeped in tradition, were unhappy. They wrote tons of protest letters. The President held firm. So did they.

"We will celebrate *two* Thanksgivings," they declared.

"One Thanksgiving too many," Congress decided. In 1941, a Congressional act set the fourth Thursday apart for the holiday.

To Think and Pray About: I am thankful for this special day. But I would not have minded two. Jesus' example was to thank God at *every* meal. So, for those who love Thanksgiving as I do, may I suggest that we celebrate it three times a day? I think God would welcome the celebrations. Look all around you at this autumn beauty and you will find so many other things to thank Him for. Take time out for little prayers of praise—or pray standing up if your schedule is demanding (and be thankful that you are able to stand!).

Our Election

Colossians 3:12-14

HAVE YOU made out your sample ballot? For months now we have been bombarded with political ads, debates, and accusations between candidates. True or false, we can vote as we choose.

Freedom. It all began with God who gave to mankind the freedom of choice.

Now, freedom is unique. It frees us—while binding us completely. As the old saying goes: "Man was never so free as when he learned that he was not free at all."

As election day approaches, we should be informed, praise the Lord for our freedoms, and guard them. Do you think of going to the polls as a duty or a privilege? Search your heart and ask if you feel the same way about going to church. There is a strong relationship as we are the "elect"!

The following excerpt seems appropriate to share:

> Freedom cannot be put into a bottle or sliced or weighed in pounds. You cannot reduce it to print, or encompass it, define it or explode it. It is teasingly remote in one way, but deeply personal and prescient and immanent in another. *Freedom is a gift of God to all men everywhere for all time.* You can try to sell it or exchange it for security, but what you get in the deal is slavery or slow death... Freedom is not negotiable. You got it when you were born and you will have it until you die...
>
> —Reprinted in *Sunshine* magazine
> from *The Better Way*

To Think and Pray About: Do you feel free to choose, to love, to give and receive, to speak up, to refuse to answer questions which incriminate or embarrass you? Free to marry the man of your choice as opposed to having an "arrangement" by families? Free to plan the size of your family and how the little ones will be brought up? Never forget that God gave you a greater freedom—that of choosing to respond to His gift of love.

Am I What I Seem to Be?

November 6   1 Samuel 16:7
                                                Matthew 5:14-16

DO YOU know the motto of your state? It—as well as the mottos for some of the other states—might prove to be the inspiration you need for the day.

I was checking out the motto of my former home state recently and became intrigued with the mottos of the entire 50. One in particular caught my attention. I read it over and over: *To be rather than to seem.* North Carolina can be proud!

As I went about my work the rest of the day those words kept returning. So loud and clear was the message that I almost laid my lip gloss down without applying it as I stood before the mirror. Was I touching myself up for some particular reason or was I putting on a false face for others?

I applied the gloss! You see, I believe that there is a far deeper spiritual meaning in the motto than something as superficial as lip gloss.

What I did think about was: How sincere a person am I? Do I say *Yes* to the needs of others just so they will think I am "nice"? In other words, am I overly concerned with what outsiders *think* or what God *knows* me to be?

The saying goes that we are three persons in one: 1. the person we perceive ourselves to be; 2. the person others perceive us to be; and 3. the person we *are.* It would be foolish to ask if God would have a problem with the "perceiving who we really are."

To Think and Pray About: How can we go about aligning the three perceptions? May I suggest that we take a look inside ourselves today? There needs to be a God-centered place within which is filled to overflowing with tenderness, care, and mercy. A place called the heart, the part of us where our Creator abides in pure and unconditional love. Only His presence can purify our thoughts and deeds. *And Lord, we know that one day You will take account of what we were not what we seemed to be. Prepare our hearts.*

Gift of God—and the Gideons

S O MANY of our freedoms have disappeared that one wonders how long the Gideons can continue to place Bibles in hotel and motel rooms.

In my school days, teachers began the day by praying. When I taught, pressures had begun; but I could "allow" children to recite the Lord's Prayer. Now, both are gone—including the "moment of silence" which came later. Let's look back with the aid of a speech made 50 years ago as W.A. Richardson presented a copy of the Holy Bible to a country school.

> This Book contains the mind of God, the state of man, the way of Salvation, doom of sinners, and happiness of believers. Its doctrines are holy, its precepts are binding, its histories are true, and its decisions are immutable.
>
> Read it to be wise, believe it to be safe and practice it to be holy. It contains light to direct you, food to support you and comfort to cheer you.
>
> It is the *traveler's map*, the pilgrim's staff, the pilot's compass, the soldier's sword and the Christian's character. . . .
>
> Christ is its grand subject, our good its design, and the glory of God its end. It should fill the memory, rule the heart, and guide the feet. Read it slowly, frequently, prayerfully, it is a mine of wealth, a paradise of glory, and a river of pleasure. It is given you in life, will be opened at the judgment, and be remembered forever.

To Think and Pray About: The expression "Times have changed" bothers me. More significant is, have *we*? We know that God's Word is as changeless as Himself. We feel so helpless sometimes. But we have God on our side. The Gideons can no longer distribute Bibles within classrooms, but they can make them available outside. Never, with the Bible as our guide, would we deny the rights of others.

Thelma Thinskin

November 8   Ephesians: 3:14-21
John 21:16

E VERYONE KNOWS A THELMA THINSKIN. The words caught my eye. After all, I might be one. I read on: "Picture her as a hostess. She is fretful and nervous about how people will react to her performance. She is super-conscious of what others say and think and often reacts at slight innuendo."

Scary, isn't it? This Thelma sounds like an extreme person; but we women may carry a few of her recessive genes which began with Mother Eve's bloodline. The article further described Cousin Thelma as triggering over-cautiousness in others. Since people never know what nerve they may touch with a comment on religion, politics, or social trends, they are guarded. Eventually, Thelma must be very choosy in cultivating friends. After all, she takes every comment personally, is responsive to slights, and in need of constant praise. When rebuffed, she becomes moody and sulks.

Yes, I've known some Thelmas. Does this fragile, transparent complexion of mine mean I'm looking one in the face each time I see my reflection? I hurried to my bathroom's three-way mirror (see how insecure I am!). But wait—would I want to be *under*sensitive? Supposing we create Theadora Thickskin. Thea would be less attuned to others, seeking relationships which would promote her goals. She'd *use* others, being more "thing-oriented" than people-oriented. So . . .

As we hurry about, let's be *ourselves*. The Lord has need of us just as we are. He certainly had an opportunity to create us in a different image. We women are the "chosen ones"—the homemakers, the earth-shakers, and the trendsetters. As our mood goes, so goes the mood of those at our table!

To Think and Pray About: There is a cure for the Thelmas and the Theas. All they need do is reach out to others. This is the time of elevating our thoughts heavenward, praising our loving Provider for our special role in His world.

Life Beyond the Dinner Table

Genesis 12:1-3   November 9

AS THE BIG DAY approaches, there is too little time to pay attention to sky-brushing palms, avocados swinging like green bells from branches already abloom with next year's fruit, rippling silver of the sand dunes...gold and scarlet of the sugar maples... and fallen red-leaves-faded-pink like braided rugs. Pumpkin and pecan pies crowd out the beauty painted around us no matter where we live. Crowd out the real meaning of Thanksgiving, too. Our minds are riveted to monumental decisions: "Frozen turkey or fresh?" "Oyster dressing or Grandma's old fashioned cornmeal stuffing?" And (alas!) "Can Willie Mae keep those hyperactive twins leashed at least during the prayer?"

Thanksgiving is a family day—no doubt about it. On my first Thanksgiving away from home I was in school, very young, and very homesick—marking off the days on my calendar until the holiday, home, and family. Then came the storm which clogged the roads with snow and iced the power lines so that they drooped like Cousin Edgar's belly after one of our feasts. Small wonder when there was twice as much food as we needed so that everybody had to keep passing everything. Half had to stay in orbit due to space. Then belts had to be adjusted as we all ate too much.

You see that was the year that I learned Thanksgiving, like God, is everywhere. That it is a state of mind. And that "family" had a much broader definition than I had assigned to it.

It all began with a truck, driven by my church minister, and jam-packed with students like me who were stranded. "Come on y'all!" they were yelling, "We're heading for the Cranes—they've shoveled the white stuff off the road that far for us refugees of all ages—bundle up and *hurry*! We're starved." So was I!

To Think and Pray About: Each of us can share our bountiful blessings—the news that there is life beyond the dinner table! How can you share?

A Pound of Flesh

ABBY'S angry. No, *mad* says it better. She's biting her nails, gnashing her teeth, and tearing her new perm. Two of her friends said Abby actually frothed at the mouth as she glared at a chocolate chip cookie, broke off just a bite (one with a chocolate drop, of course), then hurled it across the room.

What on earth?

Abby wouldn't tell. But Casandra happened to be in the adjoining room when the doctor took Abby to task because she'd gained half a pound in three days.

" 'Not much,' you say? That's nearly a pound a week. Add it up and the sum's 52 pounds a year."

Startling, isn't it? But pennies make dollars and little raindrops fill an ocean. The same is true of habits, isn't it? Left unchecked, a little habit blows itself, genie-like, into enormous proportions. And have you ever noticed how much easier it is to take on a pound of that unwanted flesh than to shake it off? Of course, it's the same with any habit—so easy to form, so hard to break.

So, knowingly, dare we sin "a little"? Jesus instructed His apostles to be "as wise as serpents and as harmless as doves" (Matthew 10:16).

If we can avoid the little traps, we are more likely to escape the kind of pit into which Eve fell. One wonders what biblical history might have been had she been "as wise as the serpent" instead of listening to him. Instead, she violated God's commandment. We can suppose that Eve's disobedience was unpremeditated; but ours? The "little white lie," the passing of a malicious rumor, the lying in wait for hubby and planning in advance the tongue-lashing? Caution!

To Think and Pray About: Satan would love that "pound of flesh." Grind him with your heel by handing the temptation to God.

A Lasting Peace

1 Timothy 2:2   November 11
Romans 14:17-19

TODAY our President will lay a wreath on the tomb of the Unknown Soldier—unknown but to God. On that gray November eleventh, in 1921, which marked the beginning of the somber observance of our fallen heroes, the date was called Armistice Day. World War I was over. The war to end all wars, weeping Americans promised one another.

Only it didn't happen that way. Wars and rumors of wars were to follow. ". . . they shall seek peace and there shall be none" (Ezekiel 7:25).

A big lump will form in my throat today as I watch the ceremony in Arlington National Cemetery. I shall weep for the first Unknown Soldier and those entombed beside him because the ultimate victory for which they died has not come. I shall weep because laying of a wreath is not enough. I shall weep that the other holidays we observe in honor of our country and its honored dead are not enough either—touching though they are. Parades . . . 21-gun salutes . . . rockets bursting in air . . . saluting our flag . . . and certainly not the three-day weekends which spell out more bloodshed on the highways than our nation sacrificed to keep our country free. I do not apologize for my tears. Perhaps we weep together . . .

Under the sad circumstances of continued hostilities, it seemed fitting to change Armistice Day to Veterans' Day. And yet a bit of the armistice must remain if we are to bring meaning to this day. The word means the suspension of hostilities between two belligerent powers. And the world has not learned from the bitter heartbreak of those treaties as long as we mistrust one another and even violate the terms.

To Think and Pray About: Will ever there be a lasting peace? *Can* there be? Only in an "armistice" with God when we put on the new armor, and follow the true Prince of Peace, His Son.

Temperance at Thanksgiving?

November 12

1 Corinthians 9:25
Proverbs 23:20,21

CONSIDER THE GLUTTON. Once upon a time he or or she could hide the paunch of other Thanksgivings by tucking a napkin beneath the jowls. (Yes, *jowls*. Henry Fairlie wrote that the glutton was like a hog at its swill, ignoring companions, "he does not chew but champs and chomps, crunches and craunches. He crams, gorges, wolfs, and bolts. He might as well be alone—only companions cannot ignore him. Even if they can avert their eyes from the spectacle they are unable to block their ears to the noise.") Oh, my goodness!

Have you laid down the shovel? Do—otherwise, we can't talk (and mouths do serve more than one purpose). If we insist on a trough, we will miss the beauty of the moment, the fellowship with companions, and the glory of praise for which Thanksgiving is set aside.

Just one more biscuit and gravy . . . a wee sliver of pumpkin pie? Listen to the doctor talking to his patient: "Overweight can be a factor in heart disease, contribute to strokes—push you over the edge." Listen to Paul talking to the Philippians (4:5): "Let moderation be known unto all men. The Lord is at hand."

Before you start on a guilt trip, remember there's a bit of the glutton within us all. Maybe our plenteous society invites it. Or maybe overeating is simply the result of the temptations we mortals must face and conquer. Dare we stretch the warnings and our stomachs? We're sure to become uncomfortable. We may have to jog it off. We *could* become addicts.

Thanksgiving Day is a celebration of praise to God for our land of plenty. God, who supplied it, would not have us feel guilty for our plenty. Neither would He have us focus on stomachs instead of His boundless goodness and grace. Right?

To Think and Pray About: Let's regard our guests as more important than the fare.

A God-Controlled Day

Romans 15:1-6   November 13

J UST WATCHING and listening to Jed Keyes as he goes
about the daily business of operating his little repair shop
is a real lifter. The silver-haired gent has fixed up ailing clocks
and turned off the wrath of customers with a soft word more
years than I am old. He is blessed with the patience of Job—
and all these years I've wondered how he did it. *He* doesn't
control his days, I learned.

One November day last year I was in Jed's shop to pick up an
old clock he keeps running for us after other tinkers have
declared it terminally ill. I was in no rush as the drizzle outside
had turned into a downpour. Maybe it was the weather or
maybe every day is like that winter day. Either way, person
after person came in complaining about the damp and what it
was doing to their rheumatism, arthritis, or allergies—not to
mention groves, dams, and roads. Jed was unruffled, just
nodding and waiting for their general complaints to zoom in
on his service. They did.

"This work was guaranteed," one man said.

"For a year, that's right," Jed answered.

"Well, it's been 360 days. I'd like a refund for the remaining
five. The clock stopped this morning."

Then, "You said this chain looked strong. It broke..."

"The parts you ordered were to be here today, rain or
shine..."

Jed listened to each complaint patiently, explained what he
thought the problem might be, promised he would check the
manufacturer's guarantee, see what happened to the ship-
ment.

"Jed," I said between customers, "how do you stay so self-
controlled?"

"God-controlled," he corrected gently.

To Think and Pray About: Good things happen when God is
in control. As little frustrations arise today, pray for a "God-
controlled day!"

A Glimpse of Heaven

WATCHING the astronauts land the space shuttle *Columbia* in the desert that bright November 14th, I noted their expressions of humility combined with sheer joy. They had visited outer space, faced its dangers bravely, and triumphantly reentered the earth's atmosphere. Out there they were strangers. Now they were home.

Crowds rushed to meet the two men. Some were laughing. Some were weeping. And some were singing. A wonderful welcome home!

How alone they must have felt in that alien territory, I thought. *How helpless.* And surely the thought must have crossed their minds that they might never be reunited with family and friends. How many doubts they must have suffered. And I suspect that more important than the scientific advancement may have been the personal triumph of the glad reunion. The reward made it all worthwhile.

It occurred to me as I conquered the lump in my throat that we, too, are strangers—even on this planet which we call "home." Like those brave men, we have an assignment, a mission to fulfill. But, in a spiritual sense, heaven is our home and something inside which I know God placed there makes me long to leave the earth's gravitational pull and soar to the Father's throne.

I like to think about that when I feel helpless and alone or when I miss the loved ones who have gone on before me. When doubts cross my mind, I picture a host of angels waiting on the ramparts to welcome me. I am no longer lonely—or afraid. That reward will make all the trials worthwhile.

To Think and Pray About: But in the meantime, each of us has an assignment. What do you think yours is? How are you fulfilling it? Do you give God a daily progress report? Our journey home began at birth, but it is not enough to enjoy the flowers along the way. We must also hate the weeds!

"Grow Bags" Are Dirt Cheap

Psalm 147:7,8   November 15
Psalm 149

L ITTLE MARCY lives in a condo. Mom and Dad work. But they are quality parents. Understanding the risks of an eight-year-old's loitering with the growing number of "latch-key kids," they gave her a reason to rush home—"gardening."

The family ordered a "grow bag" from a Finnish magazine for growing herbs on their balcony. Their daughter was so fascinated that they helped her start a similar project in a plastic vegetable bag. Together they discovered it worked as well.

"The only problem is," Marcy's mother laughs, "that our Marcy has become such a dedicated gardener that she has converted the third grade class from reading to doing!"

"Not really," Marcy's teacher explains. "Actually, the two go hand-in-hand. The other children are reading everything they can get regarding gardening."

Marcy's directions are a riot. But children understand one another. No laughs, just shining eyes and small hands eager to dig into the dirt. "Well, first you gotta have a window," Marcy tells them. "You use bread wrappers or something and fill 'em with that smelly Bandini or potty (*potting*) soil. Fill it up to here (*two or three inches from the top*), then bend the top down twice—better sew it—and seal it with tape. Cut a big X in the top and pour in gallons of water before you plant the seeds. Sun makes 'em grow and grow. . . ."

"And now," says little Marcy with pride, "my Sunday School teacher's a gardener and we're looking up Bible verses about plants—which ones to eat or feed camels."

To Think and Pray About: Wouldn't a "grow bag" be a wonderful idea for a shut-in? And who knows what else may grow from the sharing? Some people are unaware of the Bible's horticulture. And that could lead to more reading, for:

> How can one feel close to God who's never known
> the feel of sod?
>   —J.M.B.

Happy Endings

THIS HAS BEEN a day of the "Ten Plagues." Just try and get a blouse on over a cast (designed like a suit-of-armor—only worse, as it flanges out at the bottom like an inverted mushroom). Then after 30 minutes of the wiggle-and-twist to find that you have the blouse on wrong-side-out! What is there to do but, holding back a few expletives, try again? This time it goes a bit easier as the weary wearer can pull from the bottom up—except, with both hands held captive, the phone rings. I am programmed to answer—even if I have to back up to the instrument, giving no thought as to how I plan to say "Hello." Need I go on about dropping the phone . . . pulling the blouse on again (backwards) . . . and, hair qualifying me for some punk-rock group, greeting my husband? Did he have to laugh? Did I have to cry? And why didn't either of us smell the stir-and-bake cake timed for 20 minutes and left for 55?

How did I get into this jam? The physical therapist had warned me to wear loose button-down garments, but I had wanted to look the best I could in this torture chamber, show my husband I was still *me*, a woman again!

Ah, yes, the Ten Plagues. Remember how frighteningly vivid some teachers made them? But wait! They ended "happily ever after." Bloody rivers cleared. Frogs, lice, flies, and locusts (ugh!) died. As we mature, those stories lose some of their glamor, but not their significance. It is so easy to become enslaved to life's plagues.

Oh—my day? Well, George picked up the dead phone (it was he calling anyway to ask if I liked lemon jelly doughnuts—no need for that cremated cake). He said I could put a paper bag over my head . . . so happy ending.

To Think and Pray About: The Christian thinks of the still-celebrated feast of the Passover as a sacrifice, knowing that Christ is the Deliverer. He came. He will return. Now what happier ending would I ask?

Forgiving the Forgetful

L ETTY WAS TO BRING a pound of coffee to our Bible study. She didn't. Lydia's daughter was to babysit so young mothers could attend. She didn't. The custodian was to turn on the heat a half hour in advance. He didn't. No coffee to warm us on the rare morning that the lawn was tipped with frost. And, of course, eight cooing babies can be a blessing— unless one tries to listen to a leader.

The morning went badly in other ways, too. Six of our members asked for prayer, each saying that the person who was the object of concern had made no commitment to the Lord.

Are you impatient with people who make promises then break them or who seek God only in a crisis?

We were studying the Book of Exodus and I was trying hard to imagine the fury of Moses when he heard the unholy merrymaking of the Israelites so soon after their deliverance. Would there be room in my heart for forgiveness?

As we attempted to put some sense into an hour which started out awkwardly, the words of Longfellow crossed my mind:

> The little I have seen of the world teaches me to look upon the errors of others in sorrow, not in anger. When I take the history of one poor heart that sinned and suffered and think of the struggles and temptations it has passed through, the brief pulsations of joy, the feverish inquietude of hope and fear, the pressure of want, the desertion of friends, I would fain leave the soul of my fellowman with Him from whose hands it came.

I wished I could thank that gentle poet for briefly paying my heart a visit. What right had I to be critical? I did not know the circumstances; and, even so, who was I to judge?

To Think and Pray About: If we always remember God then we will leave judgment in His hands when others neither hear, heed, nor remember.

Not Guilty?

November 18   Romans 13:1,7,8,10

"JANE socked me!" Junior screams. "He broke my crayon!" Junior's sister accuses.

"Your dog chased my cat!" "Your cat was in my dog's yard!"

How many ways can we put the burden of blame on each other? On places? On things? On the world—except for the one inhabitant called *me*?

Insurance companies report lawsuits over somebody's stairway, bathtub, crack in the pavement, icy street, scatter rug, moving vehicle, *parked* vehicle, pot that boils over! Never "*I* did it." He...she...they...it did it. Then, there's the hoop-skirt approach that covers all and touches nothing: "The devil made me do it!"

Some lawyers laugh and grow fat over the meanness in us that is unwilling to negotiate, to bend, to compromise. Others try to mediate. Fred is a true peacemaker. Sometimes successful. Most often, not. He has to surrender the case to a judge he prays will be able to bring angry friends together, mend broken homes, lead each party to see the other side, and believe that justice will be served. How successful is Fred's prayer?

"Oh, it would be answered if people would allow it! We could settle out of court; but most would rather bump their heads than climb down."

Ultimately, our judge is God because He alone knows our hearts. What kind of judge is He?

God is good (Psalm 100:5)...God is compassionate (Psalm 145:9)...God is gracious (Titus 2:11)...God is merciful (Titus 3:5)...God is patient (2 Peter 3:9)...God is kind—and *stern* (Romans 11:22).

To Think and Pray About: Do the words console or do they make you fearful? Don't answer now. Wait until someone rear-ends your new Volvo. Or, to be less dramatic, when you are to meet a friend's plane which flies by Mars time!

If for One Day

Romans 12:1   November 19
Psalm 55:16-18

I F FOR ONE DAY you who smoke can refrain, you can do it for a week, a month, a year, and for a lifetime. And that lifetime will be longer. You will have more time to spend with those you love and those who love you. If you are an unmarried reader, wouldn't more time for planning that perfect wedding and all the "happily-ever-afters" be a nice bonus? Young mothers, you want to see that dumpling baby grow up. And grandmothers, don't you know that the best is yet to come? None of the above motivate you? Remember there is a certain thoughtfulness of others that the Lord would have us observe. Research shows that "secondhand" smoke is as damaging to nonsmokers as smoking is to the smoker. So, you see, we are at your mercy. A few (and I am among them) have conditions which make inhaling smoke life-threatening.

Funny thing about us Christians: We care about others—even those we have yet to meet. Statistics frighten us where human life is concerned. So bear with us, for we want you to live to lead a full life.

Remember this today—the Annual Great American Smoke-out. An amusing name. But there is nothing amusing about cancer. Breast cancer used to be the biggest killer for women. Now it's lung cancer; and the correlation between smoking and the disease is too startling to quote. Well, you can help snuff it out—just by snuffing that cigarette in your hand. The best Thanksgiving gift to yourself and others.

To Think and Pray About: Should we castigate others about a dangerous habit when we have faults of our own that need snuffing out? Pick out one that once felt wrong but now looks harmless because it has become a part of you. Identifying it is the first step to a cure. What's more, it will help in your understanding of those who smoke. Imagine a roped-off section that says: NO _____ and move into it—if for one day!

The Greatest Engineer

ADMITTEDLY, there are times when teachers want to use Afredo's native tongue on him: "*Cierre usted la boca!*" (which translates into "Shut your mouth!") when he starts talking about bridges. Afredo's a bright youngster—gifted really—and is wisely channeling his creativity and steel-trap memory the right direction. Engineering!

He was the student who bombarded my unwilling ears with what he called the "Great Debate." And it was from him that I came up with a thought which outstripped the debate about which was the world's longest bridge. But, first, Alfredo...

"Do you know where the Mackinac Bridge is?" Michigan, I thought. He looked surprised that I, a *woman* teacher, would know so much. And that was my undoing. "Right!" He beamed. "It joins the upper and the lower peninsulas and the total length of the bridge is five miles. Of course, the total length of steel superstructures is three-and-a-half (*of course!*)."

Alfredo went on to tell me the miles (in feet, mind you!) of the suspension bridge, length of center span, miles of cable wire used..."

The boy went on comparing engineering marvels. But I did not hear. Bridges in general, I was thinking, join two sides of a river, bay, or sections of ground. But the *greatest* bridge spans a wider gulf—that between us and God. Jesus, our Wonderful Bridge, who descended to fulfill the dreams and prophecies of thousands of years. The Engineer who masterminded that bridge paid far more dearly than calculators can measure.

To Think and Pray About: Other bridges have failed. Winds collapsed a Washington bridge. Quakes buckled a California bridge. And the Mackinac, strong as it is, would go up in vapor in an atomic explosion. Can Jesus fail? No! He came to redeem man, woman, and child—the old and the strong, the powerful and the weak, the gifted like Alfredo and the ignorant and uneducated! How can you point out that bridge to others today—and make them see that they need no ferry?

Liberation

Hebrews 3:12   November 21
Psalm 40:1,3

"ALL GOOD THINGS come to an end," so they say. What about the bad ones? I was beginning to think I would never be a free woman again. "Three months," the orthopedic surgeon had promised. I waited to be delivered. But the grafts and fusions did not knit-and-purl . . . not in six months either . . . and now, nine months after the trauma which rendered me helpless, I was ready to crawl from the cocoon of fiberglass. But, downcast and poor in spirit, I no longer clung to illusions of emerging a butterfly. The pain had not lessened. The muscles had atrophied. Fly! I'd do well to walk.

The doctor (none too gently) began my release aided by a nurse whose face was carved in stone. I tried to make a joke and saw that my words were as exciting as a dial tone that says your party's hung up. I tried to pray: *Out of the depths, oh Lord . . .*

This will never do, Lord. Maybe I'd better sing. Isn't that the way to conquer fear of the dark? (Was that the sound of a buzz saw— like magicians use for sawing women in half?) I hummed (Ouch! They'd hit the bone!), then I belted out the first line I recalled from "That Old-Time Religion": "It was good for the Hebrew children . . ."

But what about Moses' flock who became so divided, dissatisfied, and fearful? What was it my pastor had said? "It's easy to criticize them until one sees the same pattern emerge among Hebrew Christians. And what of people today? Afraid of the dark . . . distrustful . . . doubting . . . wanting to 'turn back'? *We do not walk alone . . .*"

Ordeal finished, I stood—grasping a chair with one hand, God's hand with the other. Oh, the pain—but I took a step. So what if I were made from spare parts from an older model? Wasn't it good that somebody *was* older! God had glued me together.

To Think and Pray About: We walk on the legs of faith! God only asks us to believe that!

Never Again—Until Next Year

November 22   Psalm 78:4
1 Corinthians 13

"THE STORM'S OVER!" Felicia said tiredly. She called to let me know that the last guest had gone home and that she somehow had survived. "But never again—never, *never*, NEVER!"

Coming from the East, the families are sure that it never rains in California. Well, the tide comes in! And there they are stranded in the ark as it were—with two of every kind of animal! Bertie's kid brings this shaggy dog they claim is house-broken, so why does he demand to go out six times a night? Tracks all over the white carpet—looks like they belong to Big Foot! They all begin yelling, "When's dinner?" before using the bathroom . . . which is tragic, since the plumbing fails and Fred's out of Drano and refuses to call a plumber on a holiday, says they can go down to the "Y" or make do. Sylvia's opposed to the rod, so Buster and Butch upset the gravy in a free-for-all. All eyes closed during prayer, that mongrel observes, so he pulls the uncarved turkey right off the dinner table. "No, I'm *not* making it up!"

I am still laughing when Felicia calls back. She's found a note in the cookie jar signed by every single guest (even a dog's footprint!). All except the "creepers and crawlers" wrote a line. "You are the true peacemaker" (Uncle Jed). And "Your just full of the holy Sprite!" (Becky, age seven). Now, Felicia's laughing with me. Oh well, she guesses her blood pressure will stabilize by next year.

Of course it will! And so will yours and mine. The noise will drive the cat crazy . . . Cousin Ike will tell the same story he told last year and that big-mouthed Billie Joseph will ask if it happened twice . . . Coralee's hair will be too red . . . Maddy'll wear a Junior Miss size when she's now a 12 . . . Uncle Amos will light that pipe . . . but they're *family*!

To Think and Pray About: Once a year, consider the extended family. "Love never faileth!"

Little Guideposts

1 John 1:9   November 23
Luke 1:79

"KNOW WHERE YOU ARE GOING—and get there!" The words caught my eye as I attempted to sort outdated materials from my *Guidelines for Writers* file. Hmmm ... the date was over a decade ago; but there was nothing outdated in the advice which followed. The wise editor had offered some guidelines for writers which would work well in dealing with others. Test these:

• Be realistic and believable, yet imaginative and surprising. People are complex, not simple (*simple* has two meanings—right?).

• Be natural and conversational, avoiding stilted language which talks down. You do not know it all!

• Be purposeful—trying to make a difference in the understanding, appreciation, or conduct of each person you "meet."

• Be sure to center on Christ in everyday experiences, situations, and problems. Would what you share help *you* cope? Then it will help others if you communicate clearly.

• Be on guard against heavy moralization, preaching, or "sermonizing" tones and attitudes. Show how we learn from each other. Ever be the gentle learner.

Wouldn't the world be brighter if we apply these rules to everyday goings-in and comings-out? Would we all be "glad of life"?

Throw that away? Of course not. And, oh, what about this? Another editor wrote: "We are trying to elevate the role of womanhood ... the thinkers ... homemakers ... community and church leaders ... teachers ... business partners ... We could go on and on."

To Think and Pray About: Yes, and so could we. No matter—we are more alike than different whether we hold executive positions or babies. We are already "elevated" in God's eyes—justified through Christ.

The Grandmother of Many

"AND what are *you* doing for Thanksgiving, Mrs. Bellwood?"

The slight emphasis on "you" tattled. The rest of us who were busily filling baskets for the less fortunate had great plans for the family day. But poor Mrs. Bellwood was less fortunate than those for whom we prepared the food. She had no family.

But then the grandmother-aged lady surprised us all. While struggling to stuff a can of macadamia nuts into a corner of her basket, she spoke loudly and clearly.

"I plan for as many members of my family as I'm able to pack into my house this year!"

Mrs. Bellwood must have read the unasked questions on our faces. "You see," she smiled as she rose to put a hand to her back, "I have a large spiritual family...my Sunday school class...my Brownie troop...my Surrogate Grandmother's Club children...and this year I've included a dozen children from the orphanage."

My heart was deeply touched. This wonderful woman was providing a family day for little ones who scarcely knew the meaning of the word. And, in so doing, she had provided me with a whole, bright, new concept of the season. What a wonderful way to say: "Praise ye the Lord!"

To Think and Pray About: Think about the real meaning of Thanksgiving then discuss it with your family and friends. Consider the poor, the homeless, and the shut-ins. As a family project or a project among friends, consider inviting the wayfaring strangers for a meal. And wouldn't it be wonderful to take a dish of dainties to those who are house-bound? Guarantee: This will be your happiest Thanksgiving ever. Take Mrs. Bellwood's word for it!

"Seeing" the Feast

Mark 8:18-25   November 25
Psalm 119:18

TODAY was my father's birthday. It often fell on Thanksgiving and that doubled our dining pleasure. Now he is feasting at the Lord's table. I miss him so much; but I envision his partaking of the spiritual fruits—eating slowly, the way he and I always did.

Others were always ready for dessert before Daddy and I were well into the main course. They teasingly said we were obsessed with food. No! that would be idolatry. Secretly, we wondered if it were not the other way around. It seemed to us that the other diners bolted down the meal, smelling but scarcely tasting and certainly not seeing. I suppose our family and friends recognized the blessings of the carefully prepared meal as a source of nourishment; but I believe that most of them gobbled those blessings so fast that food was near-tasteless and colorless—a vehicle for gratifying hunger.

Daddy and I shared something special. We appreciated the delicate flavors, noted the texture—crisp or creamy—and made glad the heart of the hostess by paying attention when a dish was steaming or chilled.

If we are thankful—*truly* thankful—for the banquet spread before us, shouldn't we drink in the beauty and thank God for that, too? But we should dine with more than our eyes? True, let's put those tastebuds to work this year. But first, let's feed the eyes. Just before the prayer or just after, let's feast our eyes on the burgundy sparkle of the cranberry juice. Notice its complement to the gold-brown of the turkey and delight in its contrast to the green vegetables and yeasty rolls. For a fleeting, prayerful moment entertain the thought that the appearance is almost too beautiful to spoil. Now, with thankful heart, dig in and enjoy. But between bites do *see!*

To Think and Pray About: Consider a family discussion on the matter of eating well especially on the day set aside to praise God for His goodness—which in some cases goes untasted and unseen.

Exercise in Futility

November 26

Philippians 4:5
1 Timothy 4:7

THANKSGIVING. That special day set aside to praise our Maker for abundant life in this land of plenty. But a time when most of us take in more calories than we burn up!

Recognizing this, a friend enclosed what she called her "Exercises in Futility" with a holiday greeting. "Here are some calorie-burning activities and the number of calories per hour they consume," she wrote. I read it and laughed. Then I reread it soberly. Engaging in such a "strenuous workout" requires no physical strength, I realized; but (warning!) they can be hazardous to your spiritual health.

- Beating around the bush when talking 75
- Climbing the walls when upset......................... 150
- Passing the buck (when you're guilty) 25
- Dragging your heels (when there's work)................ 100
- Pushing a point with a friend......................... 250
- Hitting the nail on the head (to get even) 50
- Bending over backwards (to overpersuade) 75
- Balancing the books (in your favor)................... 23
- Eating crow (just for the show) 225
- Climbing the ladder of success (stepping
  on others)... 750
- Adding fuel to the fire (by criticizing)................ 150
- Jumping to conclusions 100
- Throwing your weight around (depending
  on size) 55-300
- Making mountains out of molehills 500
- Wading through paperwork (but not doing
  the job).. 300
- Jumping on the (wrong) bandwagon 200
- Running around in circles (getting nowhere) 500
- Carrying your own burdens (when God is
  so near!) 1000

To Think and Pray About: Isn't it time we stopped stuffing our lives with "junk food"? Take a long, hard look at how you burn up calories in your daily life. Now make a list showing how to "exercise" in ways that will be pleasing to God.

Millie's Soup Kitchen

Psalm 107:1-9
Proverbs 10:21,22

November 27

AFTER THANKSGIVING, my friend, Millie—who works at home like me—makes the most wonderful soup of the year. You see, Millie always runs a soup kitchen. For her family. For her friends. And for the hungry. I copied her idea a long time ago and it works wonders for the working woman and miracles for others as well.

Unfortunately, I am unable to share Millie's recipe. She has none. It is one of those need-is-the-mother-of-invention dishes to avoid waste—both of time and money. Anyway, the fun of it is that there is never, never a repetition. It differs with each serving.

But I can share the idea as my friend shared it with me. Then you are free to (as she puts it) "marry" every leftover to the pot.

On the day following the big feast, Millie starts a new pot with a wave of leftovers. She boils the bones of the riddled bird for a broth base. From there, it's anybody's guess what bits and pieces she tosses in—tomatoes, corn, lima beans, gravy. Ask her, "What more?" and she'll reply, "What more did you have?"

The next day she's apt to add carrots, mushroom stems, the spinach Junior hates—combining them for a new flavor each day. Leftover bacon? Great. Same with eggs, any style. And, of course, scraps of bread make great croutons to add at the last moment. Seasonings are up to individual tastes. Millie keeps hers mild, because this dish is designed for her "good neighboring" policy. And what a service she performs with it. She's never flustered when hubby brings a business associate home for lunch. There's soup. No brown-bag lunches at her house. If there's a committee meeting, she brings on the soup. New neighbors? "I've been unable to get over," Millie may say, "but here's something to warm your insides."

To Think and Pray About: There are so many ways of serving—with soup and other things! Consider starting a "bits and pieces" jar. Call that friend who's recovering from surgery. She'd love an outing and your soup.

So—Why Not Be Philosophical?

November 28   Psalm 40:1-8

L ETTY FLARED UP LIKE A ROCKET when Jim brought the turkey home. The fact that it was on special for 39 cents a pound made absolutely no difference. They'd had turkey for a week—and besides, this critter wouldn't fit into their oven. Letty wanted Jim to return the bird. Jim was astounded. One just didn't return a *turkey*. What reason could he give—except that his wife had turned husband-beater? Letty didn't know and to her husband's relief admitted that he had a point—but only because there were no refunds on sale merchandise. Could I, oh please, *would* I, let them borrow my oven? To borrow a built-in oven means you're to cook the turkey. Yes, it would fit into my oven, but it would *not* fit into my schedule. And my oven was just as busy. At the moment, it was baking a whole ham. Then there was a birthday cake to bake . . . and dinner.

Silently, I counted to ten. To fifteen. Letty was waiting on the telephone with indrawn breath, like a child who's been good all year—and knows that you know. "Bring it over," I said in tired resignation just as my own husband entered cheerfully to ask, "What's for lunch?"

I turned the oven up in spite of the directions on the wrapper the ham came in. The oven grumbled and the kitchen filled with smoke. Minutes later, after George had used the fire extinguisher and removed the shrunken ham (how much water do they pump into these hams anyway?), I sat down to feel sorry for myself.

My husband is just opposite to Jim. He's happiest when there's a crisis. He came in whistling in short order and replaced the once-charred broiler, now buffed and shining.

"No great work ever gets done in a hurry." He's always making scientific discoveries like that. "Take your poetry—or this ham (*yeah, take it!*), it all has to be done by degrees."

To Think and Pray About: I needed patience and perseverance. We all do! Milton did not write *Paradise Lost* at a sitting. Shakespeare did not compose *Macbeth* in a day. And how long do you suppose our prophets and gospel writers worked for us?

Prepare Him Room

2 Peter 3:1-8   November 29

I T ALL BEGAN around Halloween. Out with the masks. In with the trappings of Christmas. Thanksgiving, with a scattering of greeting cards and grocery-store specials, was sandwiched between.

Rehearsals began for the choirs. And the search was on for stored robes, staffs, and angel wings. The Christmas program, you know. My heart always goes out to the ministers who must pull up their liturgical socks and polish their sermons to keep step with the secular world.

And how can the rest of us fit all the preparations inside the "inns" of our hearts? At first, it is fun. And then by Christmas the world is frazzled. Too late, we realize that we miss the real spirit of the holy season because we prepared for all except Jesus!

I'm not sure how to avoid the problem. Maybe it is a matter of attitude. In which case, we might consider *adding* to the preparations. We all love the Christmas greens, the plum puddings, the little social whirls . . . the shopping . . . the whispered secrets. But not in a mindless way which places a Child in the manger as a part of the decorations, forgetting His glorious gift of salvation which, though we feed the hungry and clothe the poor, may be a bumbling, uncertain, and unclear message to our non-Christian friends.

This comes to mind today as I realize that Advent has come again and will be with us until Christmas Day. This is a time of preparation of the heart for His coming (and His *staying*) in our hearts. Advent is a time of watching, waiting, *longing* for the Good News. But do those outside our Christian Family know the story? *And do we sometimes forget?*

To Think and Pray About: Oh, keep up the wonderful traditions—*please do!*—but let's prepare Him room in the hearts of as many as possible outside our church family. Let the choirs keep singing the angel songs, but what about a simple carol sung by neighbors as we exchange cookies over the fence? Let the children continue to reenact the nativity scene; but let's make sure they include a friend who doesn't know the story.

It Is a Time...

I T IS A TIME for meditation, Lord, as we turn our calendars to the final month of this year. Let it be a glorious month, Lord, one in which we bring our gifts to Your cradle and Your cross—and, finally, to Your throne of grace. For tomorrow we cross the threshold of Your blessed birthday, a time for remembering in a way pleasing in Your sight—a way which will delight Your eye and gladden Your heart. How countless are the ways in which You do this for us.

It is a time for remembering summer's gentle breezes as we watch the last leaf flutter to the breast of Mother Earth, there to await Your blanket of snow. Their life span seems so short, in recollection. But those green leaves of summer, turned gold by autumn's kiss, are but one of the reminders of what each of us can do in life's brief journey to bring brilliance and comfort into the lives of those around us. Forgive us when we failed.

It is a time for strolling the silent forest, breathing deeply of the crisp air, expanding our lungs and our horizons. Searching for a blossom. Searching our hearts and our conscience for those things left undone, preparing ourselves for the best we have to offer others—in Your name.

It is a time for readying ourselves for winter's ice. Let each heart be a storehouse of Your love. And guide us, Lord, to mete that love to all though often our patience be tried. We will be jostled by busy shoppers. We will be tempted to give more than we can afford—too often to those not in need. Prepare us as You prepare nature to remember that new life awaits—because of Your Gift! Be with us, Lord, as we pop corn, polish apples, and gather family and friends before the fireplace that Your gift is for *all*. Send us the stranger, the tired, the poor—together with a humble spirit—borrowed of Your love. Give us of Your *giving*. *It is a time!*

My Christmas Prayer

D EAR LORD, we praise You for this blessed season and the glimpse of heaven that Christmas brings to earth. It is such a busy time, Lord, that we tend to forget the greatest thing of all, preparation of our hearts—ours and those of others—for Your coming. Let us set aside a time for prayer, the kind that reaches into the recesses of the mind and 2000 years beyond, to explore and see—as little children—the miracle unfolding before us. Then, and only then, Lord, will we be equipped to seek out old friends, forgotten strangers, and one or two whom the world has rejected. Lead us to reenact Your gift gently by word and deed. Practicing soft answers. Mending differences. Listening . . . understanding . . . forgiving. And seeing Your forgiveness when we grow impatient with too much to do in too short a time. Remind us that the true gift is love as demonstrated by Your divine love—the priceless gift which will shine on when the strands of colored lights are stored away and the candles of Advent have burned low.

Bless us with a quietness of mind. It is in this quiet that we will feel Your presence near, filling our hearts with the peace and joy that You offer in abundance. For we know that, as You chose Mary to the highest calling any woman has ever known, You likewise elected the rest of us to lend that quiet, unquestioning spirit to those around us. Remind us that we, too, are "chosen" to perpetuate that quiet though the stresses rub us raw.

Bless us, too, with patience as excitement turns to frenzy and tramples us with thoughtless feet. Let us remember Your little band of believers who were patient when the waiting for a King seemed futile. Strengthen our fibers of endurance.

Let our faith remain unfaltering, our hope and courage strong. Bind us in the ribbons of tolerance and love.

The Glowing

I N A SPECIAL WAY we can recreate the spirit of Christmas. "Come Thou Long-Expected Jesus" we can sing together while decorating the tree. The words of the old hymn define the Advent season, reminding us that a weary, troubled world awaited the Messiah. We, too, are weary. We, too, are troubled. And we, too, await His reappearance. There was an urgent sense of anticipation then. That same sense remains with us as a common thread which binds together Christian and Jew. Christmas is (and should be!) a time of joy coupled with sobriety of thought.

With that blessed air of anticipation, we can rekindle that flame of expectation which has not been (and never will be!) extinguished by the now-organized Atheists' Group which acts as a watchdog for those "blatantly religious" nativity scenes and the lighting of candles on the menorah. (*Yes, Lord, they can tear down our banners and lock You from our classrooms. But they cannot lock You out of our hearts!*) One way to keep the flame glowing in the home is to weave a circle of evergreens (the circle represents the infinity of Christ) and adorn it with five candles for the Advent wreath. Traditions vary, but generally the candles are purple (prophecy), rose (joy), and white (the center candle representing Christ—"The Lord has come!"). Meditations are somber, but underneath there are joyful ripples of anticipation. What a beautiful way to prepare our hearts for Him!

To Think and Pray About: "I am the light of the world. . . ." Why do we light one purple candle? To remind us of the hope of the prophets awaiting the coming of our Lord to bring us the gift of life! We have that gift. Let us share it again . . . again . . . and again, sharing each other's hopes and honoring one another's dreams.

The Total Person

Ephesians 5:20   December 3

THE QUESTION from *Pioneer Teacher* set my husband and me to laughing: "Did you know that one out of every two Americans wears glasses? Which just goes to show how important ears are!"

One word led to another and we found ourselves remembering the "Little Moron" stories, popular some 40 years ago.

"What would happen if you had both your ears cut off?"

"I couldn't see. My hat would fall over my eyes."

Jokes aside, we set to talking about the marvel of having the senses of taste, smell, sight, and hearing—operative because of special organs connected with the brain. And I guess that touch has to do with the sensory nerves of the skin. It is, then, the *brain* that smells, sees, hears, and feels . . . even tastes.

The human body is another of God's miracles, we agreed. He has planned every little detail so that the mind unfolds simultaneously with the growing body. Cultivation of these wonderful gifts, will develop their usefulness. The remarkable thing is that when (with few exceptions) one sense is lost or impaired at least one other sense becomes sharper.

We need to marvel anew at these wonderful machines the Creator has designed to house the living soul He breathed into us. It serves to remind us that, just as the organs of sense depend upon the alertness of the brain for efficiency, we depend upon Him for "signals" to guide us through our Christian lives. How thankful I am for a creative Lord who left nothing to chance, putting together a "total person" with many parts—so many which can serve His purpose in a multitude of ways.

To Think and Pray About: Stores are offering toys which are so realistic that they amaze us. Among them are robots which can do just about anything—except think and breathe. As we Christmas shop, let's give some thought to our earthly body God created so perfectly. Manufacturers can imitate but they can never duplicate God's total person—*you!*

God Knows My Address!

Luke 15:4-7
Matthew 28:20

TWO KINDERGARTEN CHILDREN were discussing Santa Claus. Johnny wished his gift-giving friend had a compass—or at least a road map.

Peter said Santa Claus needed none.

Johnny was unconvinced. "But we're going to my grandma's this Christmas. Can Santa find me in somebody else's house?"

"*God* could," Peter replied.

What a spirit-lifting thought! Not just for the holidays, but for every day. In whatever place, in whatever circumstance, God can find us. He finds us and He walks with us every step of the way whether it's in "somebody else's house" or in some dark valley of depression, fear, and loneliness that our feet have not walked before. God will seek us out and bring us safely home.

"If I ascend up into heaven, thou art there: if I make my bed in hell, behold, thou art there.

"If I take the wings of the morning and dwell in the uttermost parts of the sea;

"Even there shall thy hand lead me . . .

"Yea, the darkness hideth not from thee; but the night shineth as the day: the darkness and the light are both alike to thee. . . ."

—Psalm 139:8-12

To Think and Pray About: God sent His Son to the world to knock on the door of every heart. Somehow on this, the season set apart to celebrate His holy birth, I sense that He knocks a little louder. How do you plan to spend the holidays? Traveling? Take Jesus with you. How do you plan to show your love to Him and to those around you? Remember that to be loved is the happiness of receiving. To love in return is the joy of giving. Give Him your heart and live in the blessed assurance that wherever you are there will He be also.

The Real Meaning of Christmas

Romans 6:23; 13:10   December 5

GREAT AUNT Lulu was known in our family more for her "horse sense" than her generosity. All the same, she linked up, unknowingly, with my son Bryce to remind me of the real meaning of Christmas.

Back when Bryce was four, he could have used something a little more tangible than the elderly relative's good wishes. Or so I thought when I opened her greeting card. "I suppose the others will be sending presents. Tell Bryce that I send my love instead," she wrote.

Tell a little boy *that*? Why, that Lady Scrooge! How filled with Christmas spirit could she get! Mean thoughts just tumbled over themselves; but I held my tongue, dreading to share the words.

To my surprise, however, Bryce showed no disappointment. "What did we send her, Mommy?" he asked instead.

"A shawl, some of the lemon bread she likes—"

"And some love?" the wise little boy inquired.

I felt a sense of shame. There had never been any real affection between Aunt Lulu and me. She was undemonstrative, frugal to a fault, and always ready with advice—and (*face it, June*) unloved.

And what about *me*? How filled with the proper spirit of Christmas was I when I equated the glorious season with "things" that a lonely, faraway member could give?

"We'll write her a love letter, you and I," I promised. My son let out a childish squeal of delight. And suddenly I knew that I loved her very much.

To Think and Pray About: Is there a member of your family or an unappealing neighbor or casual acquaintance whom you have made no effort to understand? Jesus came to a hostile world but gave the greatest gift of all! Seek out that person and, remembering His gift of love, give of yourself. This is His birthday—and all He asks for is our love for Himself and for others.

Giving to Those Who Gave

MARION and I were baking fruitcakes. As we paused to have coffee, snatches of our eight-year-old sons' conversation drifted into the kitchen. The boys were concerned, it seemed, with how to stretch their allowances to cover their Christmas gift list.

"I don't know about the new teacher," my Bryce said thoughtfully. "Do you think she'll give *us* anything?"

Marion's Chris was not sure either. "But about the kids, it's easy. I'll just look at last year's list."

"You mean the ones we gave to?"

"Nope," Chris replied, "not unless they gave to me."

Marion and I exchanged looks of motherly horror. Was all our "more blessed to give" teaching for naught? My friend was about to leave her nut chopping, go into the den, and give a review lesson when I caught her sleeve. I had had the strangest thought. . . . Wasn't there one exception to giving in accordance to what we had received? That the Giver of all good things and the gift He gave us 2000 years ago should be the gauge for our giving? For the gift of His Son is what Christmas is all about!

And *that* was what we told our children.

To Think and Pray About: What can we give to God then? Our hearts. And to His other children? Ourselves. Not because we love as we ought, but because He does! Jesus was the Son of God. We are His children, too. He gave so much and we can do so little? True, but to each of us God gave a gift that made us special. *You* are special. *I* am special. How can we share those "specialties" so that the trappings of Christmas will not dim the glory of salvation? Thank Him for the origin of giving!

A Gift of Warmth

James 2:15-18   December 7

FOLKS around us in the little East Texas community called it "the year of the boll weevil." Cotton crops failed. Gardens surrendered to the broiling sun, and hopes for a gift-giving Christmas died on the vine as well. We'd do well to survive the winter.

"But it won't be Christmas without gifts," I complained, the way a little girl will to a visiting aunt.

"There'll be gifts aplenty—that's Christmas!" she said.

I understood the why of no purchased gifts, although it hurt. But, gifts or not, my spirits lifted as Christmas drew closer. Mama spiced the house with homemade mincemeat pie and Daddy brought in a sweet-smelling cedar tree. We began singing carols at school and rehearsing the Christmas pageant at church. It even snowed!

All gifts, Auntie pointed out. *But not the kind that warm the heart,* I thought. Aloud, I said: "Not the kind that warm the hand," and shook my head sadly in recollection of last year's red mittens I was dipping my hands into. "Three busted fingers..."

Christmas morning brought some gifts, after all. How my parents managed remains a mystery, but there was no question about my aunt. And hers was the "warmest" gift of all!

Beneath the tree lay a beautiful pair of like-new mittens. Why, the mends didn't show at all. But missing from the bottom of Auntie's sweater was a scalloped edging of red yarn. Tears filled my eyes. But she only said (making it sound true): "Those doodads were forever getting in the way of my knitting." *Ah, memories of love...*

To Think and Pray About: Make this a storytelling season. Keep pleasant memories alive. And remember the greatest story of all. How can you put into practice the art of giving of yourself more than you expect to receive? This is one way in which Jesus lives in our hearts!

My Favorite Christmas Pudding

WOULDN"T IT BE FUN for us to make a world-wide recipe book? If each of us put down the ingredients that go to make up a beautiful Christmas and shared it... oh, wouldn't it be fun?

My Favorite Christmas Pudding began with an idea from *Sunshine* magazine—and I let it grow. And so can you:

Take some Human Nature, as you find it,
(The Commonest Variety will do);
Put a little Graciousness behind it,
And add a lump of Charity, or two.

Squeeze in just a drop of Moderation,
Half as much of Frugality (or less);
Add some very fine Consideration,
Straining off all of Poverty's distress.

Pour some Milk of Human Kindness in it,
Put in all of the Happiness you can;
Stir it up with Laughter every minute,
Season with Goodwill Toward every man.

Set it on the Fire of Heart's Affection,
Leave it stand till Jolly Bubbles arise;
Sprinkle it liberally with Sweet Kisses;
For Confection, sweeten with Loving Eyes.

Flavor it with Children's Merry Chatter;
Frost it with the Snow of White Winter Dells;
Place it on a Holly-garnished Platter,
And serve it with the Song of Christmas Bells.

This should make more than enough for Family;
So may God grant that you're willing to give
A Slice of the Glow to each one you know
So that Christmas forever will live!

                                                            J.M.B.

To Think and Pray About: Add other ingredients to my pudding, remembering that Jesus embodies the best gift of all—infinite love. How can we share it?

The Second Candle

Micah 5:2   December 9
John 8:1,2

YOU WOULD LIKE to write an article—no, a book—
title of which would be *Madness at the Mall!* No readers maybe. But my, oh my! What you would get off your
chest—besides these packages.

The line at the cash register has trickled down at the rate of
a leaky faucet to 12 and you are number 11. Your feet hurt. You
feel a little crazed. All around you the holiday cheers have
turned to sneers.

The woman ahead of you has two carts more heavily laden
than Santa's sleigh, and the man at the head of the line wants
to make a check using a theater stub for identification. The
cashier needs a price check then change for a 100 dollar bill.
The mumbling in the crowd grows louder and you wonder
desperately if there's someone trained in mob control. At this
point the electronic cash register balks and the frustrated
operator says there may be a delay.

You know it is no nightmare when someone stomps on your
arch to beat the crowd to another line. Your sanity is ebbing
away. Drained and maimed you stand there, noting with some
faraway part of your brain that the Gift Wrap Center is under
siege. So you will do your own...as well as dinner. Oh,
to be foisted away—with family...ready to light the second
candle...

To Think and Pray About: "I am the light of the world." Why
do we light two candles tonight? The first purple one reminds
us of the hope of the prophets (and renews our own). The
second, sometimes called the "Bethlehem Candle," reminds
us of the light and warmth that came in the midst of the dark,
cold night (and into our own hearts at this sacred moment). In
little Bethlehem plans were made to receive the blessed babe
in a world of conflict, confusion, and bewilderment. Your
fatigue dissipates in the glow. You know that when the night is
darkest and you are in need of peace, your faith still points to
the warmth of the stable—over which there hangs a star.

Great Expectations

M Y MOTHER is 90 now—going on 100! She will reach that century mark, she "expects."

I say *expects* because Mama expresses herself that way. She expects to hear from a family member. She expects her lima beans will sprout... it will be an early spring... the revival meetings are going to make a change in her community (and that company is coming "if the rooster crows thrice"!). In other words, she expects the best.

Such thinking gave me a delightful childhood. When Mama expected something, it was destined to happen. Other people's mothers *thought* this or that. Mama *expected* it. Thinking had to do with a process of the brain, she said. It had its place in school. But expecting? That was of the spirit. And she could quote enough passages from the Bible to back up her conviction.

I have been thinking of my mother today as I address greeting cards "expecting" to have a wonderful Christmas. I am following my mother's star just as shepherds followed the Star of Bethlehem 2000 years ago. Because we *expect* good things to happen, we take a positive attitude. And yes, in a very real sense, we help to bring them about. Else why would we pray?

To Think and Pray About: How about you? Do you hold great expectations for the holy season ahead? We will be celebrating the miracle of the holy birth, expected by the prophets eons before the appearance of our King. Discuss ways in which you can prepare for His return. But first, invite Him in for the holidays! *Come into our hearts, Lord Jesus. We are expecting You.*

'Tis the Night of...

1 Corinthians 9:6-15   December 11

'Tis the night of the program and all through the halls
The school is reechoing with juvenile squalls.
The heavenly choir all have colds in the head
And their teachers resemble the walking dead.
One shepherd is wheezing (allergic to wool),
And the stage curtain sticks and refuses to pull.
Now the littlest shepherd is losing his shoes,
And the amateur light crew has blown its third fuse.
St. Joseph gets thirsty and goes to the fountain,
So his beard falls apart (that you can count on).
Oops! One of the Wise Men forgets his lines;
(His I.Q., if any, is seventy-nine).
"Now, angels, please hold up your heads when you sing."
"Oh, Teacher—oh, Teacher I've busted a wing!"
"Shh-h-h! Chorus, please turn without rattling a page,
And spit out that gum before you're on stage...
Keep away from the scenery, you're going to spoil it."
"Oh, Teacher—oh, Teacher, I gotta go to the toilet!"
Need we go on? Every year you go through it,
And vow it's the last time you'll ever go through it...
But somehow we do, though we grumble about it,
For, say what you will, it's not Christmas without it!

OF ALL the gifts we give at this time of year, the Christmas program may be one of the greatest! Teachers in the public schools are perpetuating a tradition—one which grows more threatened each year (*Hang in there!*). And Sunday school teachers are making the holy birth "come alive" for children—as well as building memories that will linger long after they have crossed the borders of childhood. Adults "out there" will relive their own youth... parents and grandparents will glow... and, most important of all, who knows just who among those guests has never seen the nativity scene reenacted... never heard the story... never felt the stir that comes into their hearts tonight?

To Think and Pray About: "O Come, O Come, Emmanuel" proclaims: "God with us!"

You Just Can't Win

ARE YOU A NEW TEACHER? A new homemaker? New cook? New wife or mother? Other? All of the above? (Mercy!) Well, let us veterans share a few words of advice: You just can't win.

What a cheerful earful to start your day! We are all there, have been, or are en route. Since I was all of these (and ever the writer as well), let me explain the dilemma of the teacher:

> If you are a brand new teacher, you lack experience.
> If you have been teaching all your life, you are in a rut.
> If you seldom admit a mistake, you are arrogant.
> If you admit a mistake, you ought to go back to farming.
> If you write anything, you are neglecting your job.
> If you don't write anything, you never had a thought to share.
> If you give plenty of high grades, you have no standards.
> If you give low grades, you are a stone heart.
> If you use a few notes, you are not original.
> If you don't use a few notes, you are unprepared.
> If you can quote some facts, you are a show-off.
> If you keep up with sports, you are illiterate.
> If you stand while teaching, you are oratorical.
> If you sit while teaching, you are lazy.
> If you are young, you need seasoning.
> If you are older, you've seen better days.

To Think and Pray About: So how's your sense of humor? A sense of humor can pull you from the quagmire time after time. It will help you turn Godward instead of inward.

So...You're the Boss?

Ephesians 6:5-10   December 13

MY HUSBAND, also a teacher, saved a copy of "The School Administrator's Dilemma" (revised from Phi Delta Kappa, and distributed by his principal at a faculty meeting). That was in 1955, when administrators were largely men. Time has changed that, so let's change, too (using feminine gender instead of masculine—that is, *he* to *she*).

Women in the other work places—can you laugh with us, knowing that some of it is true? But knowing, too, that we can cope.

> If she's friendly with clerical staff, she's a politician.
> If she keeps to herself, she's a snob.
> If she makes decisions quickly, she's arbitrary.
> If she has no immediate answer, she can't make up her mind.
> If she works on a day-to-day basis, she lacks foresight.
> If she has long-range plans, she's a daydreamer.
> If her name appears in the newspaper, she's a publicity hound.
> If no one has ever heard of her, she's a nonentity.
> If she requests a large budget, she's against economy.
> If she doesn't ask for more money, she's a timid soul (or stark mad).
> If she tries to eliminate red tape, she has no regard for the system.
> If she insists on going through channels, she's a bureaucrat.
> If she speaks the language of education, she's a cliché expert.
> If she doesn't use jargon, she's illiterate.
> If she's late for work, she's taking advantage of her position.
> If she's there early, she's an eager beaver (or spying).
> If she holds weekly staff meetings, she's desperate for ideas.
> If she doesn't, she has no regard for teamwork.
> If she takes her briefcase home, she's trying to impress others.
> If not, she's lazy.

To Think and Pray About: Apply this to your daily life and have a laugh.

As It Was—and Ever Will Be

December 14

John 1:1
Micah 5:2; Psalm 90:2

THIS IS A SEASON of great joy. There will be parties of varying themes. I remember one in particular. Perhaps the account will be of help in planning a party of your own.

My husband and I were excited over the invitation to attend a "Christmas As It Was" party. The hosts had shopped all year to make "an old-fashioned Christmas." Children wore granny gowns and busily strung cranberries. Their mothers ladled out cider and spiced punch. And a ceiling-high tree was ringed by homemade doughnuts. It was all there, including the mingled scent of pine and freshly ground coffee. Why, then, did I feel disappointed?

George, noting my lackluster mood, slowed down as we drove home and stopped at one of the local churches where a small group had gathered to enjoy the nativity scene on the lawn. "They never change, do they?" he said, rolling down the windows so we could hear the carols coming from the church chimes. "I guess tonight's party just failed to go back far enough."

That was it, I realized. It's one thing to go back to earlier generations to emulate, appreciate, and perpetuate the ways of our ancestors. It's quite another to go back to the roots of Christmas—to feel the loving arms reach from a manger and hold us close to the heart of God and know that they recognize no time line.

No, they never change—those carols. They bring us the same message year after year about the star which still beckons from a billion light-years away, its energy unspent. My heart fills up with wonder at Christmas as it was, Christmas as it is, and Christmas as it ever will be!

To Think and Pray About: Christmas is a celebration of divine love. Love that goes beyond gift and feast. Without it, the season is but a touch of tinsel. Share the priceless gift of God's love. Only in this way (through simple things, their influence unmeasured) can the real meaning survive.

The Third Candle

James 2:5
John 8:12

December 15

FORMER CALIFORNIA SENATOR JOHN STULL shared an account which brings back the angels to sing for the shepherds every Christmas! Angels need little encouragement—just listening hearts like the shepherds possessed.

It was Christmas 1949, and the then-junior naval officer, his wife, and their toddler, Sinara, lived in a battleship-gray Quonset hut in Alameda, California. The Stulls forgot the sloping walls of the cramped quarters and bought a much-too-large tree which would fit only in the center of the room. That left space enough to get around it—if one crawled. That was fine with Sinara. All else could have been as gray as the hut.

"What a wonderful, memorable Christmas!" John recalls. "Another couple from the destroyer bought our daughter a tiny plaid skirt and red pullover. We woke Sinara and switched her from Dr. Denton's to her first grown-up outfit and laughed as happily as she. That was the year she got her first tricycle. The little outfit and the trike are among our red roses of memory. But there's another—so special."

The family went to the ship for dinner and when they came back it was late and dark. Walking by a dimly lighted Quonset, they heard a radio playing carols. It was then that the father felt a gentle tug of his lapel by his daughter's small hand as he cradled her in his arms.

"Daddy," the child whispered breathlessly, "listen! The angels are singing to the shepherds—telling them about the Baby Jesus."

To Think and Pray About: "I am the light of the world. . . ." Why do we light the third (and last) of the violet candles along with the other two? To remind us again of hope and faith and to add joy! The shepherds on the barren hills heard the singing first. How undeserving they must have felt. We are no more deserving. But that is the beauty of Christmas. Somebody cares!

The First Nativity Scene

December 16

Micah 5:1-4
Revelation 3:20

LOOK! My first Christmas card this year.

But isn't the nativity scene more like Walt Disney would have arranged it? Soft-eyed donkeys stand guard in the shadows. Cows bend their knees in adoration. And fleecy sheep, scrubbed as if going to the fair, peek into a manger so clean you can almost smell the sweet straw. How unreal.

We continue to send out these works of highly skilled artists year after year. And they are a joy to receive. But, just for a moment, let's steal away to view the first nativity scene.

Little Bethlehem, smallest in Judah, is abuzz with confusion. (That part, at least, coincides with today's world!) Roads leading from the barren hills (no snow) are clogged with those who are traveling to pay taxes. Inside the city, narrow streets are crowded with hawking vendors. Inns overflow. Latecomers must sleep on their mantles on the ground.

Still, a weary-faced Joseph keeps knocking at every door while Mary's frightened eyes follow her husband. She *must* have a bed! The sleepy innkeeper turns palms upward.

"Beggars, thieves—and now an expectant mother!"

But Joseph is grateful for the stable he offers. Never mind the acrid smell of the animals, the mire, the filth. Just a shelter for the holy birth!

Should this glimpse disillusion us? No, just erase fantasy and remind us that Jesus was born in pain and died in shame to save an unclean, uncaring world. And that now it is He who is knocking—knocking at the door of every heart. What a wonderful thing it would be if the entire world said: "There is room!"

To Think and Pray About:

We praise You, Lord, for Your saving Word,
The greatest greeting ever heard;
Cleanse us, Lord, from each sin—
Our hearts are open; please come in!   —J.M.B.

I Gave

John 3:16   December 17
Acts 20:35

A S a child I enjoyed the after-Christmas activity teachers provided. It went like this.

Teacher: "What did you receive this year?"

Children: "A sleepy doll . . . roller skates . . . this super new game . . ."

Gifts changed as we grew up. But answers were the same in that they were prefaced with: "I got . . . I got . . . I got . . ."

And then one year an innovative teacher wrote on the chalkboard: "What did you *give* this Christmas?"

We are not born knowing that it is more blessed to give. We must learn the secret through giving—a special brand of giving, that which is motivated by unselfish love. When we love as we ought, we give as we ought—straight from the heart. Otherwise, our gifts are but the tinkling cymbals Paul cautions us against. This learning takes time.

So this Christmas I am concentrating on giving to those I love because they are family or friends. And more! I am giving little anonymous gifts here and there to those whom I do not know well because of the great love God placed inside me when He gave the gift which changed the world. Jesus is His name!

To Think and Pray About: Would you like to make this *truly* "Christmas Around the World"? The gifts can be small—something tangible like a slip from your Christmas cactus or a gift of yourself offered in some little service. Together we can change "I got . . . I got . . . I got . . ." to "I gave . . . I *gave* . . . I GAVE!" *Merry Christmas, Lord!*

How Much Is Enough?

TWO MEN were discussing the possibility of one's leaving his present job after the holidays. "I'd take a cut, but—" he hesitated.

"Cut in salary? How much is enough?" the other asked.

How much *is* enough? I didn't hear the first man's reply; but the question brought to mind Goethe's "Nine Requisites for Contented Living":

> *Health* enough to make work a pleasure;
> *Wealth* enough to support my daily needs;
> *Strength* enough to battle with difficulties
>   and overcome them;
> *Grace* enough to confess my sins and forsake
>   them;
> *Patience* enough to toil until some good is
>   accomplished;
> *Charity* enough to see some good in my neigh-
>   bor;
> *Love* enough to move me to be useful and help-
>   ful to others;
> *Faith* enough to make real the things of God;
> *Hope* enough to remove all anxious fears con-
>   cerning the future.

Just how much money is adequate these days depends on one's standard of living, I guess. For some, it would be enough to buy a yacht; for others, to meet the payments on a secondhand car. But these are material things.

To Think and Pray About: If we had all Goethe's qualities, we would be rich indeed—spiritually. And, of course, we do have physical needs. And so we work. But is what we earn "enough," or do we need to reexamine how we use it?

What a Good Lunch!

PULLING OUT the Christmas boxes, I found a book Bryce used to love, Shigeo Watanabe's beginning-eater book. Bear's messy—but very delicious—solution excited him with each reading. Could be this would be a nice gift (or reference for yourself) for the child who has reached that first lunch "All by myself, please, Mommy."

You see, Bear's all set to eat a good lunch, but it's not easy. The soup spills over his bib. The jam spreads all over the table. And the spaghetti just can't be tamed. "Eating," Bear finally admits, "is just harder than I thought. What do I do now?"

Children can empathize with such a story. Mothers can sympathize—with each other! Learning to eat alone takes time, patience, and understanding. And, from adults, it takes love. I sat down and read the now-dilapidated book for the umpteenth time, smiling as I always did at the tale—but wondering why I'd kept it.

Maybe it is to remind me that a number of new Christians (particularly younger ones) sometimes find that life after commitment is harder than they thought. Do others truly understand this? Are they patient, helpful, and—above all—*loving*, the way God would have us love?

You've seen it happen. Young men and women accept Christ with zest. They see a "good lunch" spread before them and are sometimes eager to "make a go" of the adventure alone. It can't be done, of course. The very profession of faith commits our lives to God. But they, like Bear, find eating (from Christ's table) is just harder than they thought.

To Think and Pray About: In what ways can we help? There's a fine line of caution here, so the challenge is great. We have "shepherds" in our church—volunteers who make themselves available to the new members of the "flock." Mostly, we answer questions, let new members know of our church's services, and make sure that each is invited to enjoy the "good lunch." It works!

A Trip Around the World— for Purification

December 20   Mark 14:22-24

TODAY'S MAIL brought a unique invitation. *You are invited to take a trip around the world,* it said. A dress-up affair, they explained, "in which you are to appear in all or part of a costume befitting your heritage. Be prepared to explain how your ancestors would have spent the holiday."

Fun! After all, I needed to know how my German George and his English-Irish wife would have dressed. Research led me all over the world ahead of schedule.

On New Year's Eve Japanese people await the sound of the night watch gong. December was a bustling month. Men hurried to pay debts while women scrubbed their houses, preparing both heart and home for cleansing of the 108 human weaknesses set down by Buddha. The gong will ring 108 times.

On to Spain and Portugal where the bells will ring only 12 times. With each strike, revelers will pop 12 grapes into their mouths at once, one for each happy month ahead.

The morrow will be more solemn in Greece. The day coincides with the Greek Orthodox feast of St. Basil, the "Bearer of Blessings." Children, bearing green boughs (with which to tap the occupants of each home to bring good fortune) will serenade each house. There will be gifts.

In Ecuador, fire and noise chase away evil spirits as families create scarecrow-like figures. In Iceland, communities gather in song around a bonfire.

Around the world, the new year calls for a new beginning. The giant ball will come down in Times Square ... bells will peal from London to Lagos to La Paz. *And our church will serve communion at midnight.*

To Think and Pray About: Do you agree that we need to know more of one another's cultures? Do you agree that a new year is a new beginning? What better way to start it than at the table of the Lord. Join us. No costume is required.

The Visitor

Revelation 3:20,21   December 21
Psalm 18:1

ARE YOU EXPECTING GUESTS for the holidays? Yes? Then chances are that you're ready. Silver's polished . . . corners dusted . . . menus planned.

Once upon a time a very special Person came—and found the world unprepared. Just suppose, it happened again.

> If Jesus came to your house to spend a day or two,
> If He came unexpectedly, I wonder what you'd do.
> Oh, I know you would lodge Him as an honored Guest,
> And all the food you served Him would be the very best;
> And you would reassure Him you're glad to have Him there,
> That serving Him in your house is joy beyond compare!
> But when you saw Him coming, would you meet Him at the door
> With arms outstretched in welcome to the blessed Visitor?
> Or would you wish to tidy up before you let Him in?
> Or hide some books to let the Bible lie where they had been?
> Would you turn off the radio and hope He hadn't heard?
> And wish you hadn't uttered that last, loud, hasty word?
> Would you rush to hide your records and put some hymnals out?
> Could you bid Jesus come right in—or would you rush about?
> I wonder if the Savior spent a day or two with you,
> Would family conversation keep up the usual pace?
> And would you find it hard each meal to say a table grace?
> Would you sing songs you always sing and read the books you read?
> And let Him know the things on which your mind and spirit feed?
> Would you take Jesus with you each place you planned to go?
> Or would you maybe change your plans for just a day or so?
> Would you be glad to have Him meet your very closest friends?
> Or would you hope they'd stay away until His visit ends?
> Would you be glad if He would stay forever on and on?
> Or would you sigh with great relief when the Savior's gone?
> It might be interesting to think of things that you would do
> If Jesus came in Person to spend some time with you.
>
> —Author unknown

To Think and Pray About: Santa is a spirit of Christmas; but Jesus is the Spirit! We hear a lot about putting Christ back in Christmas; but our concern should be putting Him into our *lives*—living through Him, with Him, in Him, and for Him.

Sand Castles

M Y HUSBAND AND I weren't the only ones to make an unsound investment, but I felt that maybe losses didn't mean as much to others. We'd worked so hard, been so hopeful. Suddenly, domino-fashion, our dreams toppled. I strolled down to the beach, half hoping a giant fish would swallow me up. But it wasn't a fish I saw. It was the figure of a man on the leeward side of a little mound. Was he building a sand castle? *Child's play,* I thought—wondering why he bothered.

But, drawing closer, I realized this was no ordinary sand castle. There were spiral staircases, parapets, and turrets. The upper levels of the structure even had tiny stained glass windows that caught up the early sunlight. I was fascinated. But, alas, even as I admired what the artist had done, a wave lapped dangerously near the lovely castle.

The builder's eye caught mine and he turned palms upward. "I knew it was ephemeral. From the beginning, I knew it couldn't last."

"Then why bother?" I asked. "Doesn't the transitory nature of such a masterpiece bother you?"

"I'm an airline pilot," the young man said, consulting his watch. "I'm under a lot of stress—and this is a good lesson of how to let go."

My own problem dwindled. This man's investment was far greater than mine. It was in human lives! And yet, he steadied his hands by pursuing a hobby, something he could let go of just as he'd let go of his work. Suddenly I was able to let go completely of the niggling worry that had interfered with this glorious day. I walked away with the morning sun warm on my back. I had let go of my sand castle.

To Think and Pray About: Today marks the Winter Solstice. As Old Sol moves farthest south, our daylight minutes will increase. "The darkest hour is just before the dawn."

Christmas Is...

Christmas is the holly with berries round and bright,
Like little glowing candles that decorate the night.
Christmas is the carols floating in the air,
The notes near-reaching heaven, as if in chanted prayer.
Chrismas is the children in warm and snuggly beds
With dreams that they believe in adrift in sleepy heads.
Christmas is the whisper of gently falling snow;
And the same sweet Story we learned so long ago.

                                             J.M.B.

AND CHRISTMAS IS so much more! It is the day-to-day living, the *giving* after the "gift-giving" is done. It is the faith we have in all that is good throughout the world. It is the love and the laughter between friends. It is *remembering* the guileless wonder of children and the light of faith in young eyes on Christmas morning. It is the sweet joy of triumph that comes when you somehow (*I wonder how I pulled it off, Lord!*) are responsible for uniting a family in person or in spirit. It is the tender-sweet knowledge that you are loved by someone and (*thank You, Lord!*) that you have someone to love.

It is more yet. Christmas is prayer unlimited and belief in the Power unlimited to answer those prayers. Prayer for the wayward member of your family. Prayer for the peoples all over the world who have less than you. And prayer for the unrelenting courage to carry on with a smile.

To Think and Pray About: Christmas can be likened to the words of Rabbi Magnin: "Life can be beautiful for those who have eyes to see and ears to hear; for eyes that perceive the invisible and ears that hear the music of the Sphere. God has given us life to be lived with enthusiasm and joy. He has endowed us with minds to think and hearts to feel. It is up to us to enjoy our journey."

The Fourth Candle

December 24

Matthew 26:28
John 8:12

I AM REMEMBERING an incident which, although not personal, touched my heart—and the lives of this entire community last year. A high-school football player was badly injured and in need of blood donors. At a time when fellow students yearned to be home, they trooped *en masse* to contribute. "All but a very few showed," the principal said. One of those "very few" was a lad our family knew. Zack—shy and ashamed to ask questions—backed into a corner muttering, "No way."

The other students alienated Zack, labeling him "chicken." The athlete failed to respond to transfusions. The need for blood grew. And suddenly Zack appeared. "Take all you want— I'm ready to give all of mine," the boy said, rolling up his sleeve.

Afterward, white-faced, he lay very still. "Are you okay?" the nurse inquired. "Yes—but when am *I* going to die?"

No special recognition came to Zack, yet he was willing to give more than the others that his friend might live. And that is the spirit of Christmas.

This beautiful season the shadow of the cross hangs over the cradle. Jesus was born to die—to give His all to a world that scorned Him. As we engage in our personal traditions tonight, let us remember that the most important part of Christmas is the first six letters.

To Think and Pray About: "I am the light of the world. . . ." Why do we add the lighting of the rose candle to the first three tonight? The Angel's Candle is the candle of love—for it has come! There is always an air of mystery on Christmas Eve. It began for us in childhood and we pass the glory along. For the angels sang: "Glory to God in the highest, and on earth peace, good will toward men." This is the great mystery: How can a little child bring peace to a troubled world? It happens when that little child becomes the Holy Child who is born in our hearts.

The Candle in the Center

Luke 2:1-14   December 25
John 8:12

T HE TURKEY is in the oven—and I made the dressing myself. For the first time in *three years!* So the fifth
candle of Advent is glowing in my heart.

Thank You, dear Lord, for the power of healing—not only
my bones but my soul. Forgive me, Lord... I did not wait
patiently for You... I wanted instant healing. At first, I
expected it (as if it were my birthright). It was easy to smile
then, languishing, secretly enjoying those words of praise
about how brave I was. But weeks became months and months
became years. I became fearful and fretful. I tasted of depression and despair as over and over the specialists shook their
collective heads. And then, when they agreed that I was to
wear the yoke of pain for the rest of the journey, I tumbled
head-over-foot down, down, down. "Just take me away from
the whole ugly scene, Lord—You know I can't handle this...
this broken body, this broken spirit."

Was that what You waited to hear, Lord? Were You, in Your
infinite wisdom, teaching me patience... reminding me that
it was Your timing—not mine?

You did not mend me as I had demanded. But You gave me a
gift that doctors are unable to give—the power (Yours!) to
deal with it... to function... to rise above it... and to be
whole though my body be broken. A bit of the spring has gone
from my walk, Lord, but there's eternal spring in my heart! I
sense the budding promise within each person I see in a
wheelchair, walking on crutches, carrying a cane—and most
especially those afflicted with "castrophobia."

To Think and Pray About: "I am the light of the world...."
Why do we light all five of the candles this day? To remember
hope... faith... joy... peace... and now, the white candle is
for You, Lord, the *light* of the world... the *gift of life.* Yours is
the brightest of all, Lord, for all the others are but a part
of You. Through adversity, You have gifted me with all of
these... in the center of my heart.

'Twas the Day After Christmas

Luke 11:13
Proverbs 15:1

THERE should be a National Boxing Day. Held on December 26, its purpose would be for boxing up slippers for the same foot, kiddie computers to be assembled (instructions missing) . . . you know, the "it's too small" . . . "I have six" . . . (*you name it*).

Christmas is a time of love-giving. Somehow we have fallen into the "gift exchange" practice which all too frequently involves no love at all. So that requires the *second* gift exchange which sends the recipient trooping back (often sheepishly, hoping not to see the giver). The only way to avoid the return is to poke the gift into a closet—or to be a thoughtful giver. Of course, even when we choose carefully no amount of time, love, or money invested can assure us that the person will *like* the gift.

I probably belong in the *Guinness Book of World Records* when it comes to looking out for "As Is," "No Refunds," "All Sales Final," etc. when I shop. You see, I am married to the world's most successful complainer! George returns everything, puts up a good story, and hangs around until the store manager decides he's bad for business and makes an exchange, usually reminding him that by law he is not required to do so.

And the store manager is right! That is why it's wise to shop carefully. So shop with caution, hang onto the receipts, and know that your gift will be doubly appreciated if you tuck in a note of explanation.

Now, what if *you* are the boxer? If a toaster won't toast, you have a legitimate claim. If a sweater says "Do Not Wash," and you avoid dry cleaning, you *may* get an exchange. But you probably know all this. This is only a reminder to be gentle when you "approach the bench." Ask yourself: "Would the person behind me know I'm a Christian?"

To Think and Pray About: *Keep that Christmas Spirit!*

An Odd-Ball Music Box

Psalm 33:1-4; 34:27,28; 40:1-3   December 27

S O SOME of your gifts were—well, *peculiar?* Maybe you can make use of them. Think about it as you read about Fred and Sara.

"It's still Christmas at our house," Fred said gloomily.

It was well past the "grand opening" when he and Sara spent a quiet evening with George and me ("to get away from the noise," they said). Noise? They have no children, dogs, or . . .

Sara interrupted my thinking with a giggle. "I shouldn't have told his Aunt Bertha to stop knitting us those heavy sweaters for California winters. She sent us this oddball music box—"

"That won't shut up! Even though I threatened to bury it or take its insides out. It was okay at first, but *now* I've had to close the windows to keep the neighbors from leaving town."

"We put it in the back bedroom closet and bolted the door. But it just goes on playing 'Joy to the World'!"

Sort of funny. And a kind of dilemma. But sad, too, I thought as I made coffee. Poor determined little musicmaker. Playing on and on in that dark closet without an audience. Giving out the joyful news of the Savior's birth repeatedly to ears that would shut it out instead of *shouting* it out. And somehow I hoped that our friends would not throw the little thing away when the batteries ran down.

Shouldn't we all sing along with it no matter what the calendar says? And without closing our windows? The world needs to know the good news . . . and somebody out there may be listening.

To Think and Pray About: Choose a favorite carol and sing it all the year through as part of your daily devotional or while you are peeling potatoes. Me? I have no objection to being an "oddball music box." May the Lord recharge our batteries so we can sing out the joyful news!

Book Mark Reminders

" A RESOLUTION is a good mental process," I read as
the year fades away. "It forces us to assess what is
important in our lives, define goals, and decide how to achieve
them." Well, yes . . .

During the year I have been considering adding a third
devotional to my daily reading of two. There are some little
five-liners which shed some light on a passage of Scripture.
Just, I decided, what my husband and I needed. We could read
them together—only he preferred to read them alone. So my
problem was to have the book close-at-hand when he needed
it. The first day I read the devotional and laid the book beside
George's favorite chair. Then *I* forgot where it was. The
second day I read the book and left it where I was sitting and *he*
couldn't find it. The third day I forgot to read it at all. (I
suppose you have gathered that I like to experiment with my
resolutions to see if they will work. If not, I discard them!)

Now, there was nothing wrong with the editor's suggestion—and I had followed it up to a point. I'd fallen down on
the last point which was how to achieve my goal. It was a call
from my friend, Irene, that reminded me how to follow through
successfully.

"I'm reading my new book of devotionals in a sneak preview," she said. "Want to guess what my bookmark is?" I am
no good at guessing games, so she told me. "Each year I make a
secret resolution, seal it in an envelope, and use it to mark my
place. As I read, I recall the resolution and do whatever I've
assigned myself."

To Think and Pray About: New Year's Day is ideal for resolutions, but so is every other day! Maybe the little written-down
resolution would be a good reminder for those we love as well
as ourselves. It will serve to remind me, also, of God's day-to-
day renewal inside me. We might give the "how-to" a try.
And, above all, let us resolve to seek daily renewal in God's
sight.

Dear Lord, We Need a Word
With You . . .

DEAR LORD, we need a word with you. A new year opens its gates before us—another chance, another challenge, another reminder that, although the silver bells of Christmas are silent, we are to continue spreading the Christmas meaning to the ears of a wavering world of unbelief. We feel so helpless sometimes, Lord, so small . . . so filled with doubt and questioning fear of our abilities, quaking like the shepherds who watched their fields by night when the good news came. Oh Lord, renew our faith in things unseen and give us courage to act on that faith. We want to accomplish so much for You, Lord. Why is it that we "mess up"? Is it because we make so many promises we can't keep—instead of living in Yours and knowing that they are sufficient for all our needs? Put us back together, Lord, mend us . . . make us acceptable to do the job that lies ahead.

It seemed so easy, Lord, when we were surrounded by the warmth of Christmas. Now it looks so hard since the carols are hushed and so many tedium-filled days lie ahead.

Perhaps that is our problem, Lord. We are trying to cling to Christmas-now-past instead of stepping boldly into the new year. Remind us, then, that the Child who came at Christmas no longer lies in Bethlehem's manger, that He is at the right hand of His Father's throne above our universe. Forgive us when we forget that Christmas was only a beginning and that Jesus' intervention in our human situation continued through His death and resurrection. For, as we fold away tissue and ribbons and reenter the mainstream of life-as-usual, we lose sight that the true miracle is yet to come! So we must not stand looking into the heavens from which Jesus descended, made His loving sacrifice, and ascended again. Rather, let us praise You that we will never be alone again. And that we must be about Your business here until His return—some new year!

Before Parting

Dear Friends, you are a part of me—intangible and dear—
That make mosaics of my heart and keep your presence near.
I owe so much to all of you life scatters here and there,
I want to write my feelings down and send them everywhere.
I try to write one giant verse including every friend;
Alas! Each day brings more to say—my musings know no end.
And so instead of verse I choose a universal prayer:
"Please bless each reader for me, Lord—and let them know I care!"
                                                    J.M.B.

BEFORE PARTING, let's take a look over our shoulders at the past year.

To Think and Pray About: How far *have* we come? Can you:

1. See an idea of your own taken over by another—and not feel bitter?
2. Overhear critical words of your best effort—and bear no grudge?
3. Surrender a position, knowing you're better qualified—without hurt?
4. Watch another commit an act which is against your standards—and avoid self-righteousness?
5. Listen to another argue a point of view—and respect his right?
6. See a deliberate snub—and make allowances?
7. Suffer nagging pain, disguising your discomfort for the sake of theirs—without being a martyr?
8. Give of yourself to help another—without feeling superior?
9. Win—and not feel smug?
10. Give your heart, soul and body to your Creator—knowing that it is no gift at all (you belonged to Him all along)?

All of these? Oh, my friend, you are ahead of most of us! SOME of these? You need not be ashamed. NONE? Don't despair—praise God for another year to try again!

Journey's End

Together we've come to the journey's end
And pages gleam white ahead
While behind our course a few shadows fall
Across the pages unread.
May regrets be but a lump in the throat
For all that you've left undone
And the length of the way seem shorter now,
The race you ran feel well-run.
Consider the joy of setting the goal,
Hold fast to visions you've seen;
Together we've reached the brow of the hill—
Forget the stumbles between!
You've learned to get up and laugh at yourself,
For God would not let you fail;
He set a new goal that led higher yet,
Guiding you on the new trail.
Are your eyes now dry for bubbles that burst?
Did you comfort others too?
Have you met new friends who lent you a hand
While you learned to tunnel through?
Now . . . a book, like a road, somewhere must end . . .
What parting words can I say?
Just: "We clung to faith as we journeyed on—
Then smiled at the end of the way."   J.M.B.

AS WE FACE another year, let us pray for (and expect) growth in our spiritual lives. We need not notch the door to mark our increasing stature. Often growth is indiscernible. Great writers begin with the alphabet. Famous musicians once labored over "middle C." Gifted artists must learn to draw a straight line. We need to search our Bibles for enlightenment. Read and grow.

To Think and Pray About: And now . . . "The Lord bless thee, and keep thee; The Lord make his face shine upon thee, and be gracious unto thee; The Lord lift up his countenance upon thee, and give thee peace" (Numbers 6:24-26).

Shalom!

Other Good
Harvest House Reading

QUIET MOMENTS FOR WOMEN
by *June Masters Bacher*

Though written for women, this devotional will benefit the entire family. Mrs. Bacher's down-to-earth, often humorous experiences have a daily message of God's love for you!

THE DAILY GOSPELS
Come to Know Jesus Like You've Never Known Him Before
by *F. LaGard Smith*

Spend one month getting to know Jesus as you've never known Him before. With these 31 daily devotionals, you'll capture the entire scope of Jesus' ministry in one unified, chronological presentation of the Gospels of Matthew, Mark, Luke, and John. F. LaGard Smith, compiler of *The Narrated Bible*, invites you to get into the heart of the Gospels and learn how your life can be enriched and changed through Jesus' life and teaching.

IN TOUCH WITH GOD
How God Speaks to a Prayerful Heart
by *Marie Shropshire*

Knowing how to have life-giving fellowship with God in the midst of life's challenges is the key to fulfillment in the Christian walk. From this personal journal we learn that there is no difficulty or wound that is out of reach of His healing touch.

THE NARRATED BIBLE—In Chronological Order
by F. LaGard Smith

Dr. Smith's narrative combines with the New International Version in chronological order to guide you easily through the incredible unfolding drama from Creation to Revelation. Reading sections for each day of the year.

INSIGHTS FOR TODAY
The Wisdom of the Proverbs
by F. LaGard Smith

A convenient topical study and devotional reading of the Proverbs. Available in rich bonded leather, *Insights for Today* is an ideal aid to studying the wisdom which Proverbs offers.